METHUEN · ENGLISH · TEXTS

GENERAL EDITOR · JOHN DRAKAKIS

JOHN DONNE

Selected Poetry and Prose

METHUEN · ENGLISH · TEXTS

GENERAL EDITOR · JOHN DRAKAKIS

JOHN CLARE: *Selected Poetry and Prose* ed. Merryn and Raymond Williams
JOSEPH CONRAD: *Selected Literary Criticism and The Shadow-Line* ed. Allan Ingram
JOHN DONNE: *Selected Poetry and Prose* ed. T. W. and R. J. Craik
ANDREW MARVELL: *Selected Poetry and Prose* ed. Robert Wilcher

Forthcoming

JOHN DONNE

Selected Poetry and Prose

Edited by
T. W. and R. J. Craik

METHUEN · LONDON AND NEW YORK

First published in 1986 by
Methuen & Co. Ltd
11 New Fetter Lane
London EC4P 4EE

Published in the USA by
Methuen & Co.
in association with Methuen, Inc.
29 West 35th Street
New York, NY 10001

Typeset in Great Britain by
Scarborough Typesetting Services
and printed by
Richard Clay, The Chaucer Press,
Bungay, Suffolk

British Library Cataloguing in
Publication Data

Donne, John
Selected poetry and prose. –
(Methuen English texts)
I. Title   II. Craik, T. W.
III. Craik, R. J.
828'.309   PR2248

ISBN 0 416 40220 8

Library of Congress Cataloging in
Publication Data

Donne, John, 1572–1631.
John Donne: selected poetry and prose.
(Methuen English texts)
Bibliography: p.
I. Craik, T. W. (Thomas Wallace)
II. Craik, R. J.   III. Title.   IV. Series.
PR2246.C73   1986   821'.3
86–18019

ISBN 0 416 40220 8 (pbk.)

To Marguerita Eva Sowter
and to the memory of
James Garfield Sowter

Contents

Epithalamions, or Marriage Songs

Devotions

Sermons (extracts)

Introduction

John Donne was born, in the first half of 1572, in Bread Street in the City of London. He died, aged 59 or thereabouts, on 31 March 1631, in the Deanery of St Paul's Cathedral, within a quarter of a mile of his birthplace.

Though he died a clergyman of the Church of England, he had been born into a Catholic family and brought up in the Catholic religion. The history of religion in sixteenth-century England had been one of fluctuation. Henry VIII had retained Catholic doctrine and worship while rejecting the temporal and religious authority of the Pope and himself assuming the title of supreme head of the Church of England. Under his son Edward VI Protestantism was established, but after his short reign Henry's elder daughter Mary reintroduced Catholicism and strictly enforced it, only to have her own work undone when she also soon died, since the accession of Henry's younger daughter Elizabeth was marked by the restoration of Protestantism. All these changes in the national religion had political causes and consequences. An important consequence of Elizabeth's Protestantism was that in 1570 the Pope excommunicated her and absolved her subjects of their allegiance, an act which virtually placed those of her subjects who were Catholics in a position of having to choose between their faith and their ruler and which made them an object of suspicion to the government. This

1

suspicion was intensified from 1580 onwards, when Jesuits began to be sent to England to make converts to Catholicism and to stiffen Catholic resistance. It was into this world of insecurity and danger that Donne was born.

Donne's father, christened John like his own eldest son, was a prosperous member of the Ironmongers' Company. A Londoner by birth, he claimed descent from the ancient Welsh family of Dwn of Kidwelly in Carmarthenshire, probably with justification, though the genealogy has not been traced. His son used the arms and crest of the family, which appear in his earliest portrait and on his funeral monument. The name Donne is pronounced so as to rhyme with 'done': the poet puns on the name and the word in two of his poems included in this selection.

Donne's mother Elizabeth was the youngest daughter of John Heywood, a copious poet and brilliant writer of interludes and farces, by his wife Joan, who was the daughter of John Rastell (himself the author of one interlude, though a printer by profession) and his wife Elizabeth More, sister of Sir Thomas More. Besides being the witty and philosophical author of *Utopia*, More was a strong anti-Protestant controversialist writer, and was in matters of conscience a man of the utmost integrity, going to the block rather than subscribe to Henry VIII's headship of the Church of England and to the act of succession which declared the king's marriage to Katharine of Aragon invalid and his daughter Mary illegitimate. John Heywood, Donne's grandfather, voluntarily exiled himself to Louvain in 1564 rather than accept the official religion of England; Heywood's brother Thomas, a former monk who had remained in England, was executed in 1574 for celebrating mass; his sons Ellis and Jasper, Donne's uncles, both resigned Oxford fellowships to join the Jesuits, and Jasper returned to England as a Catholic missionary in 1581, was captured in 1583 and condemned to death, but eventually had his sentence commuted to exile. Donne's mother visited Jasper Heywood in the Tower, but that her 12-year-old son accompanied her is only a modern biographer's inference.

In January 1576 his father died, aged about 43, and within six months his mother, then aged about 31, married Dr John Syminges, a successful physician in his fifties and a widower. Two years after his

2

death in 1588 she again remarried, and by 1595 she and her third husband Richard Rainsford had settled at Antwerp in order to practise their religion freely.

Not long after Donne's father's death his eldest sister Elizabeth died (1577?), to be followed by his two younger sisters Mary and Katherine, both of whom died in 1581. This reduced the family to three children: Donne's elder sister Anne, his younger brother Henry, and himself. Anne married in 1585. In the previous year her two brothers had entered Oxford, of which university their stepfather was a graduate. Their previous education had been at home, doubtless under Catholic tutors.

It was not unusual to enter a university so young, and in their case a particular reason was to avoid having to subscribe to the Thirty-Nine Articles of Religion (a statement of Protestant doctrine) in the Book of Common Prayer which had been issued in 1559; students were required to subscribe to these Articles at the age of 16. There was no question of taking a degree, for that would have required an oath acknowledging the royal supremacy in matters of religion. After three years at Oxford, Donne and his brother are believed to have spent two or three more at Cambridge – without, for obvious reasons, being affiliated to a college – pursuing a general education. Later still they may have gone abroad to Italy and Spain. If so, they must have gone under Catholic auspices, since England was at war with Spain from 1587 to 1604.

In 1592 Donne entered Lincoln's Inn after a preliminary year at Thavie's Inn. The Inns of Court, all in the City of London, were where young gentlemen commonly finished their education, studying some law, irrespective of whether they intended to practise or merely to manage their estates, and enjoying the pleasures of town. In his first year Donne was elected Master of the Revels at Lincoln's Inn, to organize the Shrovetide entertainments. The chronicler Sir Richard Baker, who had been his fellow student there, later recalled him as 'not dissolute [i.e. careless in dress] but very neat; a great visiter of ladies, a great frequenter of plays, a great writer of conceited [i.e. clever] verses'. His inheritance under his father's will, when he was 21, added to his independence. But a few months later his brother Henry, who was probably still at Thavie's Inn, was arrested when a Catholic priest was found in his rooms; he admitted that the priest had heard his confession and had absolved him. The priest was executed; Henry Donne died in prison, of plague, while awaiting trial for harbouring him.

The fate of his brother, his mother's removal to Antwerp, the inheritance of about £750 and the necessity of finding a career (all branches of public service being closed to professed Catholics) must have urged him to take stock of the religion in which he had been brought up, and it is recorded that he read deeply in divinity at this time. It is not known when he decided to renounce Catholicism and adopt Protestantism as his religion. It is evident that he was conforming to the religion of the state by 1597 or early 1598, since otherwise he would not have been given employment, as he then was, by a statesman; and in 1602 he was able to maintain to his father-in-law that 'that fault . . . of loving a corrupt religion' which his detractors ascribed to him was a mere slander. But conformity and conviction are not the same thing, and it is uncertain whether Donne's renunciation of his Catholic faith was anything more than an act of prudence.

In 1596 and 1597 Donne, like many other young gentlemen, volunteered to serve in two military expeditions by sea against the Spaniards. The commander was the Earl of Essex (still not quite 30 years old when the first expedition sailed), in whose service Donne's Oxford friend Henry Wotton was a secretary. Besides the prospect of adventure and prize money Donne may have hoped for employment in Essex's service too. But on his return a different prospect opened. Sir Thomas Egerton, the father of one of his companions on the second voyage, had recently been appointed Lord Keeper of the Great Seal of England, and his son recommended Donne to him as a secretary. In this post Donne continued, with justified expectation of eventual promotion to important public office, until in December 1601 he inadvertently ruined his career.

Among the young people in Egerton's household when Donne joined it was Ann More, then aged about 14, the niece of Egerton's newly married second wife, who was bringing her up in London. During the next two years, perhaps in January 1600, when Lady Egerton died and Ann was preparing to return to her father's estate near Guildford, she and Donne exchanged a promise of fidelity. In

4

October 1601 her father, Sir George More, came to London for a session of Parliament, and Ann came with him. She and Donne met in secret. Realizing that Sir George would not willingly consent to their marriage – he was, indeed, looking for a suitable husband for Ann – they decided to marry secretly, and did so in December, Donne's Lincoln's Inn friend Christopher Brooke giving away the bride and his brother Samuel Brooke performing the ceremony. Ann then returned home with her father, and Donne awaited an opportunity to break the news to him. In February, being ill with a fever, he did so by letter. Sir George, in great anger, caused Donne and the Brookes to be imprisoned, persuaded Egerton to dismiss Donne from his post, and tried to get the marriage declared invalid. Though he soon decided not to have the three men prosecuted, accepted the legality of the marriage, and even asked Egerton, without success, to employ Donne again, he did not readily forgive the couple, and he refused to pay Ann's dowry of £800 until some four years later.

Donne and his wife were in great difficulty, with no income and hardly any capital. Ann's cousin Sir Francis Wolley and his wife offered them a home in their house at Pyrford, about 8 miles from Guildford. In 1606, by which time they already had three children, they rented 'a little thin house' at Mitcham, less than 10 miles from London. Donne vividly describes their situation:

> I write from the fire-side in my parlour, and in the noise of three gamesome children, and by the side of her, whom because I have transplanted into a wretched fortune, I must labour to disguise that from her by all such honest devices as giving her my company and discourse; therefore I steal from her all the time which I give this letter.
>
> (From a letter to Sir Henry Goodyer, quoted by R. C. Bald, *John Donne: A Life*, p. 156)

A fourth child was born, early in 1607,

> with extreme danger of her whom I should hardly have abstained from recompensing for her company in this world with accompanying her out of it.
>
> (From a letter probably to Sir Henry Goodyer, quoted by Bald, p. 157)

That is, if she had died, he would have been moved to die too, either of grief or by his own hand. He himself was often ill. All this time – in fact, from his dismissal in 1602 to his ordination in 1615 – he attempted to find salaried employment, but could secure nothing.

The recognized way to obtain preferment – employment or promotion in the service of the state – was by patronage. By recommending oneself to a nobleman or to some other high official one might be presented with an office that he had at his disposal. Donne was acquainted with many members of the court circle, including Sir James Hay (later Viscount Doncaster and the Earl of Carlisle) and Sir Robert Carr (later Viscount Rochester and the Earl of Somerset), both of whom were favourites of James I, who had come to the throne in 1603. For Carr's marriage in 1613 Donne wrote an epithalamion. Among his close friends he numbered Lucy, Countess of Bedford, who was one of the queen's ladies-in-waiting and also the patroness of other writers, including Ben Jonson. A number of Donne's poems are addressed to her. A patron not only was able, perhaps, to secure one preferment, but could also make one gifts of money and supply one with social invitations. Donne was prepared to spend long periods away from home if necessary. He travelled on the continent for nearly a year with a young Kentish knight, Sir Walter Chute, in 1605–6, and for nine months with Sir Robert Drury (in whose daughter's memory he had written *The First Anniversary: An Anatomy of the World*) in 1611–12. During the latter journey he is supposed to have had his famous vision (related in the fourth (1675) edition of Izaak Walton's *Life of Donne*) of his wife with a stillborn child in her arms. On his return he and his family moved from Mitcham to a house in Drury Lane next door to Sir Robert's.

In 1610 Donne recommended himself to James I by writing a prose work called *Pseudo-Martyr*. The events leading up to it were as follows. On his accession James had remitted the laws against Catholics, such as fines for non-attendance at church, but in the following year he had reimposed them. The result was the Gunpowder Plot of 1605, itself followed by severer penalties and also by a new oath of allegiance requiring Catholics to repudiate the doctrine that rulers excommunicated or deprived by the Pope might be deposed or murdered by their subjects. The king had written a defence of the oath in 1607, to which the Jesuits had retorted. The theme of Donne's book was that Catholics, while retaining their religion, might with conscience take the oath; if they refused to do so they would be 'false martyrs'. The legal penalty for refusal, it should be noted, was not death but imprisonment. Donne supported his view by theological and legal argument. His motives in writing the book were almost certainly twofold: he hated the Jesuits, whom he saw as promoters of political unrest, and against whom in the following year he wrote a short ironical prose satire, *Ignatius his Conclave*; and he wanted to bring himself to the king's notice. The king, though pleased, conceived the fixed idea that Donne should go into the church. Donne, who would have been better pleased with state employment, held out until 1615, when he consented to be ordained, was appointed a royal chaplain and was given an honorary doctorate of divinity by Cambridge at the king's command.

His biographer Walton writes that though he was given benefices in the country 'he could not leave his beloved London, to which place he had a natural inclination', so he placed curates in them. In 1616 he was appointed divinity reader at Lincoln's Inn, where he preached frequently, as well as at court and elsewhere. His financial troubles were now over, but in 1617 his wife died after giving birth to a stillborn child. In 1619 he went to Germany for eight months as chaplain to Viscount Doncaster (formerly Sir James Hay, his patron), whose mission, as royal ambassador, was to try to avert the approaching wars of religion there. In 1621 he was made Dean of St Paul's. He survived a serious illness in 1623, and continued to attract large congregations to his sermons, the last of which he delivered only a few weeks before his death. Also during his last illness he superintended the design of his funeral monument, standing upright in his shroud so that his likeness could be drawn. An engraving prefixed to his last sermon, published posthumously under the title *Death's Duel*, shows him just as he then was; his monument (still to be seen in St Paul's Cathedral, having survived the destruction of Old St Paul's in the Fire of London) shows him in better flesh and, being originally sited to face the east, seems to represent the resurrection of the body, always an idea on which he delighted to dwell.

Donne lived in three reigns, those of Elizabeth I (1558–1603), James I (1603–25) and Charles I (1625–49). In the last sixteen years of his life (1615–31), after his ordination, he wrote few poems, and, of course, all his sermons. As a poet he belongs to that continuous Elizabethan and Jacobean period which saw the works of Sidney, Spenser, Marlowe, Shakespeare, Jonson and Webster. The mere list of some major authors shows the rich variety of the literature, ranging through the epic, lyric and dramatic forms, and extending from the idealistic to the satiric and from the idyllic to the macabre.

In 1590, when Donne was 18 years old and would soon be a writer himself, there were published Sidney's prose romance *Arcadia*, the first three books of Spenser's *Faerie Queene* and Marlowe's two *Tamburlaine* plays. In 1591 were published Sidney's cycle of sonnets and songs, *Astrophil and Stella*, and Sir John Harington's translation of Ariosto's epic romance *Orlando Furioso*. In 1592 a flood of sonnet sequences inspired by Sidney began, with Constable's *Diana* and Daniel's *Delia*; and Nashe's *Piers Penniless his Supplication to the Devil* started a new wave of fantastic prose writing, packed with grotesque imagery and delivered with extrovert self-assurance. Shakespeare's first published poem, *Venus and Adonis*, appeared in 1593, and his *Lucrece* in 1594. His first plays to be published (though not the first to be acted) were *Richard II*, *Richard III* and *Romeo and Juliet*, all in 1597. Also in 1597 Joseph Hall published the first volume of his satires, in which he claimed to be the first 'English satirist'. This claim may not have been justified, but satire certainly came into fashion, and in June 1599 the Archbishop of Canterbury and the Bishop of London ordered the suppression and burning of many books, principally of satires and epigrams. One of these was 'Davyes Epigrams, with Marlowes Elegys', the epigrams being by Sir John Davies and Marlowe's elegies being his English versions of Ovid's *Amores*.

Among Donne's earliest poems are satires, epigrams and elegies. It was natural that a young man educated at the universities should have begun by imitating classical authors – Horace and Juvenal,

Martial and Ovid. In one epigram Donne borrows the whole idea from Martial:

> Thy father all from thee by his last will
> Gave to the poor: thou hast good title still.

In another the wit is his own:

> 'I am unable', yonder beggar cries,
> 'To stand, or move.' If he say true, he lies.

From the start, though working within a tradition, Donne proclaims himself an original writer. In Satire 1 ('Away, thou fondling motley humorist'), while probably remembering Horace's satire (Book 1, satire 9) about the tiresome acquaintance who meets the poet in the street and refuses to be shaken off, he devises a quite different situation and gives the acquaintance a quite different character. The topical allusions to performing animals suggest a date of 1593. His Satire 3, which is wholly original, probably belongs to the next few years.

Internal evidence from topical allusions (such as ll. 9–10 of 'Love's war') suggests that the *Elegies* are likewise early poems dating from Donne's Lincoln's Inn days. He may have seen in manuscript Marlowe's translations of Ovid into couplets (Marlowe had died in 1593 and the elegies may date from his Cambridge days in the 1580s), but he could read Ovid for himself and may have decided that Ovid's dramatic monologues would make good models for independent English poems of the same type. Some of the *Elegies* derive from non-Ovidian sources (for example, 'The anagram' and 'The comparison', which draw on Italian traditions of paradox and of satirical inversion), but in the Ovidian ones like 'Jealousy', 'Nature's lay idiot' and 'The perfume' Donne invents vividly dramatic situations involving the speaker, the mistress and others. These situations are expressed with plenty of contemporary Elizabethan local colour. One elegy, 'His picture', strongly suggests that the speaker is leaving for the Cadiz expedition of 1596.

The two verse letters 'The storm' and 'The calm' belong to the Islands Expedition of 1597. In their heightened descriptions and use of arresting similes they may reflect the extravagance of Nashe, who describes a battle between the French and the Swiss as follows in *The Unfortunate Traveller* (1594):

> All the ground was strewed as thick with battle-axes as the carpenter's yard with chips; the plain appeared like a quagmire, overspread as it were with trampled dead bodies. In one place might you behold a heap of dead murdered men overwhelmed with a falling steed in stead of a tombstone; in another place a bundle of bodies fettered together in their own bowels; and as the tyrant Roman emperors used to tie condemned living caitiffs face to face with dead corses, so were the half-living here mixed with squeezed carcases long putrefied.

Donne owes little to Spenser, with whom he has little in common, but Spenser's 'Epithalamion' (1595) was probably the stimulus for Donne's 'Epithalamion made at Lincoln's Inn'. The typically Spenserian alexandrine as the refrain to each stanza was adopted not only here but in Donne's two later wedding poems for the Lady Elizabeth and Count Palatine and for the Earl of Somerset (both 1613). The final alexandrine turns up again in each stanza of *The Progress of the Soul* (dated by Donne 16 August 1601), a bizarre mock-epic which is as far from Spenser's idealistic gravity as it could possibly be, but does resemble *The Faerie Queene* in telling an absorbing story in stanza form.

The *Songs and Sonnets*, Donne's lyric poems which express a variety of moods concerned with love, were first collected under that title in the second edition (1635) of his poems; in the first edition, published in 1633, two years after Donne's death, they had been dispersed through the volume. None of them is a sonnet in the sense of a fourteen-line poem with a regular pattern of rhymes: in the sixteenth and early seventeenth centuries the term was used both in this strict sense and in a looser sense virtually identical with the term 'song'. *Songs and Sonnets* had been the title of a poetical miscellany of works, including some true sonnets, by Wyatt, Surrey and others published by Richard Tottel in 1557 and known as *Tottel's Miscellany*. A manuscript used by Donne's editor of 1635 had grouped the poems together as 'sonnets and songs'.

The evidence does not suggest that Donne himself had collected these poems together at any time, in the way that he had probably collected his *Elegies* and *Satires*, or that he thought of them collectively as his *Songs and Sonnets*. Even their individual titles are certainly not all his own, for many are untitled both in the manuscript collections and in the 1633 edition, and some of them have different titles in different manuscripts.

Unlike *The Progress of the Soul*, none of the *Songs and Sonnets* bears a date, and their dating must be a matter of conjecture, which is made more difficult by the scarcity of those topical references which make it easier to date the *Elegies* and *Satires*. Occasionally it is possible to establish the earlier limit: the poem called 'Twickenham Garden', though it is not so titled in all the manuscripts, is so titled in enough of them to give good reason for dating it after the Countess of Bedford, Donne's patroness, acquired Twickenham Park in 1607; 'The undertaking' must have been written after the publication in 1599 of a book describing 'specular stone' as a mineral no longer in existence; references in 'The canonization' to the face of 'the king' stamped on coins, and in 'The sun rising' to 'the king' as riding out to hunt in the morning, imply dates after 1603 for those poems. The later limit can be established for 'The expiration' and 'Break of day', printed in song-books of 1609 and 1612 respectively, and for 'Lovers' infiniteness', thoroughly rewritten, but not by Donne, in a different stanza form for a song-book of 1612. But it is not possible to determine how much later than their earlier limits or how much earlier than their later ones these poems were written. Ben Jonson's remark to his friend William Drummond of Hawthornden that Donne had 'written all his best pieces ere he was twenty-five years old' (that is, by 1597) must be understood as an overstatement meaning that he had written many good poems by that time. Modern critical opinion assigns the *Songs and Sonnets* to a long period, from about 1594 to about 1614. Helen Gardner, in her edition of 1965, has argued that they can be divided, on grounds of content and form, into poems written in or before 1600 and poems written in or after 1602. Her argument, though a strong one in terms of artistic development, is open to the objection that Donne may in particular poems have reverted to an earlier way of writing.

Donne's originality as a writer of love-poems and poems about love is so unquestionable that he is sometimes supposed to have thrown overboard all the existing traditions. This is not so. Many of his poems are based on situations of unrequited love, going back to Petrarch (1304–74) and beyond, and treated in English poetry by Chaucer, Wyatt, Sidney and Sidney's successors. Another misconception is that English love-poetry before Donne was wholly trite and derivative: this can, and should, be corrected by attentive reading in (for example) *The Oxford Book of Sixteenth Century Verse* (ed. E. K. Chambers, Oxford, 1932). Even the dramatic opening that is so characteristic of him can be found already in Wyatt:

> What, no, perdy! ye may be sure.
> Think not to make me to your lure . . .
>
> ('What, no, perdy!')

and in Sidney:

> As good to write, as for to lie and groan;
> (*Astrophil and Stella*, sonnet 40)

and in Drayton:

> Since there's no help, come let us kiss and part.
> Nay, I have done; you get no more of me.
>
> (*Idea*, sonnet 61)

It has also its counterpart in the drama of the 1590s:

> Sweet Helen, make me immortal with a kiss.
> Her lips suck forth my soul; see where it flies!
> Come, Helen, come, give me my soul again . . .
> (Marlowe, *Doctor Faustus*, V. i. 99–101)

But this is not to deny the distinctiveness of Donne's personal tone.

His religious poems also, apart from 'Good Friday, 1613. Riding westward' and 'A hymn to Christ, at the author's last going into Germany', have to be dated by conjecture. The sonnet on the death of his wife must belong to 1617 or later, but some of the others may be as early as 1609, as Helen Gardner argues in her edition of 1952. Donne's were not the first holy sonnets: in 1595, at the height of the fashion for love-sonnets, Barnaby Barnes, who had published love-sonnets and love-lyrics in 1593, published *A Divine Century of Spiritual Sonnets*, two of which can be read in *The Oxford Book of Sixteenth Century Verse*. Barnes's religious sonnets, however, are very different from Donne's, being smooth and undramatic. 'The Cross' is the earliest of Donne's religious poems printed in the present selection. It may date from 1603–4, when the Puritans unsuccessfully petitioned the king to suppress the sign of the cross in baptism, or it may be much earlier and reflect Donne's views on this well-known Puritan opposition to the cross in any shape or form that savoured of Catholicism. (Nashe writes in 1594 of an army captain, punningly, that his purse was 'verily a puritan, for it kept itself from any pollution of crosses'.) A relatively early date is indicated by Donne's fondness for sustained word-play on different senses of the word 'cross', which may be compared with Shakespeare's similar word-play on 'I', 'aye' and 'eye' in *Romeo and Juliet* (III. ii. 45–51) or on Gaunt's name and the adjective 'gaunt' in *Richard II* (II. i. 72–83), both relatively early plays written in the 1590s. Donne's fondness for word-play, like Shakespeare's, never deserted him entirely, and his pun on 'Donne' and 'done' in what may have been his last poem, 'A hymn to God the Father', invites the same question that Richard II puts to Gaunt immediately after his punning speech:

Can sick men play so nicely with their names?

Donne evidently could, and his word-play is one aspect of that virtuosity which, true to the Elizabethan tradition in which he had first formed his style, he always cultivated.

A NOTE ON THE TEXT

It may be useful to discuss three aspects of the present edition: the selection, the text and the notes.

Though Donne's prose works are more abundant than his poetical ones, the emphasis in this selection is on the poetry. This is partly because the bulk of his prose is in the form of sermons, a form of literature little read nowadays and, particularly in Donne's time, one which presupposes a good deal of biblical and theological knowledge

13

in the auditor or reader. It is hoped that enough extracts from the *Sermons* have been included to give the modern reader a notion of Donne's range of content and style. The autobiographical *Devotions* are selected in order to include the beginning and the end of the sequence together with the most powerful of the intermediate ones. No other selections are made from Donne's prose. His youthful *Paradoxes and Problems* contain nothing that is not more wittily represented in his youthful poetry. His work of public argument, *Pseudo-Martyr*, and his work of private argument, *Biathanatos*, a discussion of the ethics of suicide, show the same reasoning power and illustrative readiness as the *Devotions* and *Sermons*, and are less amenable to selection. His very distinctive and amusing satire on the Jesuits, *Ignatius his Conclave*, besides calling for historical knowledge in the reader, is rather too long to be given in full and would not lend itself to condensation. His personal correspondence, though stamped with his personality in every line, is not (unlike his sermons, which he prepared for publication) part of his properly literary work.

When one thinks of Donne one first thinks of him as a poet, and in this volume it has been possible to include nearly half his poetry. The principle of choice has been to select his most representative and his most important poems and groups of poems. The *Songs and Sonnets* (placed first, and arranged alphabetically by titles, for ease of reference) are given almost in their entirety: only nine have been omitted. The handful of epigrams are omitted, but two of them are quoted earlier in this introduction. The *Elegies* and *Satires* have been chosen to show Donne's flexibility in both forms: the first Satire is very different from the third, and, though the *Elegies* present many common features, a generous selection of them will show that Donne never writes the same poem twice but achieves variety within a mode. Two (the two best) of Donne's epithalamions are selected, again partly because of the difference within similarity that they display. The fanciful and satirical mock-epic, *The Progress of the Soul*, which never got, and probably never could have got, beyond its first canto, is given in its entirety. So is the first of Donne's long elegiac poems, *An Anatomy of the World*, but not his second poem in what he may then have intended to be a series of *Anniversaries*, nor any of the shorter elegies which he wrote for various persons. Only four of his verse letters are included, the two vividly describing a storm and a calm at sea, and two others showing Donne respectively in informal and in ceremonious mood. Of the religious sonnets the cycle *La Corona* has had to be left out, but most of the rest are included, and so are 'The Cross' and 'Good Friday, 1613. Riding westward', which have the same rhymed-couplet form but were composed several years apart and can be as valuably contrasted as compared. There has not been room to include *A Litany* or the verse translation of *The Lamentations of Jeremiah*, both distinctive Donne-like poems, but the three intensely personal hymns are all included.

All the selected poetry and prose is given in a modernized text, of which more will be said later. Because very little of Donne's poetry was published during his lifetime (and of that little he seems to have superintended the printing only of his two *Anniversaries*), and because very much of it circulated in manuscript then and later, numerous variant readings exist. Some of these, but only a few, have been mentioned in the notes; in an edition of this kind it would have been impossible, and inappropriate, to list them all. Nevertheless, careful thought has been given to all the variant readings and to the arguments that have been advanced in favour of them: the editors' object has been to print an accurate text of what they believe Donne wrote, though they are well aware that many of the readings must continue to be debatable. A typically debatable reading occurs in the second stanza of 'Twickenham Garden', where some texts give the final couplet as

> Make me a mandrake, so I may groan here,
> Or a stone fountain weeping out my year,

while other texts have 'so I may grow here'. Both 'groan' and 'grow' make sense and can therefore be defended; some modern editors choose the one and some the other. The present editors prefer 'groan' because the image of the groaning mandrake is parallel to that of the weeping fountain in the following line, because the two images correspond to the sighs and tears mentioned in the opening line of the poem, and because they have found contemporary evidence (referred to in the notes) that mandrakes were believed to groan while rooted in the earth as well as to shriek when pulled out of it. They consider 'grow' to be too colourless a word for the context, meaning no more than 'exist' or, at most, 'be fixed'; the flourishing aggressive growth of the mandrake in *The Progress of the Soul* (ll. 131–60) would not be an appropriate idea here, nor would the single word 'grow' adequately convey that idea.

Modernization of the text of any author raises difficulties for an editor, whose attempt to ease the reader's difficulties may result in well-intentioned falsification. In this edition, if old-spelling editions are compared (and it should be noted that only one poem by Donne, not included here, exists in his own handwriting), the reader will see that both spelling and punctuation have been modernized, the latter being deliberately lightened as much as possible and designed to make the sentence structure clear. The old-style spelling and punctuation work together: the former is a continual reminder of how to interpret the latter. But to modernize the spelling and retain the archaic punctuation can only result in confusion.

Elisions present a problem. The old texts usually give the elided words in full and use an apostrophe to show where elision occurs in reading. In this edition, when a modern contraction exists it has usually been introduced: thus, in 'The sun rising', l. 21, where old-spelling editions have 'She ' is all States, and all Princes, I,' this edition has 'She's all states, and all princes I'; but in 'The apparition', l. 16, it has 'I had rather thou shouldst painfully repent' because the contraction 'I'd' might be equally understood as 'I had' and 'I would' (old-spelling editions have 'I ' had'). No means exist, in a modern-spelling edition, for marking such elisions as 'Lest that preserve thee; ' and since my love is spent' ('The apparition', l. 15). The correct stressing of such lines must be left to the reader's experience; little difficulty will be found if it is remembered that, though Donne's rhythm is not *tied* to his metre, it seldom goes violently *against* it. This edition, however, does distinguish between the pronounced and unpronounced endings of verbs ('callèd', 'called'), as in 'Death, be not proud, though some have callèd thee / Mighty and dreadful, for thou art not so' (Holy Sonnet 10, ll. 1–2). Two other causes of difficulty in observing Donne's metre exist. First, the termination '-ion' is sometimes pronounced (as always nowadays) as

16

one syllable and sometimes as two. When rhyme is involved, the two-syllable pronunciation always applies:

> Whose every tooth to a several place is gone,
> To vex their souls at resurrection;
>
> (Elegy 9, 'The autumnal', ll. 41–2)

When the word occurs within the line, one's ear must be one's guide:

> When by thy scorn, O murd'ress, I am dead,
> And that thou think'st thee free
> From all solicitation from me,
> Then shall my ghost come to thy bed,
> And thee, feigned vestal, in worse arms shall see.
>
> ('The apparition', ll. 1–5)

In this passage 'solicitation' has six syllables, and l. 3 has the same metrical form as ll. 1 and 5. The second metrical difficulty is caused by the fact that in Donne's time some words were not stressed on the same syllable as today (and, in some instances, were pronounced with different sounds):

> Reason, your viceroy in me, me should defend,
> But is captived, and proves weak or untrue;
>
> (Holy Sonnet 14, ll. 7–8)

Here 'captived' must be stressed on the second syllable, and the stressed sound pronounced like that in 'capsized'. It would be obtrusive to mark such emphases in the text, and impossible to mark such sound changes, and it would occupy too much space in the notes to record them there.

The notes have been kept as brief as possible, and the editors have concentrated on clarifying Donne's meaning: agreeing with H. J. C. Grierson that 'Donne's precision is as marked as his subtlety' (*Poems*, 1912, vol. II, p. 42), and with C. S. Lewis that 'He knew what he was putting into his poem, and we cannot get out of it more than he knew he was putting in' (*Studies in Medieval and Renaissance Literature*, Cambridge, 1966, p. 143), they have assumed that there is a meaning to be found, and when they could not find it (as in 'Love's growth', ll. 17–18) they have said so. Where they find word-play they have noted it, but they have not noted such proposed word-play as they reject. For example, in 'The apparition', l. 5, the old spelling 'fain'd' cannot justify the interpretation 'wished for', which receives no support from recorded usage of the adjective or verb *fain*; 'fain'd' is simply a variant spelling of 'feigned'. There has not been room to discuss all the interpretations of meaning that previous editors and critics have proposed. For example, it is usual to explain the sun's 'flasks' ('A nocturnal upon St Lucy's Day', l. 3) as 'powder-flasks, i.e. stars, thought to store up light from the sun'. In this edition the literal meaning is accepted, but the figurative one is not, and is not recorded. Stars do not seem to give out less light in winter; on the contrary, particularly on a dark frosty night, they seem to give out more. The 'now' of l. 3 is not the day's midnight, but the year's (all the other imagery of the stanza relates to the season, not to the hour). Therefore the flasks are not actual objects in the universe described in a figurative term but are a figurative term for the sun's own energy, emitted in fitful gleams during the winter season. Another example is the opening of the last stanza of 'Twickenham Garden':

> Hither with crystal vials, lovers, come,
>> And take my tears, which are love's wine,
>> And try your mistress' tears at home,
> For all are false that taste not just like mine.

Helen Gardner's note (*The Elegies and the Songs and Sonnets*, 1965, p. 216), accepted by later editors, is as follows:

> *christall vyals.* It was believed at this time that the small glass or alabaster vessels found in ancient tombs, probably to hold perfumes, were lachrymatories or tear-bottles in which mourners at funerals caught their tears in order to deposit them as tributes to the dead.

There is no reason to suppose that in this stanza Donne had lachrymatories in mind, for the poem has to do with unrequited love, grief and metamorphosis, not with death, mourning and burial. All that

18

Donne is inviting lovers to do, when he shall have been changed into an ever-weeping fountain, is to conduct a scientific experiment; the vials (the usual word for small bottles: compare *Hamlet*, I. v. 62) are to be made of crystal because that is a proverbial type of clarity ('as clear as crystal') and therefore appropriate to the contrast of the metamorphosed lover's sincerity and the insincerity of false mistresses. Accordingly, lachrymatories are not mentioned in the notes of this edition.

Donne is a poet who has received a great amount of editorial attention. The reader who wishes to go more deeply into the questions of establishing and interpreting the text of his poems may do so by consulting the editions listed in the first section of the Select Bibliography. The second section, a list of biographical, critical and historical works, has deliberately been kept short and confined to modern books. Selections from earlier critics of Donne's poetry can be found in two of these, A. J. Smith's *Donne and the Metaphysical Poets: The Critical Heritage* and Julian Lovelock's *Donne: 'Songs and Sonnets': A Casebook*, and these selections will enable the reader to follow the changes in Donne's reputation over the years. The extracts from more modern criticism given in these two volumes and in Helen Gardner's *John Donne: A Collection of Critical Essays* will direct the reader towards other books on Donne which have not been listed here: a choice among these can be made by the reader on the basis of the extracts.

JOHN DONNE
Selected Poetry and Prose

Songs and Sonnets

AIR AND ANGELS

Twice or thrice had I loved thee
Before I knew thy face or name;
So in a voice, so in a shapeless flame,
Angels affect us oft, and worshipped be;
   Still when to where thou wert I came
Some lovely glorious nothing I did see;
   But since my soul, whose child love is,
Takes limbs of flesh, and else could nothing do,
   More subtle than the parent is
Love must not be, but take a body too,   10
   And therefore what thou wert and who
      I bid love ask, and now
That it assume thy body I allow,
And fix itself in thy lip, eye, and brow.

Whilst thus to ballast love I thought,
And so more steadily to have gone,
With wares which would sink admiration
I saw I had love's pinnace overfraught:
   Every thy hair for love to work upon
Is much too much, some fitter must be sought;   20

* Numbers in square brackets refer to pages on which notes may be found

For nor in nothing nor in things
Extreme and scatt'ring bright can love inhere;
   Then as an angel face and wings
Of air – not pure as it, yet pure – doth wear,
   So thy love may be my love's sphere;
     Just such disparity
As is 'twixt air and angels' purity
'Twixt women's love and men's will ever be.

Composed before 1615   First published 1633

THE ANNIVERSARY

All kings, and all their favourites,
   All glory of honours, beauties, wits,
The sun itself, which makes times as they pass,
Is elder by a year, now, than it was
When thou and I first one another saw.
All other things to their destruction draw;
   Only our love hath no decay;
This no tomorrow hath, nor yesterday;
Running it never runs from us away,
But truly keeps his first, last, everlasting day.   10

Two graves must hide thine and my corse;
   If one might, death were no divorce.
Alas, as well as other princes, we
(Who prince enough in one another be)
Must leave at last in death these eyes and ears
Oft fed with true oaths and with sweet salt tears;
   But souls where nothing dwells but love
(All other thoughts being inmates) then shall prove
This or a love increasèd there above,
When bodies to their graves, souls from their graves remove.   20

24

And then we shall be throughly bless'd,
  But we no more than all the rest.
Here upon earth we're kings, and none but we
Can be such kings, nor of such subjects be;
Who is so safe as we, where none can do
Treason to us except one of us two?
  True and false fears let us refrain;
Let us love nobly, and live, and add again
Years and years unto years, till we attain
To write threescore; this is the second of our reign.   30

Composed before 1615   First published 1633

THE APPARITION

When by thy scorn, O murd'ress, I am dead,
  And that thou think'st thee free
From all solicitation from me,
Then shall my ghost come to thy bed,
And thee, feigned vestal, in worse arms shall see.
Then thy sick taper will begin to wink,
And he whose thou art then, being tired before,
Will, if thou stir, or pinch to wake him, think
    Thou call'st for more,
And in false sleep will from thee shrink.   10
And then, poor aspen wretch, neglected thou
Bathed in a cold quicksilver sweat wilt lie
    A verier ghost than I.
What I will say, I will not tell thee now,
Lest that preserve thee; and since my love is spent,
I had rather thou shouldst painfully repent,
Than by my threatenings rest still innocent.

Composed before 1615   First published 1633

25

THE BAIT

Come live with me, and be my love,
And we will some new pleasures prove
Of golden sands, and crystal brooks,
With silken lines, and silver hooks.

There will the river whispering run
Warmed by thy eyes more than the sun.
And there the enamoured fish will stay,
Begging themselves they may betray.

When thou wilt swim in that live bath,
Each fish, which every channel hath,   10
Will amorously to thee swim,
Gladder to catch thee than thou him.

If thou to be so seen be'st loath
By sun or moon, thou dark'nest both,
And if myself have leave to see,
I need not their light, having thee.

Let others freeze with angling reeds,
And cut their legs with shells and weeds,
Or treacherously poor fish beset
With strangling snare or windowy net;   20

Let coarse bold hands from slimy nest
The bedded fish in banks outwrest,
Or curious traitors, sleavesilk flies,
Bewitch poor fishes' wandering eyes.

For thee, thou need'st no such deceit,
For thou thyself art thine own bait;
That fish that is not catched thereby,
Alas, is wiser far than I.

Composed before 1612   First published 1633

26

THE BLOSSOM

Little think'st thou, poor flower,
   Whom I have watched six or seven days,
And seen thy birth, and seen what every hour
Gave to thy growth, thee to this height to raise,
And now dost laugh and triumph on this bough,
      Little think'st thou
That it will freeze anon, and that I shall
Tomorrow find thee fall'n, or not at all.

Little think'st thou, poor heart,
   That labour'st yet to nestle thee,   10
And think'st by hovering here to get a part
In a forbidden or forbidding tree,
And hop'st her stiffness by long siege to bow,
      Little think'st thou,
That thou tomorrow, ere that sun doth wake,
Must with this sun and me a journey take.

But thou, which lov'st to be
   Subtle to plague thyself, wilt say,
'Alas, if you must go, what's that to me?
Here lies my business, and here I will stay.   20
You go to friends, whose love and means present
      Various content
To your eyes, ears, and tongue, and every part.
If then your body go, what need you a heart?'

Well then, stay here; but know,
   When thou hast stayed and done thy most,
A naked thinking heart, that makes no show,
Is to a woman but a kind of ghost;
How shall she know my heart, or, having none,
      Know thee for one?   30
Practice may make her know some other part,
But take my word, she doth not know a heart.

Meet me at London, then,
   Twenty days hence, and thou shalt see
Me fresher, and more fat, by being with men,
Than if I had stayed still with her and thee.
For God's sake, if you can, be you so too:
   I would give you,
There, to another friend, whom we shall find
As glad to have my body as my mind.   40

Composed before 1615   First published 1633

BREAK OF DAY

'Tis true, 'tis day, what though it be?
O wilt thou therefore rise from me?
Why should we rise, because 'tis light?
Did we lie down because 'twas night?
Love, which in spite of darkness brought us hither,
Should in despite of light keep us together.

Light hath no tongue, but is all eye;
If it could speak as well as spy,
This were the worst that it could say,
That, being well, I fain would stay,   10
And that I loved my heart and honour so,
That I would not from him that had them go.

Must business thee from hence remove?
Oh, that's the worst disease of love;
The poor, the foul, the false, love can
Admit, but not the busied man.
He which hath business, and makes love, doth do
Such wrong as when a married man doth woo.

Composed before 1612   First published 1612

THE BROKEN HEART

He is stark mad, whoever says
   That he hath been in love an hour;
Yet not that love so soon decays,
   But that it can ten in less space devour;
Who will believe me if I swear
That I have had the plague a year?
    Who would not laugh at me if I should say
    I saw a flask of powder burn a day?

Ah, what a trifle is a heart,
   If once into Love's hands it come!   10
All other griefs allow a part
   To other griefs, and ask themselves but some;
They come to us, but us Love draws;
He swallows us, and never chaws;
    By him, as by chained shot, whole ranks do die;
    He is the tyrant pike, our hearts the fry.

If 'twere not so, what did become
   Of my heart when I first saw thee?
I brought a heart into the room,
   But from the room I carried none with me;   20
If it had gone to thee, I know
Mine would have taught thy heart to show
    More pity unto me; but Love, alas,
    At one first blow did shiver it as glass.

Yet nothing can to nothing fall,
   Nor any place be empty quite;
Therefore I think my breast hath all
   Those pieces still, though they be not unite;
And now, as broken glasses show
A hundred lesser faces, so   30
    My rags of heart can like, wish, and adore,
    But after one such love can love no more.

Composed before 1615   First published 1633

THE CANONIZATION

For God's sake hold your tongue, and let me love,
   Or chide my palsy or my gout,
My five grey hairs or ruined fortune flout;
    With wealth your state, your mind with arts improve;
      Take you a course, get you a place,
       Observe his Honour, or his Grace,
Or the King's real, or his stamped face
    Contemplate; what you will, approve,
    So you will let me love.

Alas, alas, who's injured by my love?   10
    What merchant's ships have my sighs drowned?
Who says my tears have overflowed his ground?
    When did my colds a forward spring remove?
      When did the heats which my veins fill
      Add one more to the plaguy bill?
Soldiers find wars, and lawyers find out still
    Litigious men which quarrels move,
    Though she and I do love.

Call us what you will, we are made such by love;
    Call her one, me another fly;   20
We 're tapers too, and at our own cost die,
    And we in us find the eagle and the dove.
      The phoenix riddle hath more wit
      By us; we two, being one, are it.
So to one neutral thing both sexes fit.
    We die and rise the same, and prove
    Mysterious by this love.

We can die by it, if not live by love;
    And if unfit for tombs and hearse
Our legend be, it will be fit for verse;   30
    And if no piece of chronicle we prove,
      We'll build in sonnets pretty rooms;
      As well a well-wrought urn becomes

The greatest ashes as half-acre tombs.
    And by these hymns, all shall approve
    Us canonized for love:

And thus invoke us: 'You whom reverend love
    Made one another's hermitage;
You to whom love was peace, that now is rage;
    Who did the whole world's soul contract, and drove   40
        Into the glasses of your eyes
        (So made such mirrors and such spies
That they did all to you epitomize)
    Countries, towns, courts: beg from above
    A pattern of your love!'

Composed 1603–15   First published 1633

COMMUNITY

Good we must love, and must hate ill,
For ill is ill and good good still;
    But there are things indifferent,
Which we may neither hate nor love,
But one and then another prove,
    As we shall find our fancy bent.

If then at first wise Nature had
Made women either good or bad,
    Then some we might hate and some choose;
But since she did them so create   10
That we may neither love nor hate,
    Only this rests, all all may use.

If they were good it would be seen;
Good is as visible as green,
    And to all eyes itself betrays.
If they were bad they could not last;

Bad doth itself and others waste.
    So they deserve nor blame nor praise.

But they are ours as fruits are ours;
He that but tastes, he that devours,   20
    And he that leaves all, doth as well.
Changed loves are but changed sorts of meat,
And when he hath the kernel eat,
    Who doth not fling away the shell?

Composed before 1615   First published 1633

THE COMPUTATION

For the first twenty years since yesterday
    I scarce believed thou couldst be gone away.
For forty more I fed on favours past,
    And forty on hopes that thou wouldst they might last.
Tears drowned one hundred, and sighs blew out two;
    A thousand I did neither think nor do,
    Or not divide, all being one thought of you;
    Or in a thousand more, forgot that too.
Yet call not this long life; but think that I
Am, by being dead, immortal; can ghosts die?   10

Composed before 1615   First published 1633

THE CURSE

Whoever guesses, thinks, or dreams he knows
Who is my mistress, wither by this curse:
        His only, and only his purse
        May some dull heart to love dispose,
And she yield then to all that are his foes;
    May he be scorned by one whom all else scorn,
    Forswear to others what to her he hath sworn,
    With fear of missing, shame of getting, torn;

Madness his sorrow, gout his cramps, may he
Make, by but thinking who hath made him such: 10
  And may he feel no touch
  Of conscience but of fame, and be
Anguished not that 'twas sin, but that 'twas she;
 In early and long scarceness may he rot,
 For land which had been his, if he had not
 Himself incestuously an heir begot;

May he dream treason, and believe that he
Meant to perform it, and confess, and die,
  And no record tell why;
  His sons, which none of his may be,   20
Inherit nothing but his infamy;
 Or may he so long parasites have fed,
 That he would fain be theirs whom he hath bred,
 And at the last be circumcized for bread;

The venom of all stepdames, gamesters' gall,
What tyrants and their subjects interwish,
  What plants, mines, beasts, fowl, fish,
  Can contribute, all ill which all
Prophets or poets spake; and all which shall
 Be annexed in schedules unto this by me,   30
 Fall on that man; for if it be a she
 Nature beforehand hath outcursèd me.

Composed before 1615 First published 1633

THE DAMP

When I am dead, and doctors know not why,
  And my friends' curiosity
Will have me cut up to survey each part,
When they shall find your picture in my heart,
  You think a sudden damp of love
  Will thorough all their senses move,

And work on them as me, and so prefer
Your murder to the name of massacre.

Poor victories; but if you dare be brave,
    And pleasure in your conquest have,   10
First kill th' enormous giant your Disdain,
And let th' enchantress Honour next be slain,
    And like a Goth and Vandal rise,
    Deface records and histories
Of your own arts and triumphs over men,
And without such advantage kill me then.

For I could muster up as well as you
    My giants and my witches too,
Which are vast Constancy and Secretness,
But these I neither look for nor profess;   20
    Kill me as woman, let me die
    As a mere man; do you but try
Your passive valour, and you shall find then,
Naked you've odds enough of any man.

Composed before 1615   First published 1633

THE DISSOLUTION

She's dead; and all which die
    To their first elements resolve;
And we were mutual elements to us,
    And made of one another.
    My body then doth hers involve,
And those things whereof I consist hereby
In me abundant grow and burdenous,
    And nourish not, but smother.
    My fire of passion, sighs of air,
Water of tears, and earthy sad despair,   10
    Which my materials be,
But near worn out by love's security,

She, to my loss, doth by her death repair,
    And I might live long wretched so
But that my fire doth with my fuel grow.
        Now as those active kings
    Whose foreign conquest treasure brings
Receive more, and spend more, and soonest break:
This (which I am amazed that I can speak)
        This death hath with my store   20
            My use increased.
And so my soul more earnestly released,
Will outstrip hers; as bullets flown before
A latter bullet may o'ertake, the powder being more.

Composed before 1615   First published 1633

THE DREAM

Dear love, for nothing less than thee
Would I have broke this happy dream.
        It was a theme
For reason, much too strong for fantasy,
Therefore thou waked'st me wisely; yet
My dream thou brok'st not, but continued'st it;
Thou art so true, that thoughts of thee suffice,
To make dreams truths, and fables histories;
Enter these arms, for since thou thought'st it best
Not to dream all my dream, let's act the rest.   10

As lightning, or a taper's light,
Thine eyes and not thy noise waked me;
        Yet I thought thee
(For thou lov'st truth) an angel, at first sight;
But when I saw thou saw'st my heart,
And knew'st my thoughts, beyond an angel's art,
When thou knew'st what I dreamt, when thou knew'st
    when
Excess of joy would wake me, and cam'st then,

35

I must confess it could not choose but be
Profane to think thee anything but thee. 20

Coming and staying showed thee thee,
But rising makes me doubt that now
     Thou art not thou.
That love is weak where fear's as strong as he;
'Tis not all spirit, pure, and brave,
If mixture it of fear, shame, honour, have.
Perchance as torches which must ready be
Men light and put out, so thou deal'st with me;
Thou cam'st to kindle, go'st to come; then I
Will dream that hope again, but else would die. 30

Composed before 1615   First published 1633

THE ECSTASY

Where, like a pillow on a bed,
  A pregnant bank swelled up, to rest
The violet's reclining head,
  Sat we two, one another's best;

Our hands were firmly cemented
  With a fast balm which thence did spring;
Our eye-beams twisted, and did thread
  Our eyes upon one double string;

So to intergraft our hands, as yet,
  Was all our means to make us one, 10
And pictures in our eyes to get
  Was all our propagation.

As 'twixt two equal armies Fate
  Suspends uncertain victory,
Our souls, which to advance their state
  Were gone out, hung 'twixt her and me;

And whilst our souls negotiate there,
   We like sepulchral statues lay;
All day the same our postures were,
   And we said nothing all the day.   20

If any, so by love refined
   That he souls' language understood,
And by good love were grown all mind,
   Within convenient distance stood,

He (though he knew not which soul spake,
   Because both meant, both spake the same)
Might thence a new concoction take,
   And part far purer than he came.

This ecstasy doth unperplex
   (We said) and tell us what we love;   30
We see by this, it was not sex,
   We see, we saw not what did move;

But as all several souls contain
   Mixture of things, they know not what,
Love these mixed souls doth mix again,
   And makes both one, each this and that.

A single violet transplant,
   The strength, the colour, and the size,
All which before was poor and scant,
   Redoubles still and multiplies.   40

When love with one another so
   Interinanimates two souls,
That abler soul which thence doth flow
   Defects of loneliness controls.

We, then, who are this new soul, know
   Of what we are composed and made,

For th' atomies of which we grow
    Are souls whom no change can invade.

But O, alas, so long, so far,
    Our bodies why do we forbear?   50
They're ours, though they're not we, we are
    The intelligences, they the sphere.

We owe them thanks because they thus
    Did us to us at first convey,
Yielded their forces, sense, to us,
    Nor are dross to us, but allay.

On man heaven's influence works not so
    But that it first imprints the air;
So soul into the soul may flow,
    Though it to body first repair.   60

As our blood labours to beget
    Spirits as like souls as it can,
Because such fingers need to knit
    That subtle knot which makes us man,

So must pure lovers' souls descend
    To affections, and to faculties,
Which sense may reach and apprehend,
    Else a great prince in prison lies.

To our bodies turn we then, that so
    Weak men on love revealed may look;   70
Love's mysteries in souls do grow,
    But yet the body is his book.

And if some lover such as we
    Have heard this dialogue of one,
Let him still mark us, he shall see
    Small change when we're to bodies gone.

Composed before 1615   First published 1633

THE EXPIRATION

So, so, break off this last lamenting kiss,
   Which sucks two souls, and vapours both away;
Turn thou ghost that way, and let me turn this,
   And let ourselves benight our happiest day.
We asked none leave to love; nor will we owe
   Any so cheap a death as saying, Go.

Go; and if that word have not quite killed thee,
   Ease me with death by bidding me go too.
Or if it have, let my word work on me,
   And a just office on a murderer do.   10
Except it be too late to kill me so,
   Being double dead, going and bidding go.

Composed before 1609   First published 1609

A FEVER

O do not die, for I shall hate
   All women so, when thou art gone,
That thee I shall not celebrate
   When I remember thou wast one.

But yet thou canst not die, I know;
   To leave this world behind is death,
But when thou from this world wilt go
   The whole world vapours with thy breath.

Or if, when thou, the world's soul, go'st,
   It stay, 'tis but thy carcass then,   10
The fairest woman but thy ghost,
   But corrupt worms the worthiest men.

O wrangling schools, that search what fire
   Shall burn this world, had none the wit

Unto this knowledge to aspire,
   That this her fever might be it?

And yet she cannot waste by this,
   Nor long bear this torturing wrong,
For much corruption needful is
   To fuel such a fever long.   20

These burning fits but meteors be,
   Whose matter in thee is soon spent.
Thy beauty and all parts which are thee
   Are unchangeable firmament.

Yet 'twas of my mind, seizing thee,
   Though it in thee cannot persever.
For I had rather owner be
   Of thee one hour, than all else ever.

Composed before 1615   First published 1633

THE FLEA

Mark but this flea, and mark in this,
How little that which thou deny'st me is;
It sucked me first, and now sucks thee,
And in this flea our two bloods mingled be;
Thou know'st that this cannot be said
A sin, nor shame, nor loss of maidenhead,
   Yet this enjoys before it woo,
   And pampered swells with one blood made of two,
   And this, alas, is more than we would do.

Oh stay, three lives in one flea spare,   10
Where we almost, nay more than married are.
This flea is you and I, and this
Our marriage bed and marriage temple is;
Though parents grudge, and you, we're met

And cloistered in these living walls of jet.
   Though use make you apt to kill me,
   Let not to this self-murder added be,
   And sacrilege, three sins in killing three.

Cruel and sudden, hast thou since
Purpled thy nail in blood of innocence?   20
Wherein could this flea guilty be
Except in that drop which it sucked from thee?
Yet thou triumph'st, and say'st that thou
Find'st not thyself nor me the weaker now.
   'Tis true; then learn how false fears be;
   Just so much honour, when thou yield'st to me,
   Will waste as this flea's death took life from thee.

Composed before 1615   First published 1633

THE FUNERAL

Whoever comes to shroud me, do not harm
     Nor question much
That subtle wreath of hair, which crowns my arm,
The mystery, the sign you must not touch;
     For 'tis my outward soul,
Viceroy to that which, then to heaven being gone,
     Will leave this to control
And keep these limbs, her provinces, from dissolution.

For if the sinewy thread my brain lets fall
     Through every part   10
Can tie those parts, and make me one of all,
These hairs which upward grew, and strength and art
     Have from a better brain,
Can better do't; except she meant that I
     By this should know my pain,
As prisoners then are manacled when they're condemned to
  die.

What'er she meant by't, bury it with me,
>> For since I am
Love's martyr, it might breed idolatry
If into others' hands these relics came;
>> As 'twas humility
To afford to it all that a soul can do,
>> So 'tis some bravery
That since you would save none of me I bury some of you.

Composed before 1615   First published 1633

THE GOOD-MORROW

I wonder, by my troth, what thou and I
>> Did till we loved? were we not weaned till then,
But sucked on country pleasures, childishly?
>> Or snorted we in the seven sleepers' den?
'Twas so; but this, all pleasures fancies be.
If ever any beauty I did see,
Which I desired, and got, 'twas but a dream of thee.

And now good-morrow to our waking souls,
>> Which watch not one another out of fear;
For love all love of other sights controls,
>> And makes one little room an everywhere.
Let sea-discoverers to new worlds have gone,
Let maps to others worlds on worlds have shown,
Let us possess one world, each hath one, and is one.

My face in thine eye, thine in mine appears,
>> And true plain hearts do in the faces rest;
Where can we find two better hemispheres
>> Without sharp north, without declining west?
Whatever dies, was not mixed equally;
If our two loves be one, or thou and I
Love so alike that none do slacken, none can die.

Composed before 1615   First published 1633

42

THE INDIFFERENT

I can love both fair and brown,
Her whom abundance melts, and her whom want betrays,
Her who loves loneness best, and her who masques and plays,
Her whom the country formed, and whom the town,
Her who believes, and her who tries,
Her who still weeps with spongy eyes,
And her who is dry cork and never cries;
I can love her and her, and you and you;
I can love any, so she be not true.

Will no other vice content you?   10
Will it not serve your turn to do as did your mothers?
Have you old vices spent, and now would find out others?
Or doth a fear that men are true torment you?
Oh we are not, be not you so,
Let me, and do you, twenty know.
Rob me, but bind me not, and let me go.
Must I, who came to travel thorough you,
Grow your fixed subject because you are true?

Venus heard me sigh this song,
And by love's sweetest part, variety, she swore   20
She heard not this till now; it should be so no more.
She went, examined, and returned ere long,
And said, 'Alas, some two or three
Poor heretics in love there be,
Which think to stablish dangerous constancy.
But I have told them, "Since you will be true,
You shall be true to them, who're false to you."'

Composed before 1615   First published 1633

43

A LECTURE UPON THE SHADOW

Stand still, and I will read to thee
A lecture, love, in love's philosophy.
    These three hours that we have spent
    Walking here, two shadows went
Along with us, which we ourselves produced;
But now the sun is just above our head
    We do those shadows tread,
    And to brave clearness all things are reduced.
  So whilst our infant loves did grow,
  Disguises did, and shadows, flow   10
  From us and our care; but now 'tis not so.

That love hath not attained the high'st degree,
Which is still diligent lest others see.

Except our loves at this noon stay,
We shall new shadows make the other way.
    As the first were made to blind
    Others, these which come behind
Will work upon ourselves, and blind our eyes.
If our loves faint, and westwardly decline,
    To me thou, falsely, thine,   20
    And I to thee mine actions shall disguise.
  The morning shadows wear away,
  But these grow longer all the day,
  But oh, love's day is short, if love decay.

Love is a growing or full constant light,
And his first minute after noon is night.

Composed before 1615   *First published 1635*

44

THE LEGACY

When I died last (and, dear, I die
  As often as from thee I go),
  Though it be an hour ago,
And lovers' hours be full eternity,
I can remember yet that I
  Something did say, and something did bestow;
Though I be dead which sent me, I should be
Mine own executor and legacy.

I heard me say, 'Tell her anon,
  That my self' (that's you, not I)   10
  'Did kill me,' and when I felt me die,
I bid me send my heart, when I was gone;
But I alas could there find none,
  When I had ripped me, and searched where hearts should
    lie;
It killed me again, that I, who still was true
In life, in my last will should cozen you.

Yet I found something like a heart,
  But colours it and corners had;
  It was not good, it was not bad;
It was entire to none, and few had part.   20
As good as could be made by art
  It seemed; and therefore, for our losses sad,
I meant to send this heart instead of mine,
But oh, no man could hold it, for 'twas thine.

Composed before 1615   First published 1633

LOVERS' INFINITENESS

If yet I have not all thy love,
Dear, I shall never have it all;
I cannot breathe one other sigh, to move,
Nor can entreat one other tear to fall;

All my treasure, which should purchase thee,
Sighs, tears, and oaths, and letters, I have spent;
Yet no more can be due to me,
Than at the bargain made was meant.
If then thy gift of love were partial,
That some to me, some should to others fall, 10
   Dear, I shall never have thee all.

Or if then thou gav'st me all,
All was but all which thou hadst then;
But if in thy heart, since, there be or shall
New love created be by other men,
Which have their stocks entire, and can in tears,
In sighs, in oaths, and letters, outbid me,
This new love may beget new fears,
For this love was not vowed by thee.
And yet it was, thy gift being general; 20
The ground, thy heart, is mine; whatever shall
   Grow there, dear, I should have it all.

Yet I would not have all yet,
He that hath all can have no more,
And since my love doth every day admit
New growth, thou shouldst have new rewards in store.
Thou canst not every day give me thy heart:
If thou canst give it, then thou never gav'st it.
Love's riddles are that though thy heart depart
It stays at home, and thou with losing sav'st it; 30
But we will have a way more liberal
Than changing hearts, to join them; so we shall
   Be one, and one another's all.

Composed before 1612   *First published 1633*

LOVE'S ALCHEMY

Some that have deeper digged love's mine than I,
Say where his centric happiness doth lie.
    I have loved, and got, and told,
But should I love, get, tell, till I were old,
I should not find that hidden mystery;
    Oh, 'tis imposture all.
And as no chemic yet the elixir got,
    But glorifies his pregnant pot
    If by the way to him befall
Some odoriferous thing, or med'cinal,   10
  So lovers dream a rich and long delight,
  But get a winter-seeming summer's night.

Our ease, our thrift, our honour, and our day,
Shall we for this vain bubble's shadow pay?
    Ends love in this, that any man
Can be as happy as I can, if he can
Endure the short scorn of a bridegroom's play?
    That loving wretch that swears
'Tis not the bodies marry, but the minds,
    Which he in her angelic finds,   20
    Would swear as justly that he hears
In that day's rude hoarse minstrelsy the spheres.
  Hope not for mind in women; at their best
  Sweetness and wit, they're but mummy, possessed.

Composed before 1615   *First published 1633*

LOVE'S DEITY

I long to talk with some old lover's ghost
  Who died before the god of love was born:
I cannot think that he who then loved most
  Sunk so low as to love one which did scorn.
But since this god produced a destiny,

47

And that vice-nature custom lets it be,
    I must love her that loves not me.

Sure, they which made him god meant not so much,
    Nor he in his young godhead practised it,
But when an even flame two hearts did touch,   10
    His office was indulgently to fit
Actives to passives. Correspondency
Only his subject was; it cannot be
    Love, till I love her that loves me.

But every modern god will now extend
    His vast prerogative as far as Jove.
To rage, to lust, to write to, to commend,
    All is the purlieu of the god of love.
O, were we wakened by this tyranny
To ungod this child again, it could not be   20
    I should love her who loves not me.

Rebel and atheist too, why murmur I,
    As though I felt the worst that love could do?
Love might make me leave loving, or might try
    A deeper plague, to make her love me too,
Which, since she loves before, I'm loath to see;
Falsehood is worse than hate; and that must be,
    If she whom I love should love me.

Composed before 1615   First published 1633

LOVE'S DIET

To what a cumbersome unwieldiness
And burdenous corpulence my love had grown,
    But that I did, to make it less,
    And keep it in proportion,
Give it a diet, made it feed upon
That which love worst endures, discretion.

48

Above one sigh a day I allowed him not,
Of which my fortune and my faults had part;
 And if sometimes by stealth he got
 A she-sigh from my mistress' heart,
And thought to feast on that, I let him see
'Twas neither very sound, nor meant to me.

If he wrung from me a tear, I brined it so
With scorn or shame, that him it nourished not;
 If he sucked hers, I let him know
 'Twas not a tear which he had got;
His drink was counterfeit, as was his meat;
For eyes which roll towards all weep not, but sweat.

Whatever he would dictate, I writ that,
But burnt my letters; when she writ to me,
 And that that favour made him fat,
 I said, 'If any title be
Conveyed by this, ah, what doth it avail,
To be the fortieth name in an entail?'

Thus I reclaimed my buzzard love, to fly
At what, and when, and how, and where I choose;
 Now negligent of sport I lie,
 And now, as other falconers use,
I spring a mistress, swear, write, sigh and weep,
And, the game killed or lost, go talk and sleep.

Composed before 1615 First published 1633

LOVE'S EXCHANGE

 Love, any devil else but you,
Would for a given soul give something too.
 At court your fellows every day
Give th' art of rhyming, huntsmanship, and play,
 For them who were their own before;

49

Only I have nothing which gave more,
But am, alas, by being lowly, lower.

I ask not dispensation now
To falsify a tear, or sigh, or vow;
    I do not sue from thee to draw   10
A *non obstante* on nature's law;
    These are prerogatives, they inhere
    In thee and thine; none should forswear
Except that he Love's minion were.

Give me thy weakness, make me blind
Both ways, as thou and thine, in eyes and mind;
    Love, let me never know that this
Is love, or that love childish is.
    Let me not know that others know
    That she knows my pain, lest that so   20
A tender shame make me mine own new woe.

If thou give nothing, yet thou'rt just,
Because I would not thy first motions trust;
    Small towns which stand stiff till great shot
Enforce them, by war's law condition not.
    Such in love's warfare is my case,
    I may not article for grace,
Having put Love at last to show this face.

This face by which he could command
And change the idolatry of any land,   30
    This face which wheresoe'er it comes
Can call vowed men from cloisters, dead from tombs,
    And melt both poles at once, and store
    Deserts with cities, and make more
Mines in the earth, than quarries were before.

For this Love is enraged with me,
Yet kills not. If I must example be

To future rebels, if th' unborn
Must learn by my being cut up and torn,
   Kill and dissect me, Love, for this   40
   Torture against thine own end is:
Racked carcasses make ill anatomies.

Composed before 1615   First published 1633

LOVE'S GROWTH

I scarce believe my love to be so pure
   As I had thought it was,
   Because it doth endure
Vicissitude and season, as the grass;
Methinks I lied all winter, when I swore
My love was infinite, if spring make it more.
But if this medicine love, which cures all sorrow
With more, not only be no quintessence,
But mixed of all stuffs paining soul or sense,
And of the sun his working vigour borrow,   10
Love's not so pure and abstract as they use
To say which have no mistress but their Muse,
But as all else, being elemented too,
Love sometimes would contemplate, sometimes do.

And yet not greater, but more eminent,
   Love by the spring is grown;
   As, in the firmament,
Stars by the sun are not enlarged, but shown.
Gentle love-deeds, as blossoms on a bough,
From love's awakened root do bud out now.   20
If, as in water stirred more circles be
Produced by one, love such additions take,
Those, like so many spheres, but one heaven make,
For they are all concentric unto thee;
And though each spring do add to love new heat,

As princes do in times of action get
New taxes, and remit them not in peace,
No winter shall abate the spring's increase.

Composed before 1615   First published 1633

LOVE'S USURY

For every hour that thou wilt spare me now,
    I will allow,
Usurious God of Love, twenty to thee,
When with my brown my grey hairs equal be;
Till then, Love, let my body reign, and let
Me travel, sojourn, snatch, plot, have, forget,
Resume my last year's relict, think that yet
    We'd never met.

Let me think any rival's letter mine,
    And at next nine   10
Keep midnight's promise; mistake by the way
The maid, and tell the lady of that delay;
Only let me love none, no, not the sport;
From country grass to comfitures of court
Or city's *quelque-choses*, let report
    My mind transport.

This bargain's good; if when I'm old, I be
    Inflamed by thee,
If thine own honour, or my shame, or pain,
Thou covet, most at that age thou shalt gain.   20
Do thy will then, then subject and degree
And fruit of love, Love, I submit to thee;
Spare me till then, I'll bear it, though she be
    One that loves me.

Composed before 1615   First published 1633

THE MESSAGE

Send home my long-strayed eyes to me,
Which, O, too long have dwelt on thee.
Yet since there they've learned such ill,
    Such forced fashions
    And false passions
      That they be
      Made by thee
Fit for no good sight, keep them still.

Send home my harmless heart again,
Which no unworthy thought could stain.   10
But if it be taught by thine
    To make jestings
    Of protestings,
      And cross both
      Word and oath,
Keep it, for then 'tis none of mine.

Yet send me back my heart and eyes,
That I may know and see thy lies,
And may laugh and joy when thou
    Art in anguish   20
    And dost languish
      For some one
      That will none,
Or prove as false as thou art now.

Composed before 1615   *First published 1633*

NEGATIVE LOVE

I never stooped so low as they
Which on an eye, cheek, lip, can prey;
  Seldom to them which soar no higher
  Than virtue or the mind to admire;

For sense and understanding may
  Know what gives fuel to their fire.
My love, though silly, is more brave,
For may I miss whene'er I crave,
If I know yet what I would have.

If that be simply perfectest   10
Which can by no way be expressed
  But negatives, my love is so.
  To all which all love I say no.
If any who decipher best
  What we know not, ourselves, can know,
Let him teach me that nothing; this
As yet my ease and comfort is,
Though I speed not, I cannot miss.

Composed before 1615   First published 1633

A NOCTURNAL UPON ST LUCY'S DAY, BEING THE SHORTEST DAY

'Tis the year's midnight, and it is the day's,
Lucy's, who scarce seven hours herself unmasks;
  The sun is spent, and now his flasks
  Send forth light squibs, no constant rays;
    The world's whole sap is sunk:
The general balm th' hydroptic earth hath drunk,
Whither, as to the bed's-feet, life is shrunk,
Dead and interred; yet all these seem to laugh,
Compared with me, who am their epitaph.

Study me then, you who shall lovers be   10
At the next world, that is, at the next spring:
  For I am every dead thing
  In whom Love wrought new alchemy.
    For his art did express
A quintessence even from nothingness,

From dull privations, and lean emptiness;
He ruined me, and I am re-begot
Of absence, darkness, death; things which are not.

All others from all things draw all that's good,
Life, soul, form, spirit, whence they being have;   20
 I, by love's limbeck, am the grave
 Of all that's nothing. Oft a flood
  Have we two wept, and so
Drowned the whole world, us two; oft did we grow
To be two chaoses, when we did show
Care to aught else; and often absences
Withdrew our souls, and made us carcasses.

But I am by her death (which word wrongs her)
Of the first nothing the elixir grown;
 Were I a man, that I were one   30
 I needs must know; I should prefer,
  If I were any beast,
Some ends, some means; yea plants, yea stones detest,
And love; all, all some properties invest;
If I an ordinary nothing were,
As shadow, a light and body must be here.

But I am none; nor will my sun renew.
You lovers, for whose sake the lesser sun
 At this time to the Goat is run
 To fetch new lust, and give it you,   40
  Enjoy your summer all;
Since she enjoys her long night's festival,
Let me prepare towards her, and let me call
This hour her vigil and her eve, since this
Both the year's and the day's deep midnight is.

Composed probably before 1615 First published 1633

THE PARADOX

No lover saith 'I love', nor any other
 Can judge a perfect lover;
He thinks that else none can, nor will agree
 That any loves but he:
I cannot say I loved, for who can say
 He was killed yesterday?
Love with excess of heat, more young than old,
 Death kills with too much cold;
We die but once, and who loved last did die,
 He that saith twice, doth lie: 10
For though he seem to move and stir a while,
 It doth the sense beguile.
Such life is like the light which bideth yet
 When the light's life is set,
Or like the heat which fire in solid matter
 Leaves behind two hours after.
Once I loved and died; and am now become
 Mine epitaph and tomb.
Here dead men speak their last, and so do I;
 Love-slain, lo, here I lie.   20

Composed before 1615 First published 1633

THE PRIMROSE

 Upon this primrose hill,
 Where, if heaven would distil
A shower of rain, each several drop might go
To his own primrose, and grow manna so,
And where their form and their infinity
 Make a terrestrial galaxy,
 As the small stars do in the sky,
I walk to find a true-love; and I see
That 'tis not a mere woman that is she,
But must or more or less than woman be.   10

Yet know I not which flower
I wish; a six, or four.
For should my true-love less than woman be,
She were scarce anything; and then, should she
Be more than woman, she would get above
All thought of sex, and think to move
My heart to study her, and not to love.
Both these were monsters; since there must reside
Falsehood in woman, I could more abide
She were by art than nature falsified. 20

Live, primrose, then, and thrive
With thy true number, five;
And women, whom this flower doth represent,
With this mysterious number be content.
Ten is the farthest number; if half ten
Belong unto each woman, then
Each woman may take half us men;
Or if this will not serve their turn, since all
Numbers are odd or even, and they fall
First into this, five, women may take us all. 30

Composed before 1615   First published 1633

THE PROHIBITION

Take heed of loving me;
At least remember I forbade it thee;
Not that I shall repair my unthrifty waste
Of breath and blood upon thy sighs and tears
By being to thee then what to me thou wast;
But so great joy our life at once outwears.
Then lest thy love by my death frustrate be,
If thou love me, take heed of loving me.

Take heed of hating me,
Or too much triumph in the victory; 10

57

Not that I shall be mine own officer,
And hate with hate again retaliate;
  But thou wilt lose the style of conqueror
If I, thy conquest, perish by thy hate.
  Then lest my being nothing lessen thee,
  If thou hate me, take heed of hating me.

    Yet love and hate me too;
So these extremes shall neither's office do;
  Love me, that I may die the gentler way;
Hate me, because thy love's too great for me;   20
  Or let these two themselves, not me, decay;
So shall I live thy stay, not triumph be.
  Lest thou thy love and hate and me undo,
  To let me live, O, love and hate me too.

Composed before 1615   First published 1633

                    THE RELIC

    When my grave is broke up again
    Some second guest to entertain
    (For graves have learned that womanhead
    To be to more than one a bed),
        And he that digs it spies
A bracelet of bright hair about the bone,
        Will he not let's alone,
And think that there a loving couple lies,
Who thought that this device might be some way
To make their souls, at the last busy day,   10
Meet at this grave, and make a little stay?

    If this fall in a time or land
    Where mis-devotion doth command,
    Then he that digs us up will bring
    Us to the bishop and the king,
        To make us relics; then

58

Thou shalt be a Mary Magdalen, and I
    A something else thereby;
All women shall adore us, and some men;
And since at such time miracles are sought,   20
I would have that age by this paper taught
What miracles we harmless lovers wrought.

    First, we loved well and faithfully,
    Yet knew not what we loved, nor why.
    Difference of sex no more we knew,
    Than our guardian angels do.
        Coming and going, we
Perchance might kiss, but not between those meals.
        Our hands ne'er touched the seals
Which nature, injured by late law, sets free.   30
These miracles we did; but now, alas,
All measure and all language I should pass,
Should I tell what a miracle she was.

Composed before 1615   First published 1633

SONG

Go and catch a falling star,
  Get with child a mandrake root,
Tell me where all past years are,
  Or who cleft the Devil's foot,
Teach me to hear mermaids singing,
Or to keep off envy's stinging,
     And find
     What wind
Serves to advance an honest mind.

If thou be'st borne to strange sights,   10
  Things invisible to see,
Ride ten thousand days and nights,
  Till age snow white hairs on thee;

Thou, when thou return'st, wilt tell me
All strange wonders that befell thee,
    And swear
    Nowhere
Lives a woman true and fair.

If thou find'st one, let me know;
  Such a pilgrimage were sweet.   20
Yet do not, I would not go,
  Though at next door we might meet.
Though she were true when you met her,
And last till you write your letter,
    Yet she
    Will be
False, ere I come, to two or three.

Composed before 1615   First published 1633

SONG

Sweetest love, I do not go
  For weariness of thee,
Nor in hope the world can show
  A fitter love for me;
    But since that I
Must die at last, 'tis best
To use my self in jest
  Thus by feigned deaths to die.

Yesternight the sun went hence,
  And yet is here today;   10
He hath no desire nor sense,
  Nor half so short a way;
    Then fear not me,
But believe that I shall make
Speedier journeys, since I take
  More wings and spurs than he.

O how feeble is man's power,
  That if good fortune fall,
Cannot add another hour,
  Nor a lost hour recall!
    But come bad chance,
And we join to it our strength,
And we teach it art and length,
  Itself o'er us t'advance.

When thou sigh'st, thou sigh'st not wind,
  But sigh'st my soul away,
When thou weep'st, unkindly kind,
  My life's blood doth decay.
    It cannot be
That thou lov'st me, as thou say'st,
If in thine my life thou waste:
  Thou art the best of me.

Let not thy divining heart
  Forethink me any ill;
Destiny may take thy part,
  And may thy fears fulfil.
    But think that we
Are but turned aside to sleep;
They who one another keep
  Alive ne'er parted be.

Composed before 1615   First published 1633

THE SUN RISING

  Busy old fool, unruly sun,
    Why dost thou thus
Through windows and through curtains call on us?
Must to thy motions lovers' seasons run?
    Saucy pedantic wretch, go chide
    Late schoolboys and sour prentices;

Go tell court-huntsmen that the king will ride;
    Call country ants to harvest offices;
Love, all alike, no season knows nor clime,
Nor hours, days, months, which are the rags of time.   10

    Thy beams so reverend and strong
        Why shouldst thou think?
I could eclipse and cloud them with a wink,
But that I would not lose her sight so long.
        If her eyes have not blinded thine,
        Look, and tomorrow late, tell me,
    Whether both th' Indias, of spice and mine,
    Be where thou left'st them, or lie here with me.
Ask for those kings whom thou saw'st yesterday,
And thou shalt hear, all here in one bed lay.   20

    She's all states, and all princes I;
        Nothing else is.
Princes do but play us; compared to this,
All honour's mimic, all wealth alchemy.
        Thou, sun, art half as happy as we,
        In that the world's contracted thus;
    Thine age asks ease, and since thy duties be
    To warm the world, that's done in warming us.
Shine here to us, and thou art everywhere;
This bed thy centre is, these walls thy sphere.   30

Composed 1603–15   First published 1633

TWICKENHAM GARDEN

Blasted with sighs and surrounded with tears,
    Hither I come to seek the spring,
    And at mine eyes and at mine ears
Receive such balms as else cure everything;
    But O, self-traitor, I do bring
The spider love, which transubstantiates all,

62

And can convert manna to gall,
And that this place may thoroughly be thought
   True paradise, I have the serpent brought.

'Twere wholesomer for me that winter did   10
   Benight the glory of this place,
   And that a grave frost did forbid
These trees to laugh and mock me to my face;
   But that I may not this disgrace
Endure, nor yet leave loving, Love, let me
   Some senseless piece of this place be:
Make me a mandrake, so I may groan here,
   Or a stone fountain weeping out my year.

Hither with crystal vials, lovers, come,
   And take my tears, which are love's wine,   20
   And try your mistress' tears at home,
For all are false that taste not just like mine;
   Alas, hearts do not in eyes shine,
Nor can you more judge woman's thoughts by tears
   Than by her shadow what she wears.
O perverse sex, where none is true but she,
   Who's therefore true, because her truth kills me.

Composed 1607–15   First published 1633

THE UNDERTAKING

I have done one braver thing
   Than all the Worthies did,
And yet a braver thence doth spring,
   Which is, to keep that hid.

It were but madness now t' impart
   The skill of specular stone,
When he which can have learned the art
   To cut it can find none.

So if I now should utter this,
  Others (because no more
Such stuff to work upon there is)
  Would love but as before.

But he who loveliness within
  Hath found all outward loathes,
For he who colour loves, and skin,
  Loves but her oldest clothes.

If, as I have, you also do
  Virtue attired in woman see,
And dare love that, and say so too,
  And forget the He and She;

And if this love, though placèd so,
  From profane men you hide,
Which will no faith on this bestow,
  Or, if they do, deride:

Then you have done a braver thing
  Than all the Worthies did,
And a braver thence will spring,
  Which is, to keep that hid.

10

20

Composed 1599–1615   First published 1633

A VALEDICTION: FORBIDDING
MOURNING

As virtuous men pass mildly away,
  And whisper to their souls to go,
Whilst some of their sad friends do say,
  The breath goes now, and some say, no,

So let us melt, and make no noise,
    No tear-floods nor sigh-tempests move;
'Twere profanation of our joys
    To tell the laity our love.

Moving of th' earth brings harms and fears,
    Men reckon what it did and meant,   10
But trepidation of the spheres,
    Though greater far, is innocent.

Dull sublunary lovers' love
    (Whose soul is sense) cannot admit
Absence, because it doth remove
    Those things which elemented it.

But we, by a love so much refined
    That ourselves know not what it is
Inter-assurèd of the mind,
    Care less eyes, lips, and hands to miss.   20

Our two souls, therefore, which are one,
    Though I must go, endure not yet
A breach, but an expansion,
    Like gold to airy thinness beat.

If they be two, they are two so
    As stiff twin compasses are two;
Thy soul, the fixed foot, makes no show
    To move, but doth, if th' other do.

And though it in the centre sit,
    Yet when the other far doth roam,   30
It leans and hearkens after it,
    And grows erect as that comes home.

Such wilt thou be to me, who must
    Like th' other foot obliquely run;

Thy firmness makes my circle just,
   And makes me end where I begun.

Composed before 1615   *First published 1633*

A VALEDICTION: OF WEEPING

     Let me pour forth
My tears before thy face, whilst I stay here,
For thy face coins them, and thy stamp they bear,
And by this mintage they are something worth,
     For thus they be
     Pregnant of thee;
Fruits of much grief they are, emblems of more;
When a tear falls, that thou falls which it bore;
So thou and I are nothing then, when on a diverse shore.

     On a round ball   10
A workman that hath copies by can lay
An Europe, Afric, and an Asia,
And quickly make that which was nothing all;
     So doth each tear,
     Which thee doth wear,
A globe, yea world, by that impression grow,
Till thy tears mixed with mine do overflow
This world, by waters sent from thee, my heaven dissolvèd
   so.

     O more than moon,
Draw not up seas to drown me in thy sphere,   20
Weep me not dead in thine arms, but forbear
To teach the sea what it may do too soon;
     Let not the wind
     Example find
To do me more harm than it purposeth;

66

Since thou and I sigh one another's breath,
Whoe'er sighs most is cruellest, and hastes the other's death.

Composed before 1615   First published 1633

THE WILL

Before I sigh my last gasp, let me breathe,
Great Love, some legacies; here I bequeath
Mine eyes to Argus, if mine eyes can see;
If they be blind, then, Love, I give them thee;
My tongue to Fame; to ambassadors mine ears;
    To women or the sea my tears.
Thou, Love, hast taught me heretofore,
  By making me serve her who had twenty more,
That I should give to none but such as had too much before.

My constancy I to the planets give;   10
My truth to them who at the court do live;
Mine ingenuity and openness
To Jesuits; to buffoons my pensiveness;
My silence to any who abroad hath been;
    My money to a Capuchin.
Thou, Love, taught'st me, by appointing me
  To love there where no love received can be,
Only to give to such as have an incapacity.

My faith I give to Roman Catholics;
All my good works unto the schismatics   20
Of Amsterdam; my best civility
And courtship to an university;
My modesty I give to soldiers bare;
    My patience let gamesters share.
Thou, Love, taught'st me, by making me
  Love her that holds my love disparity,
Only to give to those that count my gifts indignity.

I give my reputation to those
Which were my friends; mine industry to foes;
To schoolmen I bequeath my doubtfulness;   30
My sickness to physicians, or excess;
To Nature, all that I in rhyme have writ;
    And to my company my wit.
Thou, Love, by making me adore
Her who begot this love in me before,
Taught'st me to make as though I gave, when I did but
restore.

To him for whom the passing bell next tolls,
I give my physic books; my written rolls
Of moral counsels I to Bedlam give;
My brazen medals unto them which live   40
In want of bread; to them which pass among
    All foreigners mine English tongue.
Thou, Love, by making me love one
Who thinks her friendship a fit portion
For younger lovers, dost my gifts thus disproportion.

Therefore I'll give no more; but I'll undo
The world by dying; because Love dies too.
Then all your beauties will be no more worth
Than gold in mines, where none doth draw it forth;
And all your graces no more use shall have   50
    Than a sundial in a grave.
Thou, Love, taught'st me, by making me
Love her who doth neglect both me and thee,
T' invent and practise this one way t' annihilate all three.

Composed before 1615   *First published 1633*

WOMAN'S CONSTANCY

Now thou hast loved me one whole day,
Tomorrow, when thou leav'st, what wilt thou say?
Wilt thou then antedate some new-made vow?
    Or say that now
We are not just those persons which we were?
Or that oaths made in reverential fear
Of Love, and his wrath, any may forswear?
Or as true deaths true marriages untie,
So lovers' contracts, images of those,
Bind but till sleep, death's image, them unloose?   10
    Or, your own end to justify,
For having purposed change and falsehood, you
Can have no way but falsehood to be true?
Vain lunatic, against these 'scapes I could
    Dispute, and conquer, if I would,
    Which I abstain to do,
For by tomorrow I may think so too.

Composed before 1615   First published 1633

Elegies

ELEGY 1 JEALOUSY

Fond woman, which wouldst have thy husband die,
And yet complain'st of his great jealousy;
If swoll'n with poison he lay in his last bed,
His body with a sere-bark coverèd,
Drawing his breath as thick and short as can
The nimblest crotcheting musician,
Ready with loathsome vomiting to spew
His soul out of one hell into a new,
Made deaf with his poor kindred's howling cries,
Begging with few feigned tears great legacies,   10
Thou wouldst not weep, but jolly and frolic be
As a slave which tomorrow should be free;
Yet weep'st thou when thou seest him hungerly
Swallow his own death, heart's-bane jealousy.
O give him many thanks, he's courteous,
That in suspecting kindly warneth us.
We must not, as we used, flout openly,
In scoffing riddles, his deformity;
Nor at his board together being sat,
With words, nor touch, scarce looks adulterate;   20
Nor when he, swoll'n and pampered with great fare,

Sits down and snorts, caged in his basket chair,
Must we usurp his own bed any more,
Nor kiss and play in his house, as before.
Now I see many dangers; for that is
His realm, his castle, and his diocese.
But if, as envious men, which would revile
Their prince, or coin his gold, themselves exile
Into another country, and do it there,
We play in another house, what should we fear?   30
There we will scorn his household policies,
His silly plots, and pensionary spies,
As the inhabitants of Thames' right side
Do London's Mayor; or Germans, the Pope's pride.

Composed 1593–6?   *First published 1633*

ELEGY 2   THE ANAGRAM

Marry and love thy Flavia, for she
Hath all things whereby others beauteous be;
For, though her eyes be small, her mouth is great;
Though they be ivory, yet her teeth are jet;
Though they be dim, yet she is light enough;
And though her harsh hair fall, her skin is rough;
What though her cheeks be yellow, her hair's red;
Give her thine, and she hath a maidenhead.
These things are beauty's elements; where these
Meet in one, that one must, as perfect, please.   10
If red and white and each good quality
Be in thy wench, ne'er ask where it doth lie.
In buying things perfumed, we ask if there
Be musk and amber in it, but not where.
Though all her parts be not in th' usual place,
She hath yet an anagram of a good face.
If we might put the letters but one way,

In the lean dearth of words, what could we say?
When by the gamut some musicians make
A perfect song, others will undertake,   20
By the same gamut changed, to equal it.
Things simply good can never be unfit.
She's fair as any, if all be like her,
And if none be, then she is singular.
All love is wonder; if we justly do
Account her wonderful, why not lovely too?
Love built on beauty soon as beauty dies;
Choose this face, changed by no deformities.
Women are all like angels; the fair be
Like those which fell to worse; but such as she,   30
Like to good angels, nothing can impair:
'Tis less grief to be foul, than to have been fair.
For one night's revels silk and gold we choose,
But in long journeys cloth and leather use.
Beauty is barren oft; best husbands say
There is best land where there is foulest way.
O, what a sovereign plaster will she be,
If thy past sins have taught thee jealousy!
Here needs no spies, nor eunuchs; her commit
Safe to thy foes; yea, to a marmoset.   40
When Belgia's cities the round countries drown,
That dirty foulness guards and arms the town:
So doth her face guard her; and so, for thee,
Which, forced by business, absent oft must be,
She whose face, like clouds, turns the day to night,
Who, mightier than the sea, makes Moors seem white,
Who, though seven years she in the stews had laid,
A nunnery durst receive, and think a maid,
And though in childbirth's labour she did lie
Midwives would swear 'twere but a tympany,   50
Whom, if she accuse herself, I credit less
Than witches, which impossibles confess,
Whom dildoes, bedstaves, and her velvet glass
Would be as loath to touch as Joseph was,

One like none, and liked of none, fittest were,
For things in fashion every man will wear.

Composed 1593–6?   First published 1633

ELEGY 3   CHANGE

Although thy hand and faith, and good works too,
Have sealed thy love which nothing should undo,
Yea though thou fall back, that apostasy
Confirm thy love; yet much, much I fear thee.
Women are like the arts, forced unto none,
Open to all searchers, unprized if unknown.
If I have caught a bird, and let him fly,
Another fowler using these means, as I,
May catch the same bird; and, as these things be,
Women are made for men, not him, nor me.   10
Foxes and goats, all beasts change when they please;
Shall women, more hot, wily, wild than these,
Be bound to one man, and did Nature then
Idly make them apter t' endure than men?
They're our clogs, not their own; if a man be
Chained to a galley, yet the galley's free;
Who hath a plough-land casts all his seed corn there,
And yet allows his ground more corn should bear;
Though Danuby into the sea must flow,
The sea receives the Rhine, Volga, and Po.   20
By nature, which gave it, this liberty
Thou lov'st, but O, canst thou love it and me?
Likeness glues love: then, if so thou do,
To make us like and love, must I change too?
More than thy hate I hate it; rather let me
Allow her change, than change as oft as she,
And so not teach but force my opinion
To love not any one, nor every one.
To live in one land is captivity;
To run all countries, a wild roguery;   30

73

Waters stink soon if in one place they bide,
And in the vast sea are worse putrefied:
But when they kiss one bank and, leaving this,
Never look back, but the next bank do kiss,
Then are they purest; change is the nursery
Of music, joy, life and eternity.

Composed 1593–6?   First published 1633

ELEGY 4   THE PERFUME

Once, and but once, found in thy company,
All thy supposed escapes are laid on me;
And as a thief at bar is questioned there
By all the men that have been robbed that year,
So am I (by this traitorous means surprised)
By thy hydroptic father catechized.
Though he had wont to search with glazèd eyes,
As though he came to kill a cockatrice,
Though he have oft sworn that he would remove
Thy beauty's beauty and food of our love,   10
Hope of his goods, if I with thee were seen,
Yet close and secret as our souls we've been.
Though thy immortal mother which doth lie
Still buried in her bed, yet will not die,
Takes this advantage to sleep out daylight,
And watch thy entries and returns all night,
And when she takes thy hand, and would seem kind,
Doth search what rings and armlets she can find,
And kissing notes the colour of thy face,
And fearing lest thou'rt swoll'n, doth thee embrace;   20
To try if thou long, doth name strange meats,
And notes thy paleness, blushings, sighs, and sweats;
And politicly will to thee confess
The sins of her own youth's rank lustiness;
Yet love these sorceries did remove, and move
Thee to gull thine own mother for my love.

Thy little brethren, which like fairy sprites
Oft skipped into our chamber, those sweet nights,
And, kissed and ingled on thy father's knee,
Were bribed next day to tell what they did see: 30
The grim eight-foot-high iron-bound serving-man,
That oft names God in oaths, and only then,
He that to bar the first gate doth as wide
As the great Rhodian Colossus stride,
Which, if in hell no other pains there were,
Makes me fear hell, because he must be there:
Though by thy father he were hired to this,
Could never witness any touch or kiss.
But O, too common ill, I brought with me
That which betrayed me to mine enemy –   40
A loud perfume, which at my entrance cried
Even at thy father's nose; so we were spied.
When, like a tyrant king that in his bed
Smelt gunpowder, the pale wretch shiverèd,
Had it been some bad smell, he would have thought
That his own feet or breath that smell had wrought.
But as we, in our isle imprisonèd,
Where cattle only and diverse dogs are bred,
The precious unicorns strange monsters call,
So thought he good strange, that had none at all.   50
I taught my silks their whistling to forbear,
Even my oppressed shoes dumb and speechless were;
Only thou bitter sweet, whom I had laid
Next me, me traitorously hast betrayed,
And unsuspected hast invisibly
At once fled unto him, and stayed with me.
Base excrement of earth, which dost confound
Sense from distinguishing the sick from sound;
By thee the silly amorous sucks his death
By drawing in a leprous harlot's breath;   60
By thee the greatest stain to man's estate
Falls on us, to be called effeminate;
Though you be much loved in the prince's hall,

There things that seem exceed substantial.
Gods, when ye fumed on altars, were pleased well,
Because you were burnt, not that they liked your smell;
You're loathsome all, being taken simply alone;
Shall we love ill things joined, and hate each one?
If you were good, your good doth soon decay;
And you are rare, that takes the good away.   70
All my perfumes I give most willingly
T'embalm thy father's corse. What, will he die?

Composed 1593–6?   *First published 1633*

ELEGY 5 HIS PICTURE

Here, take my picture, though I bid farewell;
Thine in my heart, where my soul dwells, shall dwell.
'Tis like me now, but I dead, 'twill be more
When we are shadows both, than 'twas before.
When weather-beaten I come back, my hand
Perhaps with rude oars torn or sunbeams tanned,
My face and breast of haircloth, and my head
With care's rash sudden hoariness o'erspread,
My body a sack of bones, broken within,
And powder's blue stains scattered on my skin,   10
If rival fools tax thee to have loved a man
So foul and coarse as, O, I may seem then,
This shall say what I was: and thou shalt say,
'Do his hurts reach me? doth my worth decay?
Or do they reach his judging mind, that he
Should now love less what he did love to see?
That which in him was fair and delicate
Was but the milk which in love's childish state
Did nurse it: who now is grown strong enough
To feed on that, which to disused tastes seems tough.'   20

Composed 1596?   *First published 1633*

76

ELEGY 7

Nature's lay idiot, I taught thee to love,
And in that sophistry, O, thou dost prove
Too subtle. Fool, thou didst not understand
The mystic language of the eye nor hand;
Nor couldst thou judge the difference of the air
Of sighs, and say, 'this lies', 'this sounds despair';
Nor by th' eye's water call a malady
Desperately hot, or changing feverously.
I had not taught thee then the alphabet
Of flowers, how they devicefully being set   10
And bound up might with speechless secrecy
Deliver errands mutely and mutually.
Remember since all thy words used to be
To every suitor, 'Ay, if my friends agree';
Since household charms, thy husband's name to teach,
Were all the love-tricks that thy wit could reach;
And since an hour's discourse could scarce have made
One answer in thee, and that ill-arrayed
In broken proverbs and torn sentences.
Thou art not by so many duties his   20
That, from the world's common having severed thee,
Inlaid thee, neither to be seen nor see,
As mine, who have with amorous delicacies
Refined thee into a blissful paradise.
Thy graces and good works my creatures be;
I planted knowledge and life's tree in thee,
Which, O, shall strangers taste? Must I, alas,
Frame and enamel plate, and drink in glass?
Chafe wax for others' seals? break a colt's force,
And leave him then, being made a ready horse?   30

Composed 1593–6?   *First published 1633*

ELEGY 8   THE COMPARISON

As the sweet sweat of roses in a still,
As that which from chafed musk-cats' pores doth trill,
As the almighty balm of th' early east,
Such are the sweat-drops of my mistress' breast,
And on her neck her skin such lustre sets,
They seem no sweat-drops, but pearl carcanets.
Rank sweaty froth thy mistress' brow defiles,
Like spermatic issue of ripe menstruous boils,
Or like that scum which, by need's lawless law
Enforced, Sanserra's starvèd men did draw   10
From parboiled shoes, and boots, and all the rest
Which were with any sovereign fatness blessed,
And like vile lying stones in saffroned tin,
Or warts, or weals, they hang upon her skin.
Round as the world's her head, on every side,
Like to that fatal ball which fell on Ide,
Or that whereof God had such jealousy,
As for the ravishing thereof we die.
Thy head is like a rough-hewn statue of jet,
Where marks for eyes, nose, mouth, are yet scarce set;   20
Like the first Chaos, or flat-seeming face
Of Cynthia, when th' earth's shadows her embrace.
Like Proserpine's white beauty-keeping chest,
Or Jove's best fortune's urn, is her fair breast.
Thine's like worm-eaten trunks clothed in seal's skin,
Or grave that's dirt without and stink within.
And like that slender stalk, at whose end stands
The woodbine quivering, are her arms and hands.
Like rough-barked elm-boughs, or the russet skin
Of men late scourged for madness, or for sin,   30
Like sun-parched quarters on the city gate,
Such is thy tanned skin's lamentable state,
And like a bunch of ragged carrots stand
The short swoll'n fingers of thy gouty hand.
Then like the chemic's masculine equal fire,

Which in the limbeck's warm womb doth inspire
Into th' earth's worthless dirt a soul of gold,
Such cherishing heat her best-loved part doth hold.
Thine's like the dread mouth of a firèd gun,
Or like hot liquid metals newly run   40
Into clay moulds, or like to that Etna
Where round about the grass is burnt away.
Are not your kisses then as filthy, and more,
As a worm sucking an envenomed sore?
Doth not thy fearful hand in feeling quake,
As one which, gathering flowers, still fears a snake?
Is not your last act harsh and violent,
As when a plough a stony ground doth rent?
So kiss good turtles, so devoutly nice
Are priests in handling reverent sacrifice,   50
And such in searching wounds the surgeon is
As we, when we embrace, or touch, or kiss.
Leave her, and I will leave comparing thus;
She and comparisons are odious.

Composed 1593–6?   *First published 1633*

ELEGY 9   THE AUTUMNAL

No spring nor summer beauty hath such grace
As I have seen in one autumnal face.
Young beauties force your love, and that's a rape;
This doth but counsel, yet you cannot scape.
If 'twere a shame to love, here 'twere no shame;
Affection here takes reverence's name.
Were her first years the Golden Age, that's true,
But now she's gold oft tried, and ever new.
That was her torrid and inflaming time,
This is her tolerable tropic clime.   10
Fair eyes, who asks more heat than comes from hence,

79

He in a fever wishes pestilence.
Call not these wrinkles graves; if graves they were,
They were Love's graves, for else he is nowhere.
Yet lies not Love dead here, but here doth sit
Vowed to this trench, like an anachorit.
And here, till hers, which must be his death, come,
He doth not dig a grave, but build a tomb.
Here dwells he; though he sojourn everywhere
In progress, yet his standing house is here,   20
Here, where still evening is; not noon, nor night;
Where no voluptuousness, yet all delight.
In all her words, unto all hearers fit,
You may at revels, you at council, sit.
This is Love's timber, youth his underwood;
There he, as wine in June, enrages blood,
Which then comes seasonabliest, when our taste
And appetite to other things is past.
Xerxes' strange Lydian love, the platane tree,
Was loved for age, none being so large as she,   30
Or else because, being young, nature did bless
Her youth with age's glory, barrenness.
If we love things long sought, age is a thing
Which we are fifty years in compassing;
If transitory things, which soon decay,
Age must be loveliest at the latest day.
But name not winter-faces, whose skin's slack;
Lank as an unthrift's purse; but a soul's sack;
Whose eyes seek light within, for all here's shade;
Whose mouths are holes, rather worn out than made;   40
Whose every tooth to a several place is gone,
To vex their souls at resurrection;
Name not these living death's-heads unto me,
For these not ancient but antics be.
I hate extremes; yet I had rather stay
With tombs than cradles, to wear out a day.
Since such love's natural lation is, may still
My love descend and journey down the hill,

80

Not panting after growing beauties, so,
I shall ebb on with them who homeward go.   50

Composed 1593–9?   First published 1633

ELEGY 16   ON HIS MISTRESS

By our first strange and fatal interview,
By all desires which thereof did ensue,
By our long starving hopes, by that remorse
Which my words' masculine persuasive force
Begot in thee, and by the memory
Of hurts which spies and rivals threatened me,
I calmly beg; but by thy parents' wrath,
By all pains which want and divorcement hath,
I conjure thee; and all those oaths which I
And thou have sworn to seal joint constancy,   10
Here I unswear, and overswear them thus,
Thou shalt not love by means so dangerous.
Temper, O fair love, love's impetuous rage,
Be my true mistress still, not my feigned page.
I'll go, and, by thy kind leave, leave behind
Thee, only worthy to nurse in my mind
Thirst to come back; O, if thou die before,
From other lands my soul towards thee shall soar.
Thy else almighty beauty cannot move
Rage from the seas, nor thy love teach them love,   20
Nor tame wild Boreas' harshness; thou hast read
How roughly he in pieces shiverèd
Fair Orithea, whom he swore he loved.
Fall ill or good, 'tis madness to have proved
Dangers unurged; feed on this flattery,
That absent lovers one in th' other be.
Dissemble nothing, not a boy, nor change
Thy body's habit, nor mind's; be not strange
To thy self only; all will spy in thy face
A blushing womanly discovering grace;   30

81

Richly clothed apes are called apes, and as soon
Eclipsed as bright we call the moon the moon.
Men of France, changeable chameleons,
Spitals of diseases, shops of fashions,
Love's fuellers, and the rightest company
Of players which upon the world's stage be,
Will quickly know thee, and know thee; and, alas,
Th' indifferent Italian, as we pass
His warm land, well content to think thee page,
Will haunt thee with such lust and hideous rage   40
As Lot's fair guests were vexed. But none of these,
Nor spongy hydroptic Dutch, shall thee displease
If thou stay here. Oh stay here, for for thee
England is only a worthy gallery,
To walk in expectation, till from thence
Our great King call thee into his presence.
When I am gone, dream me some happiness,
Nor let thy looks our long-hid love confess,
Nor praise nor dispraise me, nor bless nor curse
Openly love's force, nor in bed fright thy nurse   50
With midnight's startings, crying out, 'Oh, oh,
Nurse, O my love is slain, I saw him go
O'er the white Alps alone; I saw him, I,
Assailed, fight, taken, stabbed, bleed, fall, and die.'
Augur me better chance, except dread Jove
Think it enough for me to have had thy love.

Composed 1593–6?   First published 1635

ELEGY 18   LOVE'S PROGRESS

Whoever loves, if he do not propose
The right true end of love, he's one that goes
To sea for nothing but to make him sick.
Love is a bear-whelp born; if we over-lick
Our love, and force it new strange shapes to take,
We err, and of a lump a monster make.

82

Were not a calf a monster that were grown
Faced like a man, though better than his own?
Perfection is in unity: prefer
One woman first, and then one thing in her.   10
I, when I value gold, may think upon
The ductileness, the application,
The wholesomeness, the ingenuity,
From rust, from soil, from fire ever free,
But if I love it, 'tis because 'tis made
By our new nature, use, the soul of trade.
    All these in women we might think upon
(If women had them) and yet love but one.
Can men more injure women than to say
They love them for that by which they are not they?   20
Makes virtue woman? must I cool my blood
Till I both be and find one wise and good?
May barren angels love so. But if we
Make love to woman, virtue is not she,
As beauty's not, nor wealth. He that strays thus
From her to hers, is more adulterous
Than if he took her maid. Search every sphere
And firmament, our Cupid is not there.
He's an infernal god and underground
With Pluto dwells, where gold and fire abound.   30
Men to such gods their sacrificing coals
Did not in altars lay, but pits and holes.
Although we see celestial bodies move
Above the earth, the earth we till and love:
So we her airs contemplate, words and heart,
And virtues; but we love the centric part.
    Nor is the soul more worthy or more fit
For love than this, as infinite as it.
But in attaining this desirèd place
How much they stray, that set out at the face!   40
The hair a forest is of ambushes,
Of springes, snares, fetters and manacles;
The brow becalms us when 'tis smooth and plain,

83

And when 'tis wrinkled shipwrecks us again;
Smooth, 'tis a paradise, where we would have
Immortal stay, and wrinkled 'tis our grave.
The nose like to the first meridian runs
Not 'twixt an east and west, but 'twixt two suns;
It leaves a cheek, a rosy hemisphere,
On either side, and then directs us where   50
Upon the Islands Fortunate we fall
(Not faint Canaries, but Ambrosial),
Her swelling lips; to which when we are come,
We anchor there, and think ourselves at home,
For they seem all: there sirens' songs, and there
Wise Delphic oracles do fill the ear;
There in a creek where chosen pearls do swell,
The remora, her cleaving tongue, doth dwell.
These, and the glorious promontory, her chin,
O'erpast, and the strait Hellespont between   60
The Sestos and Abydos of her breasts,
(Not of two lovers, but two Loves the nests)
Succeeds a boundless sea, but that thine eye
Some island moles may scattered there descry,
And sailing towards her India, in that way
Shall at her fair Atlantic navel stay;
Though thence the current be thy pilot made,
Yet ere thou be where thou wouldst be embayed,
Thou shalt upon another forest set,
Where many shipwreck, and no further get.   70
When thou art there, consider what this chase
Misspent by thy beginning at the face.
     Rather set out below, practise my art.
Some symmetry the foot hath with that part
Which thou dost seek, and is thy map for that,
Lovely enough to stop, but not stay at;
Least subject to disguise and change it is;
Men say the Devil never can change his;
It is the emblem that hath figurèd
Firmness; 'tis the first part that comes to bed.   80

84

Civility, we see, refined the kiss,
Which, at the face begun, transplanted is
Since to the hand, since to the imperial knee,
Now at the papal foot delights to be.
If kings think that the nearer way, and do
Rise from the foot, lovers may do so too;
For as free spheres move faster far than can
Birds, whom the air resists, so may that man
Which goes this empty and ethereal way,
Than if at beauty's elements he stay.   90
Rich Nature hath in women wisely made
Two purses, and their mouths aversely laid;
They then, which to the lower tribute owe,
That way which that exchequer looks must go.
He which doth not, his error is as great
As who by clyster gave the stomach meat.

Composed 1593–6?   *First published 1661*

ELEGY 19   TO HIS MISTRESS GOING TO BED

Come, Madam, come, all rest my powers defy;
Until I labour, I in labour lie.
The foe oft-times, having the foe in sight,
Is tired with standing though he never fight.
Off with that girdle, like heaven's zone glistering,
But a far fairer world encompassing.
Unpin that spangled breastplate which you wear
That th' eyes of busy fools may be stopped there.
Unlace yourself, for that harmonious chime
Tells me from you, that now 'tis your bed time.   10
Off with that happy busk, which I envy,
That still can be, and still can stand so nigh.
Your gown going off, such beauteous state reveals
As when from flowery meads th' hills' shadow steals.
Off with that wiry coronet and show
The hairy diadem which on you doth grow;

Now off with those shoes, and then safely tread
In this Love's hallowed temple, this soft bed.
In such white robes heaven's angels used to be
Received by men; thou angel bring'st with thee   20
A heaven like Mahomet's paradise; and though
Ill spirits walk in white, we easily know
By this these angels from an evil sprite –
Those set our hairs, but these our flesh upright.

 Licence my roving hands, and let them go
Before, behind, between, above, below.
O my America, my new found land,
My kingdom, safeliest when with one man manned,
My mine of precious stones, my empery,
How bless'd am I in this discovering thee!   30
To enter in these bonds is to be free;
Then where my hand is set my seal shall be.

 Full nakedness, all joys are due to thee.
As souls unbodied, bodies unclothed must be,
To taste whole joys. Gems which you women use
Are like Atlanta's balls, cast in men's views,
That when a fool's eye lighteth on a gem,
His earthly soul may covet theirs, not them.
Like pictures, or like books' gay coverings made
For laymen, are all women thus arrayed;   40
Themselves are mystic books, which only we
Whom their imputed grace will dignify
Must see revealed. Then since that I may know,
As liberally as to a midwife show
Thyself: cast all, yea, this white linen hence;
There is no penance due to innocence.

 To teach thee, I am naked first; why then,
What need'st thou have more covering than a man?

Composed 1593–6? First published 1669

ELEGY 20 LOVE'S WAR

Till I have peace with thee, war other men,
And when I have peace, can I leave thee then?
All other wars are scrupulous; only thou,
O fair free city, mayst thyself allow
To any one. In Flanders, who can tell
Whether the master press, or men rebel?
Only we know, that which all idiots say,
They bear most blows which come to part the fray.
France in her lunatic giddiness did hate
Ever our men, yea, and our God of late;   10
Yet she relies upon our angels well,
Which ne'er return, no more than they which fell.
Sick Ireland is with a strange war possessed
Like to an ague, now raging, now at rest,
Which time will cure, yet it must do her good
If she were purged, and her head-vein let blood.
And Midas' joys our Spanish journeys give –
We touch all gold, but find no food to live;
And I should be, in that hot parching clime,
To dust and ashes turned before my time.   20
To mew me in a ship is to enthral
Me in a prison that were like to fall;
Or in a cloister, save that there men dwell
In a calm heaven, here in a swaggering hell.
Long voyages are long consumptions,
And ships are carts for executions.
Yea, they are deaths; is't not all one to fly
Into another world, as 'tis to die?
Here let me war; in these arms let me lie;
Here let me parley, batter, bleed, and die.   30
Thine arms imprison me, and mine arms thee,
Thy heart thy ransom is, take mine for me.
Other men war that they their rest may gain,
But we will rest that we may fight again.
Those wars the ignorant, these th' experienced love,

87

There we are always under, here above.
There engines far off breed a just true fear,
Near thrusts, pikes, stabs, yea bullets hurt not here.
There lies are wrongs, here safe uprightly lie;
There men kill men, we'll make one by and by.   40
Thou nothing, I not half so much shall do
In these wars, as they may which from us two
Shall spring. Thousands we see which travel not
To wars, but stay swords, arms, and shot
To make at home; and shall not I do then
More glorious service, staying to make men?

Composed 1593–4?   First published 1802

Epithalamions, or Marriage Songs

EPITHALAMION MADE AT
LINCOLN'S INN

The sunbeams in the east are spread;
Leave, leave, fair bride, your solitary bed;
　　No more shall you return to it alone;
It nurseth sadness, and your body's print,
Like to a grave, the yielding down doth dint;
　　You and your other you meet there anon;
　　　　Put forth, put forth that warm balm-breathing thigh,
Which when next time you in these sheets will smother
There it must meet another,
　　　　Which never was, but must be, oft, more nigh;　　　　10
Come glad from thence, go gladder than you came;
Today put on perfection, and a woman's name.

Daughters of London, you which be
Our golden mines, and furnished treasury,
　　You which are angels, yet still bring with you
Thousands of angels on your marriage days,
Help with your presence and device to praise
　　These rites, which also unto you grow due;
　　　　Conceitedly dress her, and be assigned

By you fit place for every flower and jewel;   20
Make her for love fit fuel,
 As gay as Flora, and as rich as Ind;
So may she fair and rich, in nothing lame,
Today put on perfection, and a woman's name.

And you, frolic patricians,
Sons of these senators, wealth's deep oceans,
 Ye painted courtiers, barrels of others' wits,
Ye country men, who but your beasts love none,
Ye of those fellowships whereof he's one,
 Of study and play made strange hermaphrodits,   30
  Here shine; this bridegroom to the temple bring.
Lo, in yon path which store of strewed flowers graceth
The sober virgin paceth;
 Except my sight fail, 'tis no other thing;
Weep not nor blush, here is no grief nor shame,
Today put on perfection, and a woman's name.

Thy two-leaved gates, fair temple, unfold,
And these two in thy sacred bosom hold,
 Till, mystically joined, but one they be;
Then may thy lean and hunger-starvèd womb   40
Long time expect their bodies and their tomb,
 Long after their own parents fatten thee.
  All elder claims, and all cold barrenness,
All yielding to new loves be far for ever,
Which might these two dissever;
 Always all th' other may each one possess;
For the best bride, best worthy of praise and fame,
Today puts on perfection, and a woman's name.

O, winter days bring much delight,
Not for themselves, but for they soon bring night;   50
 Other sweets wait thee than these diverse meats,
Other disports than dancing jollities,
Other love-tricks than glancing with the eyes,

But that the sun still in our half-sphere sweats;
　　He flies in winter, but he now stands still.
Yet shadows turn; noon point he hath attained,
His steeds nill be restrained,
　　But gallop lively down the western hill;
Thou shalt, when he hath run the world's half-frame,
Tonight put on perfection, and a woman's name.　　60

The amorous evening star is rose,
Why then should not our amorous star inclose
　Herself in her wished bed? Release your strings,
Musicians, and dancers, take some truce
With these your pleasing labours, for great use
　　As much weariness as perfection brings;
　　You, and not only you, but all toiled beasts
Rest duly; at night all their toils are dispensed;
But in their beds commenced
　　Are other labours, and more dainty feasts;　　70
She goes a maid, who, lest she turn the same,
Tonight puts on perfection, and a woman's name.

Thy virgin's girdle now untie,
And in thy nuptial bed (love's altar) lie
　A pleasing sacrifice; now dispossess
Thee of these chains and robes which were put on
T' adorn the day, not thee; for thou, alone,
　Like virtue and truth, art best in nakedness;
　　This bed is only to virginity
A grave, but to a better state a cradle;　　80
Till now thou wast but able
　　To be what now thou art; then, that by thee
No more be said 'I may be', but 'I am',
Tonight put on perfection, and a woman's name.

Even like a faithful man content
That this life for a better should be spent,
　So she a mother's rich style doth prefer,

91

And at the bridegroom's wished approach doth lie
Like an appointed lamb, when tenderly
   The priest comes on his knees t' embowel her;   90
     Now sleep or watch with more joy; and O light
Of heaven, tomorrow rise thou hot, and early;
This sun will love so dearly
     Her rest, that long, long we shall want her sight;
Wonders are wrought, for she which had no maim
Tonight puts on perfection, and a woman's name.

Composed 1595?   *First published 1633*

AN EPITHALAMION, OR MARRIAGE
SONG, ON THE LADY ELIZABETH AND
COUNT PALATINE BEING MARRIED ON
ST VALENTINE'S DAY

Hail Bishop Valentine, whose day this is!
    All the air is thy diocese,
    And all the chirping choristers
And other birds are thy parishioners;
    Thou marriest every year
The lyric lark, and the grave whispering dove,
The sparrow that neglects his life for love,
The household bird with the red stomacher;
    Thou mak'st the blackbird speed as soon
As doth the goldfinch, or the halcyon;   10
The husband cock looks out, and straight is sped,
And meets his wife, which brings her feather-bed.
This day more cheerfully than ever shine,
This day, which might inflame thyself, old Valentine.

Till now, thou warmed'st with multiplying loves
    Two larks, two sparrows, or two doves.
    All that is nothing unto this,
For thou this day couplest two phoenixes;
    Thou mak'st a taper see

What the sun never saw; and what the Ark   20
(Which was of fowls and beasts the cage and park)
Did not contain, one bed contains, through thee –
    Two phoenixes, whose joinèd breasts
Are unto one another mutual nests,
Where motion kindles such fires as shall give
Young phoenixes, and yet the old shall live;
Whose love and courage never shall decline,
But make the whole year through thy day, O Valentine.

Up then fair phoenix bride, frustrate the sun,
    Thyself from thine affection   30
    Tak'st warmth enough, and from thine eye
All lesser birds will take their jollity.
    Up, up, fair bride, and call
Thy stars from out their several boxes, take
Thy rubies, pearls, and diamonds forth, and make
Thyself a constellation of them all,
    And by their blazing signify
That a great princess falls, but doth not die;
Be thou a new star, that to us portends
Ends of much wonder; and be thou those ends.   40
Since thou dost this day in new glory shine,
May all men date records from this thy Valentine.

Come forth, come forth, and as one glorious flame,
    Meeting another, grows the same,
    So meet thy Frederick, and so
To an unseparable union grow.
    Since separation
Falls not on such things as are infinite,
Nor things which are but one can disunite,
You 're twice inseparable, great and one;   50
    Go, then, to where the bishop stays
To make you one, his way, which divers ways
Must be effected; and when all is past,
And that you 're one, by hearts and hands made fast,

You two have one way left, yourselves to entwine,
Besides this bishop's knot, or Bishop Valentine.

But oh, what ails the sun, that here he stays
    Longer today than other days?
    Stays he new light from these to get,
And finding here such store, is loath to set?   60
    And why do you two walk
So slowly-paced in this procession?
Is all your care but to be looked upon,
And be to others spectacle and talk?
    The feast, with gluttonous delays,
Is eaten, and too long their meat they praise,
The masquers come late, and I think will stay,
Like fairies, till the cock crow them away.
Alas, did not antiquity assign
A night, as well as day, to thee, O Valentine?   70

They did, and night is come; and yet we see
    Formalities retarding thee.
    What mean these ladies, which (as though
They were to take a clock in pieces) go
    So nicely about the bride?
A bride, before a good-night could be said,
Should vanish from her clothes into her bed,
As souls from bodies steal, and are not spied.
    But now she 's laid; what though she be?
Yet there are more delays, for where is he?   80
He comes, and passes through sphere after sphere:
First her sheets, then her arms, then anywhere.
Let not this day, then, but this night be thine;
Thy day was but the eve to this, O Valentine.

Here lies a she-sun, and a he-moon here;
    She gives the best light to his sphere;
    Or each is both, and all, and so
They unto one another nothing owe;

 And yet they do, but are
So just and rich in that coin which they pay,   90
That neither would nor needs forbear nor stay;
Neither desires to be spared, nor to spare;
 They quickly pay their debt, and then
Take no acquittances, but pay again;
They pay, they give, they lend, and so let fall
No such occasion to be liberal.
More truth, more courage in these two do shine,
Than all thy turtles have, and sparrows, Valentine.

And by this act of these two phoenixes
 Nature again restorèd is,   100
 For since these two are two no more,
There's but one phoenix still, as was before.
 Rest now at last, and we,
As satyrs watch the sun's uprise, will stay
Waiting when your eyes opened let out day,
Only desired because your face we see;
 Others near you shall whispering speak,
And wagers lay, at which side day will break,
And win by observing, then, whose hand it is
That opens first a curtain, hers or his;   110
This will be tried tomorrow after nine,
Till which hour we thy day enlarge, O Valentine.

Composed 1613   First published 1633

95

Satires

SATIRE 1

Away, thou fondling motley humorist,
Leave me, and in this standing wooden chest,
Consorted with these few books, let me lie
In prison, and here be coffined, when I die;
Here are God's conduits, grave divines; and here
Nature's secretary, the philosopher;
And jolly statesmen, which teach how to tie
The sinews of a city's mystic body;
Here gathering chroniclers, and by them stand
Giddy fantastic poets of each land.   10
Shall I leave all this constant company,
And follow, headlong, wild uncertain thee?
First swear by thy best love in earnest
(If thou, which lov'st all, canst love any best)
Thou wilt not leave me in the middle street,
Though some more spruce companion thou dost meet,
Not though a captain do come in thy way
Bright parcel-gilt with forty dead men's pay;
Not though a brisk perfumed pert courtier
Deign with a nod thy courtesy to answer;   20
Nor come a velvet justice with a long

Great train of blue coats, twelve or fourteen strong,
Wilt thou grin or fawn on him, or prepare
A speech to court his beauteous son and heir.
For better or worse take me, or leave me:
To take and leave me is adultery.
Oh monstrous, superstitious puritan,
Of refined manners, yet ceremonial man,
That when thou meet'st one, with enquiring eyes
Dost search, and like a needy broker prize   30
The silk and gold he wears, and to that rate
So high or low dost raise thy formal hat;
That wilt consort none, until thou have known
What lands he hath in hope, or of his own,
As though all thy companions should make thee
Jointures, and marry thy dear company.
Why shouldst thou (that dost not only approve
But in rank itchy lust desire and love
The nakedness and bareness to enjoy
Of thy plump muddy whore, or prostitute boy)   40
Hate virtue, though she be naked and bare?
At birth and death our bodies naked are;
And till our souls be unapparellèd
Of bodies, they from bliss are banishèd.
Man's first bless'd state was naked; when by sin
He lost that, yet he was clothed but in beasts' skin;
And in this coarse attire which I now wear,
With God and with the Muses I confer.
But since thou like a contrite penitent,
Charitably warned of thy sins, dost repent   50
These vanities and giddinesses, lo,
I shut my chamber door, and come, let's go.
But sooner may a cheap whore, that hath been
Worn by as many several men in sin,
As are black feathers or musk-colour hose,
Name her child's right true father, 'mongst all those;
Sooner may one guess who shall bear away
The Infanta of London, heir to an India;

And sooner may a gulling weather-spy
By drawing forth heaven's scheme tell certainly   60
What fashioned hats or ruffs or suits next year
Our subtle-witted antic youths will wear;
Than thou, when thou depart'st from me, canst show
Whither, why, when, or with whom thou wouldst go.
But how shall I be pardoned my offence
That thus have sinned against my conscience?
Now we are in the street; he first of all,
Improvidently proud, creeps to the wall,
And so imprisoned and hemmed in by me
Sells for a little state his liberty;   70
Yet though he cannot skip forth now to greet
Every fine silken painted fool we meet,
He them to him with amorous smiles allures,
And grins, smacks, shrugs, and such an itch endures
As prentices or schoolboys which do know
Of some gay sport abroad, yet dare not go.
And as fiddlers stop lowest at highest sound,
So to the most brave stoops he nigh'st the ground.
But to a grave man he doth move no more
Than the wise politic horse would heretofore,   80
Or thou O elephant or ape wilt do,
When any names the King of Spain to you.
Now leaps he upright, jogs me, and cries, 'D' you see
Yonder well-favoured youth?' 'Which?' 'O, 'tis he
That dances so divinely.' 'O,' said I,
'Stand still, must you dance here for company?'
He drooped, we went, till one which did excel
Th' Indians in drinking his tobacco well
Met us; they talked; I whispered, 'Let us go;
'T may be you smell him not, truly I do.'   90
He hears not me, but, on the other side
A many-coloured peacock having spied,
Leaves him and me; I for my lost sheep stay;
He follows, overtakes, goes on the way,
Saying, 'Him whom I last left, all repute

For his device, in handsoming a suit,
To judge of lace, pink, panes, print, cut, and pleat,
Of all the court to have the best conceit.'
'Our dull comedians want him, let him go;
But O, God strengthen thee, why stoop'st thou so?'   100
'Why? he hath travelled.' 'Long?' 'No, but to me
(Which understand none) he doth seem to be
Perfect French, and Italian.' I replied,
'So is the pox.' He answered not, but spied
More men of sort, of parts, and qualities;
At last his love he in a window spies,
And like light dew exhaled, he flings from me,
Violently ravished to his lechery.
Many were there, he could command no more;
He quarrelled, fought, bled; and, turned out of door,   110
Directly came to me hanging the head,
And constantly a while must keep his bed.

Composed 1593?   *First published 1633*

SATIRE 3

Kind pity chokes my spleen; brave scorn forbids
Those tears to issue which swell my eyelids;
I must not laugh, nor weep sins, and be wise;
Can railing then cure these worn maladies?
Is not our mistress fair religion,
As worthy of all our souls' devotion,
As virtue was to the first blinded age?
Are not heaven's joys as valiant to assuage
Lusts, as earth's honour was to them? Alas,
As we do them in means, shall they surpass   10
Us in the end, and shall thy father's spirit
Meet blind philosophers in heaven, whose merit
Of strict life may be imputed faith, and hear
Thee, whom he taught so easy ways and near
To follow, damned? O if thou dar'st, fear this;

This fear great courage and high valour is.
Dar'st thou aid mutinous Dutch, and dar'st thou lay
Thee in ships' wooden sepulchres, a prey
To leaders' rage, to storms, to shot, to dearth?
Dar'st thou dive seas, and dungeons of the earth?   20
Hast thou courageous fire to thaw the ice
Of frozen north discoveries? and thrice
Colder than salamanders, like divine
Children in th' oven, fires of Spain and the line,
Whose countries limbecks to our bodies be,
Canst thou for gain bear? and must every he
Which cries not 'Goddess!' to thy mistress, draw,
Or eat thy poisonous words? Courage of straw!
O desperate coward, wilt thou seem bold, and
To thy foes and his who made thee to stand   30
Sentinel in his world's garrison thus yield,
And for forbidden wars leave th' appointed field?
Know thy foes: the foul Devil, he whom thou
Strivest to please, for hate, not love, would allow
Thee fain his whole realm to be quit; and as
The world's all parts wither away and pass,
So the world's self, thy other loved foe, is
In her decrepit wane, and thou loving this
Dost love a withered and worn strumpet; last,
Flesh (itself's death) and joys which flesh can taste,   40
Thou lovest; and thy fair goodly soul, which doth
Give this flesh power to taste joy, thou dost loathe.
Seek true religion. O where? Mirreus,
Thinking her unhoused here, and fled from us,
Seeks her at Rome; there, because he doth know
That she was there a thousand years ago;
He loves her rags so as we here obey
The statecloth where the prince sat yesterday.
Crants to such brave loves will not be enthralled,
But loves her only who at Geneva is called   50
Religion, plain, simple, sullen, young,
Contemptuous, yet unhandsome; as among

100

Lecherous humours, there is one that judges
No wenches wholesome, but coarse country drudges.
Graius stays still at home here, and because
Some preachers, vile ambitious bawds, and laws
Still new like fashions, bid him think that she
Which dwells with us is only perfect, he
Embraceth her whom his godfathers will
Tender to him, being tender, as wards still   60
Take such wives as their guardians offer, or
Pay values. Careless Phrygius doth abhor
All, because all cannot be good, as one,
Knowing some women whores, dares marry none.
Gracchus loves all as one, and thinks that so
As women do in diverse countries go
In diverse habits, yet are still one kind,
So doth, so is religion; and this blind-
ness too much light breeds; but unmovèd thou
Of force must one, and forced but one allow;   70
And the right; ask thy father which is she;
Let him ask his; though truth and falsehood be
Near twins, yet truth a little elder is;
Be busy to seek her; believe me this,
He's not of none, nor worst, that seeks the best.
T' adore, or scorn an image, or protest,
May all be bad; doubt wisely; in strange way
To stand inquiring right, is not to stray;
To sleep, or run wrong, is. On a huge hill,
Craggèd and steep, Truth stands, and he that will   80
Reach her, about must, and about must go,
And what the hill's suddenness resists win so;
Yet strive so, that before age, death's twilight,
Thy soul rest, for none can work in that night.
To will implies delay, therefore now do.
Hard deeds, the body's pains; hard knowledge too
The mind's endeavours reach, and mysteries
Are like the sun, dazzling, yet plain to all eyes.
Keep the truth which thou 'st found; men do not stand

In so ill case here, that God hath with his hand   90
Signed kings blank-charters to kill whom they hate,
Nor are they vicars but hangmen to Fate.
Fool and wretch, wilt thou let thy soul be tied
To man's laws, by which she shall not be tried
At the last day? O will it then boot thee
To say a Philip, or a Gregory,
A Harry, or a Martin taught thee this?
Is not this excuse for mere contraries,
Equally strong? Cannot both sides say so?
That thou may'st rightly obey power, her bounds know;   100
Those past, her nature and name is changed; to be
Then humble to her is idolatry.
As streams are, power is; those bless'd flowers that dwell
At the rough stream's calm head thrive and do well,
But having left their roots, and themselves given
To the stream's tyrannous rage, alas, are driven
Through mills, and rocks, and woods, and at last, almost
Consumed in going, in the sea are lost:
So perish souls, which more choose men's unjust
Power from God claimed, than God himself to trust.   110

Composed 1594–6?   First published 1633

The Progress of the Soul

Infinitati sacrum
16 Augusti 1601

METEMPSYCHOSIS
Poema satyricon

Epistle

Others at the porches and entries of their buildings set their
arms; I, my picture; if any colours can deliver a mind so plain,
and flat, and through-light as mine. Naturally at a new author,
I doubt, and stick, and do not say quickly, 'good'. I censure
much and tax; and this liberty costs me more than others by
how much my own things are worse than others'. Yet I would
not be so rebellious against myself as not to do it, since I love it;
nor so unjust to others as to do it *sine talione*. As long as I give
them as good hold upon me they must pardon me my bitings. I
forbid no reprehender but him that like the Trent Council for- 10
bids not books but authors, damning whatever such a name
hath or shall write. None writes so ill that he gives not something exemplary to follow or fly. Now when I begin this book,
I have no purpose to come into any man's debt; how my stock
will hold out I know not; perchance waste, perchance increase
in use; if I do borrow anything of antiquity, besides that I make
account that I pay it to posterity with as much and as good, you
shall still find me to acknowledge it, and to thank not him only

103

that hath digged out treasure for me, but that hath lighted me a
candle to the place. All which I will bid you remember (for I   20
would have no such readers as I can teach) is that the Pytha-
gorean doctrine doth not only carry one soul from man to man,
nor man to beast, but indifferently to plants also: and therefore
you must not grudge to find the same soul in an emperor, in a
post-horse, and in a mushroom, since no unreadiness in the
soul, but an indisposition in the organs works this. And therefore though this soul could not move when it was a melon, yet
it may remember and now tell me at what lascivious banquet it
was served. And though it could not speak when it was a
spider, yet it can remember and now tell me who used it for   30
poison to attain dignity. However the bodies have dulled her
other faculties, her memory hath ever been her own, which
makes me so seriously deliver you by her relation all her
passages from her first making, when she was that apple which
Eve ate, to this time, when she is he whose life you shall find in
the end of this book.

THE PROGRESS OF THE SOUL

First song

1

I sing the progress of a deathless soul,
Whom Fate, which God made, but doth not control,
Placed in most shapes; all times before the law
Yoked us, and when, and since, in this I sing.
And the great world to his agèd evening,
From infant morn, through manly noon I draw.
What the gold Chaldee or silver Persian saw,
Greek brass, or Roman iron, is in this one;
A work t' outwear Seth's pillars, brick and stone,
    And (holy writ excepted) made to yield to none.   10

2

Thee, eye of heaven, this great soul envies not;
By thy male force is all we have begot;
In the first east thou now beginn'st to shine,
Suck'st early balm and island spices there,
And wilt anon in thy loose-reined career
At Tagus, Po, Seine, Thames, and Danow dine,
And see at night thy western land of mine,
Yet hast thou not more nations seen than she,
That before thee one day began to be,
   And thy frail light being quenched, shall long, long outlive
     thee.   20

3

Nor, holy Janus, in whose sovereign boat
The Church and all the monarchies did float;
That swimming college and free hospital
Of all mankind, that cage and vivary
Of fowls and beasts, in whose womb Destiny
Us and our latest nephews did instal
(For thence are all derived, that fill this all),
Didst thou in that great stewardship embark
So diverse shapes into that floating park
   As have been moved and informed by this heavenly spark.   30

4

Great Destiny the commissary of God,
That hast marked out a path and period
For every thing; who, where we offspring took,
Our ways and ends seest at one instant; thou
Knot of all causes, thou whose changeless brow
Ne'er smiles nor frowns, O vouch thou safe to look
And show my story, in thy eternal book;
That (if my prayer be fit) I may understand
So much myself, as to know with what hand
   How scant or liberal this my life's race is spanned.   40

105

5

To my six lustres almost now outwore,
Except thy book owe me so many more,
Except my legend be free from the lets
Of steep ambition, sleepy poverty,
Spirit-quenching sickness, dull captivity,
Distracting business, and from beauty's nets,
And all that calls from this, and t'other whets,
O let me not launch out, but let me save
Th' expense of brain and spirit; that my grave
   His right and due, a whole unwasted man, may have.   50

6

But if my days be long and good enough,
In vain this sea shall enlarge or enrough
Itself; for I will through the wave and foam,
And shall in sad lone ways, a lively sprite,
Make my dark heavy poem light and light.
For though through many straits and lands I roam,
I launch at paradise and sail towards home;
The course I there began shall here be stayed,
Sails hoisèd there struck here, and anchors laid
   In Thames which were at Tigris and Euphrates weighed.   60

7

For this great soul which here amongst us now
Doth dwell, and moves that hand, and tongue, and brow,
Which, as the moon the sea, moves us; to hear
Whose story with long patience you will long
(For 'tis the crown, and last strain of my song);
This soul to whom Luther and Mahomet were
Prisons of flesh; this soul which oft did tear
And mend the wracks of th' Empire and late Rome,
And lived where every great change did come,
   Had first in paradise a low but fatal room.   70

8

Yet no low room, nor than the greatest less,
If (as devout and sharp men fitly guess)
That Cross, our joy and grief, where nails did tie
That all which always was all, everywhere,
Which could not sin, and yet all sins did bear;
Which could not die, yet could not choose but die;
Stood in the selfsame room in Calvary,
Where first grew the forbidden learnèd tree,
For on that tree hung in security
   This soul, made by the Maker's will from pulling free.   80

9

Prince of the orchard, fair as dawning morn,
Fenced with the law, and ripe as soon as born,
That apple grew, which this soul did enlive,
Till the then climbing serpent, that now creeps
For that offence for which all mankind weeps,
Took it, and to her whom the first man did wive
(Whom, and her race, only forbiddings drive)
He gave it; she to her husband; both did eat;
So perishèd the eaters, and the meat;
   And we (for treason taints the blood) thence die and sweat.   90

10

Man all at once was there by woman slain,
And one by one we're here slain o'er again
By them. The mother poisoned the well-head;
The daughters here corrupt us, rivulets.
No smallness 'scapes, no greatness breaks their nets.
She thrust us out, and by them we are led
Astray from turning to whence we are fled.
Were prisoners judges, 'twould seem rigorous,
She sinned, we bear; part of our pain is thus –
   To love them whose fault to this painful love yoked us.   100

107

11

So fast in us doth this corruption grow,
That now we dare ask why we should be so.
Would God (disputes the curious rebel) make
A law, and would not have it kept? Or can
His creatures' will cross his? Of every man
For one, will God (and be just) vengeance take?
Who sinned? 'twas not forbidden to the snake,
Nor her who was not then made; nor is 't writ
That Adam cropped, or knew the apple; yet
    The worm and she, and he, and we endure for it.   110

12

But snatch me, heavenly Spirit, from this vain
Reckoning their vanities; less is the gain
Than hazard still, to meditate on ill,
Though with good mind; their reasons, like those toys
Of glassy bubbles, which the gamesome boys
Stretch to so nice a thinness through a quill
That they themselves [do] break, do themselves spill:
Arguing is heretics' game, and exercise,
As wrestlers, perfects them; not liberties
    Of speech but silence, hands, not tongues, end heresies.   120

13

Just in that instant when the serpent's gripe
Broke the slight veins and tender conduit-pipe
Through which this soul from the tree's root did draw
Life and growth to this apple, fled away
This loose soul, old one and another day.
As lightning, which one scarce dares say he saw,
'Tis so soon gone (and better proof the law
Of sense than faith requires), swiftly she flew
To a dark and foggy plot; her her fate threw
    There through th' earth's pores, and in a plant housed her
      anew.   130

14

The plant, thus abled, to itself did force
A place where no place was; by nature's course,
As air from water, water fleets away
From thicker bodies, by this root thronged so
His spongy confines gave him place to grow,
Just as in our streets, when the people stay
To see the prince, and have so filled the way
That weasels scarce could pass, when she comes near
They throng and cleave up, and a passage clear,
   As if, for that time, their round bodies flattened were.　　140

15

His right arm he thrust out towards the east,
Westward his left; th' ends did themselves digest
Into ten lesser strings, these fingers were;
And as a slumberer stretching on his bed,
This way he this, and that way scatterèd
His other leg, which feet with toes upbear;
Grew on his middle parts, the first day, hair,
To show that in love's business he should still
A dealer be, and be used well or ill:
   His apples kindle, his leaves force of conception kill.　　150

16

A mouth, but dumb, he hath; blind eyes, deaf ears,
And to his shoulders dangle subtle hairs;
A young Colossus there he stands upright,
And as that ground by him were conquerèd
A leafy garland wears he on his head
Enchased with little fruits, so red and bright
That for them you would call your love's lips white;
So, of a lone unhaunted place possessed,
Did this soul's second inn, built by the guest,
   This living buried man, this quiet mandrake, rest.　　160

17

No lustful woman came this plant to grieve,
But 'twas because there was none yet but Eve,
And she (with other purpose) killed it quite.
Her sin had now brought in infirmities,
And so her cradled child the moist red eyes
Had never shut, nor slept since it saw light;
Poppy she knew, she knew the mandrake's might,
And tore up both, and so cooled her child's blood;
Unvirtuous weeds might long unvexed have stood;
    But he's short-lived, that with his death can do most good.   170

18

To an unfettered soul's quick nimble haste
Are falling stars and heart's thoughts but slow-paced:
Thinner than burnt air flies this soul, and she
Whom four new coming and four parting suns
Had found and left the mandrake's tenant runs
Thoughtless of change; when her firm destiny
Confined and enjailed her that seemed so free
Into a small blue shell, the which a poor
Warm bird o'erspread, and sat still evermore,
    Till her enclosed child kicked and pecked itself a door.   180

19

Outcrept a sparrow, this soul's moving inn,
On whose raw arms stiff feathers now begin,
As children's teeth through gums, to break with pain;
His flesh is jelly yet, and his bones threads;
All a new downy mantle overspreads;
A mouth he opes, which would as much contain
As his late house, and the first hour speaks plain,
And chirps aloud for meat. Meat fit for men
His father steals for him, and so feeds then
    One that within a month will beat him from his hen.   190

110

20

In this world's youth wise nature did make haste;
Things ripened sooner, and did longer last;
Already this hot cock, in bush and tree,
In field and tent, o'erflutters his next hen;
He asks her not who did so last, nor when,
Nor if his sister or his niece she be,
Nor doth she pule for his inconstancy
If in her sight he change, nor doth refuse
The next that calls; both liberty do use;
 Where store is of both kinds, both kinds may freely choose. 200

21

Men, till they took laws which made freedom less,
Their daughters and their sisters did ingress;
Till now unlawful, therefore ill, 'twas not.
So jolly that it can move this soul is,
The body so free of his kindnesses,
That self-preserving it hath now forgot,
And slack'neth so the soul's and body's knot
Which temperance straitens; freely on his she-friends
He blood and spirit, pith and marrow spends,
 Ill steward of himself, himself in three years ends. 210

22

Else might he long have lived; man did not know
Of gummy blood, which doth in holly grow,
How to make bird-lime, nor how to deceive
With feigned calls, hid nets, or enwrapping snare,
The free inhabitants of the pliant air.
Man to beget and woman to conceive
Asked not of roots nor of cock-sparrows leave.
Yet chooseth he, though none of these he fears,
Pleasantly three, than straitened twenty years
 To live, and, to increase his race, himself outwears. 220

23

This coal with overblowing quenched and dead,
The soul from her too active organs fled
To a brook; a female fish's sandy roe
With the male's jelly newly leavened was,
For they had intertouched as they did pass,
And one of those small bodies, fitted so,
This soul informed, and abled it to row
Itself with finny oars, which she did fit;
Her scales seemed yet of parchment, and as yet
   Perchance a fish, but by no name you could call it.   230

24

When goodly, like a ship in her full trim,
A swan, so white that you may unto him
Compare all whiteness, but himself to none,
Glided along, and as he glided watched,
And with his archèd neck this poor fish catched.
It moved with state, as if to look upon
Low things it scorned, and yet before that one
Could think he sought it, he had swallowed clear
This, and much such, and unblamed devoured there
   All but who too swift, too great, or well armèd were.   240

25

Now swum a prison in a prison put,
And now this soul in double walls was shut,
Till melted with the swan's digestive fire
She left her house the fish, and vapoured forth;
Fate not affording bodies of more worth
For her as yet, bids her again retire
T'another fish, to any new desire
Made a new prey; for he that can to none
Resistance make, nor complaint, sure is gone.
   Weakness invites, but silence feasts oppression.   250

26

Pace with her native stream this fish doth keep,
And journeys with her towards the glassy deep,
But oft retarded, once with a hidden net
Though with great windows, for when need first taught
These tricks to catch food, then they were not wrought
As now, with curious greediness to let
None 'scape, but few and fit for use to get,
As in this trap a ravenous pike was ta'en,
Who, though himself distressed, would fain have slain
    This wretch; so hardly are ill habits left again.   260

27

Here by her smallness she two deaths o'erpast;
Once innocence 'scaped, and left the oppressor fast;
The net through-swum, she keeps the liquid path,
And whether she leap up sometimes to breathe
And suck in air, or find it underneath,
Or working parts like mills or limbecks hath
To make the water thin and airlike, faith
Cares not, but safe the place she's come unto,
Where fresh with salt waves meet, and what to do
    She knows not, but between both makes a board or two.   270

28

So far from hiding her guests water is
That she shows them in bigger quantities
Than they are. Thus doubtful of her way,
For game and not for hunger a sea pie
Spied through this traitorous spectacle, from high,
The silly fish where it disputing lay,
And, t' end her doubts and her, bears her away.
Exalted she is, but to the exalter's good,
As are by great ones men which lowly stood.
    It's raised, to be the raiser's instrument and food.   280

29

Is any kind subject to rape like fish?
Ill unto man they neither do nor wish;
Fishers they kill not, nor with noise awake;
They do not hunt, nor strive to make a prey
Of beasts, nor their young sons to bear away;
Fowls they pursue not, nor do undertake
To spoil the nests industrious birds do make;
Yet them all these unkind kinds feed upon;
To kill them is an occupation,
   And laws make fasts, and lents, for their destruction.   290

30

A sudden stiff land-wind in that self hour
To seaward forced this bird, that did devour
The fish; he cares not, for with ease he flies,
Fat gluttony's best orator: at last
So long he hath flown, and hath flown so fast
That, many leagues at sea, now tired he lies,
And with his prey, that till then languished, dies:
The souls, no longer foes, two ways did err;
The fish I follow, and keep no calendar
   Of the other; he lives yet in some great officer.   300

31

Into an embryon fish our soul is thrown,
And in due time thrown out again, and grown
To such vastness as, if unmanacled
From Greece Morea were, and that by some
Earthquake unrooted loose Morea swum,
Or seas from Afric's body had severèd
And torn the hopeful promontory's head,
This fish would seem these; and, when all hopes fail,
A great ship overset, or without sail
   Hulling, might (when this was a whelp) be like this whale.   310

114

32

At every stroke his brazen fins do take,
More circles in the broken sea they make
Than cannons' voices when the air they tear;
His ribs are pillars, and his high-arched roof
Of bark that blunts best steel is thunder-proof:
Swim in him swallowed dolphins, without fear,
And feel no sides, as if his vast womb were
Some inland sea; and ever as he went
He spouted rivers up, as if he meant
   To join our seas with seas above the firmament.   320

33

He hunts not fish, but as an officer,
Stays in his court, as his own net, and there
All suitors of all sorts themselves enthral;
So on his back lies this whale wantoning,
And in his gulf-like throat sucks every thing
That passeth near. Fish chaseth fish, and all,
Flyer and follower, in this whirlpool fall;
O might not states of more equality
Consist? and is it of necessity
   That thousand guiltless smalls, to make one great, must die?   330

34

Now drinks he up seas, and he eats up flocks,
He jostles islands, and he shakes firm rocks.
Now in a roomful house this soul doth float,
And like a prince she sends her faculties
To all her limbs, distant as provinces.
The sun hath twenty times both crab and goat
Parchèd, since first launched forth this living boat.
'Tis greatest now, and to destruction
Nearest; there's no pause at perfection;
   Greatness a period hath, but hath no station.   340

115

35

Two little fishes whom he never harmed,
Nor fed on their kind, two not throughly armed
With hope that they could kill him, nor could do
Good to themselves by his death (they do not eat
His flesh, nor suck those oils, which thence outstreat),
Conspired against him; and it might undo
The plot of all, that the plotters were two,
But that they fishes were, and could not speak.
How shall a tyrant wise strong projects break,
   If wretches can on them the common anger wreak?   350

36

The flail-finned thresher, and steel-beaked swordfish
Only attempt to do what all do wish.
The thresher backs him, and to beat begins;
The sluggard whale yields to oppression,
And to hide himself from shame and danger, down
Begins to sink; the swordfish upward spins,
And gores him with his beak; his staff-like fins
So well the one, his sword the other plies,
That now a scoff and prey this tyrant dies,
   And (his own dole) feeds with himself all companies.   360

37

Who will revenge his death? or who will call
Those to account that thought and wrought his fall?
Th' heirs of slain kings, we see, are often so
Transported with the joy of what they get,
That they revenge and obsequies forget;
Nor will against such men the people go,
Because he's now dead, to whom they should show
Love in that act; some kings by vice being grown
So needy of subjects' love, that of their own
   They think they lose, if love be to the dead prince shown.   370

116

38

This soul, now free from prison and passion,
Hath yet a little indignation
That so small hammers should so soon down beat
So great a castle. And having for her house
Got the strait cloister of a wretched mouse
(As basest men that have not what to eat,
Nor enjoy aught, do far more hate the great
Than they who good reposed estates possess),
This soul, late taught that great things might by less
  Be slain, to gallant mischief doth herself address.   380

39

Nature's great masterpiece, an elephant,
The only harmless great thing; the giant
Of beasts; who thought no more had gone to make one wise
But to be just, and thankful, loath to offend
(Yet nature hath given him no knees to bend:
Himself he up-props, on himself relies,
And foe to none, suspects no enemies),
Still sleeping stood; vexed not his fantasy
Black dreams; like an unbent bow, carelessly
  His sinewy proboscis did remissly lie;   390

40

In which as in a gallery this mouse
Walked, and surveyed the rooms of this vast house,
And to the brain, the soul's bedchamber, went,
And gnawed the life-cords there; like a whole town
Clean undermined, the slain beast tumbled down.
With him the murderer dies, whom envy sent
To kill, not 'scape (for only he that meant
To die did ever kill a man of better room);
And thus he made his foe his prey and tomb:
  Who cares not to turn back may anywhither come.   400

41

Next housed this soul a wolf's yet unborn whelp,
Till the best midwife, Nature, gave it help
To issue. It could kill as soon as go.
Abel, as white and mild as his sheep were
(Who in that trade of church and kingdoms there
Was the first type), was still infested so
With this wolf that it bred his loss and woe;
And yet his bitch, his sentinel, attends
The flock so near, so well warns and defends,
  That the wolf (hopeless else) to corrupt her intends.   410

42

He took a course which since, successfully,
Great men have often taken, to espy
The counsels or to break the plots of foes:
To Abel's tent he stealeth in the dark,
On whose skirts the bitch slept; ere she could bark,
Attached her with strait grips, yet he called those
Embracements of love; to love's work he goes,
Where deeds move more than words; nor doth she show
Now much resist, nor needs he straiten so
  His prey, for, were she loose, she would nor bark, nor go.   420

43

He hath engaged her; his she wholly bides;
Who not her own, none other's secrets hides.
If to the flock he come, and Abel there,
She feigns hoarse barkings, but she biteth not;
Her faith is quite, but not her love forgot.
At last a trap, of which some everywhere
Abel had placed, ended his loss and fear
By the wolf's death; and now just time it was
That a quick soul should give life to that mass
  Of blood in Abel's bitch, and thither this did pass.   430

44

Some have their wives, their sisters some begot,
But in the lives of emperors you shall not
Read of a lust the which may equal this;
This wolf begot himself, and finishèd
What he began alive, when he was dead;
Son to himself, and father too, he is.
A riddling lust, for which schoolmen would miss
A proper name. The whelp of both these lay
In Abel's tent, and with soft Moaba,
   His sister, being young, it used to sport and play.   440

45

He soon for her too harsh and churlish grew,
And Abel (the dam dead) would use this new
For the field. Being of two kinds thus made,
He, as his dam, from sheep drove wolves away,
And as his sire, he made them his own prey.
Five years he lived and cozened with his trade,
Then, hopeless that his faults were hid, betrayed
Himself by flight, and by all followèd,
From dogs, a wolf, from wolves, a dog he fled;
   And like a spy to both sides false he perishèd.   450

46

It quickened next a toyful ape, and so
Gamesome it was, that it might freely go
From tent to tent, and with the children play.
His organs now so like theirs he doth find,
That why he cannot laugh, and speak his mind,
He wonders. Much with all, most he doth stay
With Adam's fifth daughter Siphatecia,
Doth gaze on her, and, where she passeth, pass,
Gathers her fruits, and tumbles on the grass,
   And, wisest of that kind, the first true lover was.   460

119

47

He was the first that more desired to have
One than another; first that e'er did crave
Love by mute signs, and had no power to speak;
First that could make love-faces, or could do
The vaulter's somersaults, or used to woo
With hoiting gambols, his own bones to break
To make his mistress merry or to wreak
Her anger on himself. Sins against kind
They easily do, that can let feed their mind
   With outward beauty; beauty they in boys and beasts do find.   470

48

By this misled, too low things men have proved,
And too high; beasts and angels have been loved.
This ape, though else through-vain, in this was wise,
He reached at things too high, but open way
There was, and he knew not she would say nay;
His toys prevail not, likelier means he tries;
He gazeth on her face with tear-shot eyes,
And up lifts subtly with his russet paw
Her kidskin apron without fear or awe
   Of Nature; Nature hath no gaol, though she have law.   480

49

First she was silly and knew not what he meant;
That virtue, by his touches chafed and spent,
Succeeds an itchy warmth, that melts her quite;
She knew not first, now cares not what he doth,
And willing half and more, more than half loath,
She neither pulls nor pushes, but outright
Now cries, and now repents; when Tethlemite
Her brother entered, and a great stone threw
After the ape, who, thus prevented, flew.
   This house thus battered down, the soul possessed a new.   490

120

50

And whether by this change she lose or win,
She comes out next, where th' ape would have gone in.
Adam and Eve had mingled bloods, and now,
Like chemics' equal fires, her temperate womb
Had stewed and formed it: and part did become
A spongy liver, that did richly allow,
Like a free conduit on a high hill's brow,
Life-keeping moisture unto every part;
Part hardened itself to a thicker heart,
    Whose busy furnaces life's spirits do impart;   500

51

Another part became the well of sense,
The tender well-armed feeling brain, from whence
Those sinewy strings which do our bodies tie
Are ravelled out, and, fast there by one end,
Did this soul limbs, these limbs a soul attend,
And now they joined: keeping some quality
Of every past shape, she knew treachery,
Rapine, deceit, and lust, and ills enow
To be a woman. Themech she is now,
    Sister and wife to Cain, Cain that first did plough.   510

52

Whoe'er thou be'st that read'st this sullen writ,
Which just so much courts thee as thou dost it,
Let me arrest thy thoughts; wonder with me
Why ploughing, building, ruling and the rest,
Or most of those arts whence our lives are bless'd,
By cursèd Cain's race invented be,
And bless'd Seth vexed us with astronomy.
There's nothing simply good nor ill alone;
Of every quality comparison
    The only measure is, and judge, opinion.   520

Composed 1601   *First published 1633*

121

Verse Letters

THE STORM

To Mr Christopher Brooke

Thou which art I ('tis nothing to be so),
Thou which art still thyself, by these shalt know
Part of our passage; and a hand or eye
By Hilliard drawn is worth an history
By a worse painter made; and (without pride)
When by thy judgement they are dignified,
My lines are such: 'tis the pre-eminence
Of friendship only t' impute excellence.
England, to whom we owe what we be and have,
Sad that her sons did seek a foreign grave   10
(For Fate's or Fortune's drifts none can soothsay;
Honour and misery have one face and way),
From out her pregnant entrails sighed a wind
Which at th' air's middle marble room did find
Such strong resistance that itself it threw
Downward again; and so when it did view
How in the port our fleet dear time did leese,
Withering like prisoners which lie but for fees,
Mildly it kissed our sails, and fresh and sweet

As to a stomach starved, whose insides meet,   20
Meat comes, it came; and swole our sails, when we
So joyed, as Sara her swelling joyed to see.
But 'twas but so kind as our countrymen,
Which bring friends one day's way, and leave them then.
Then like two mighty kings, which, dwelling far
Asunder, meet against a third to war,
The south and west winds joined, and, as they blew,
Waves like a rolling trench before them threw.
Sooner than you read this line did the gale,
Like shot, not feared till felt, our sails assail;   30
And what at first was called a gust, the same
Hath now a storm's, anon a tempest's name.
Jonas, I pity thee, and curse those men
Who, when the storm raged most, did wake thee then;
Sleep is pain's easiest salve, and doth fulfil
All offices of death, except to kill.
But when I waked, I saw that I saw not.
I, and the sun which should teach me, had forgot
East, west, day, night, and I could only say,
If the world had lasted, now it had been day.   40
Thousands our noises were, yet we 'mongst all
Could none by his right name but thunder call:
Lightning was all our light, and it rained more
Than if the sun had drunk the sea before.
Some coffined in their cabins lie, equally
Grieved that they are not dead and yet must die.
And as sin-burdened souls from graves will creep
At the last day, some forth their cabins peep,
And tremblingly ask what news, and do hear so,
Like jealous husbands, what they would not know.   50
Some, sitting on the hatches, would seem there
With hideous gazing to fear away fear.
There note they the ship's sicknesses, the mast
Shaked with this ague, and the hold and waist
With a salt dropsy clogged, and all our tacklings
Snapping like too high-stretchèd treble strings.

And from our tottered sails, rags drop down so,
As from one hanged in chains, a year ago.
Even our ordnance placed for our defence
Strive to break loose and 'scape away from thence.   60
Pumping hath tired our men, and what's the gain?
Seas into seas thrown we suck in again;
Hearing hath deafed our sailors; and if they
Knew how to hear, there's none knows what to say.
Compared to these storms, death is but a qualm,
Hell somewhat lightsome, and the Bermuda calm.
Darkness, light's elder brother, his birthright
Claims o'er this world, and to heaven hath chasèd light.
All things are one, and that one none can be,
Since all forms uniform deformity   70
Doth cover, so that we, except God say
Another *Fiat*, shall have no more day.
So violent yet long these furies be
That though thine absence starve me I wish not thee.

Composed 1597   First published 1633

THE CALM

Our storm is past, and that storm's tyrannous rage
A stupid calm, but nothing it, doth 'suage.
The fable is inverted, and far more
A block afflicts, now, than a stork before.
Storms chafe, and soon wear out themselves, or us;
In calms, heaven laughs to see us languish thus.
As steady as I can wish that my thoughts were,
Smooth as thy mistress' glass, or what shines there,
The sea is now; and, as those isles which we
Seek, when we can move, our ships rooted be.   10
As water did in storms, now pitch runs out,
As lead, when a fired church becomes one spout.
And all our beauty, and our trim, decays,
Like courts removing, or like ended plays.

124

The fighting place now seamen's rags supply;
And all the tackling is a frippery.
No use of lanterns; and in one place lay
Feathers and dust, today and yesterday.
Earth's hollownesses, which the world's lungs are,
Have no more wind than the upper vault of air.   20
We can nor left friends nor sought foes recover,
But meteor-like, save that we move not, hover.
Only the calenture together draws
Dear friends, which meet dead in great fishes' jaws:
And on the hatches as on altars lies
Each one, his own priest and own sacrifice.
Who live, that miracle do multiply
Where walkers in hot ovens do not die.
If in despite of these we swim, that hath
No more refreshing than our brimstone bath,   30
But from the sea into the ship we turn,
Like parboiled wretches on the coals to burn.
Like Bajazet encaged, the shepherd's scoff,
Or like slack-sinewed Samson, his hair off,
Languish our ships. Now, as a myriad
Of ants durst th' emperor's loved snake invade,
The crawling galleys, sea-gaols, finny chips,
Might brave our Venices, now bed-rid ships.
Whether a rotten state, and hope of gain,
Or to disuse me from the queasy pain   40
Of being beloved and loving, or the thirst
Of honour or fair death, out pushed me first,
I lose my end: for here as well as I
A desperate may live, and a coward die.
Stag, dog, and all which from or towards flies,
Is paid with life or prey, or doing dies.
Fate grudges us all, and doth subtly lay
A scourge, 'gainst which we all forget to pray.
He that at sea prays for more wind, as well
Under the poles may beg cold, heat in hell.   50
What are we then? How little more, alas,

Is man now, than before he was! he was
Nothing; for us, we are for nothing fit;
Chance or ourselves still disproportion it.
We have no power, no will, no sense. I lie:
I should not then thus feel this misery.

Composed 1597   First published 1633

TO SIR HENRY WOTTON

Sir, more than kisses, letters mingle souls,
For thus friends absent speak. This ease controls
The tediousness of my life: but for these
I could ideate nothing which could please,
But I should wither in one day, and pass
To a bottle of hay, that am a lock of grass.
Life is a voyage, and in our life's ways
Countries, courts, towns are rocks, or remoras;
They break or stop all ships, yet our state's such,
That though than pitch they stain worse, we must touch.   10
If in the furnace of the even line,
Or under th' adverse icy poles thou pine,
Thou know'st two temperate regions girded in;
Dwell there. But O, what refuge canst thou win
Parched in the court, and in the country frozen?
Shall cities, built of both extremes, be chosen?
Can dung and garlic be a perfume? or can
A scorpion and torpedo cure a man?
Cities are worst of all three; of all three
(O knotty riddle) each is worst equally.   20
Cities are sepulchres; they who dwell there
Are carcasses, as if no such there were.
And courts are theatres, where some men play
Princes, some slaves, all to one end, and of one clay.
The country is a desert, where no good
Gained (as habits, not born) is understood.
There men become beasts, and prone to more evils;

126

In cities blocks, and in a lewd court devils.
As in the first chaos confusedly
Each element's qualities were in th' other three;   30
So pride, lust, covetise, being several
To these three places, yet all are in all,
And mingled thus, their issue incestuous.
Falsehood is denizened. Virtue is barbarous.
Let no man say there, 'Virtue's flinty wall
Shall lock vice in me, I'll do none, but know all.'
Men are sponges, which to pour out, receive;
Who know false play, rather than lose, deceive.
For in best understandings sin began:
Angels sinned first, then devils, and then man.   40
Only perchance beasts sin not; wretched we
Are beasts in all but white integrity.
I think if men which in these places live
Durst look for themselves, and themselves retrieve,
They would like strangers greet themselves, seeing then
Utopian youth grown old Italian.

　　Be then thine own home, and in thyself dwell;
Inn anywhere, continuance maketh hell.
And seeing the snail, which everywhere doth roam,
Carrying his own house still, still is at home,   50
Follow (for he is easy-paced) this snail,
Be thine own palace, or the world's thy gaol.
And in the world's sea, do not like cork sleep
Upon the water's face, nor in the deep
Sink like a lead without a line: but as
Fishes glide, leaving no print where they pass,
Nor making sound, so closely thy course go,
Let men dispute whether thou breathe or no.
Only in this one thing be no Galenist: to make
Courts' hot ambitions wholesome, do not take   60
A dram of country's dullness; do not add
Correctives, but, as chemics, purge the bad.
But, Sir, I advise not you, I rather do
Say o'er those lessons which I learned of you:

Whom, free from German schisms, and lightness
Of France, and fair Italy's faithlessness,
Having from these sucked all they had of worth,
And brought home that faith which you carried forth,
I throughly love. But if myself I 've won
To know my rules, I have, and you have,

                      Donne.   70

Composed 1597–8?   *First published 1633*

TO THE COUNTESS OF BEDFORD

Honour is so sublime perfection,
And so refined, that when God was alone
And creatureless at first, himself had none;

But as of th' elements, these which we tread
Produce all things with which we're joyed or fed,
And those are barren both above our head,

So from low persons doth all honour flow;
Kings whom they would have honoured to us show,
And but direct our honour, not bestow.

For when from herbs the pure parts must be won   10
From gross, by stilling, this is better done
By despised dung than by the fire or sun.

Care not then, Madam, how low your praisers lie;
In labourers' ballads oft more piety
God finds than in Te Deums' melody.

And ordnance raised on towers so many mile
Send not their voice, nor last so long a while,
As fires from th' earth's low vaults in Sicil Isle.

128

Should I say I lived darker than were true,
Your radiation can all clouds subdue;   20
But one, 'tis best light to contemplate you:

You, for whose body God made better clay,
Or took souls' stuff such as shall late decay,
Or such as needs small change at the last day.

This, as an amber drop enwraps a bee,
Covering discovers your quick soul; that we
May in your through-shine front your heart's thoughts see.

You teach (though we learn not) a thing unknown
To our late times, the use of specular stone,
Through which all things within without were shown.   30

Of such were temples; so and of such you are;
Being and seeming is your equal care,
And virtue's whole sum is but know and dare.

But as our souls of growth and souls of sense
Have birthright of our reason's soul, yet hence
They fly not from that, nor seek precedence:

Nature's first lesson, so, discretion,
Must not grudge zeal a place, nor yet keep none;
Not banish itself, nor religion.

Discretion is a wise man's soul, and so   40
Religion is a Christian's, and you know
How these are one, her yea is not her no.

Nor may we hope to solder still and knit
These two, and dare to break them; nor must wit
Be colleague to religion, but be it.

In those poor types of God (round circles) so
Religion's types, the pieceless centres flow,
And are in all the lines which all ways go.

If either ever wrought in you alone
Or principally, then religion   50
Wrought your ends, and your ways discretion.

Go thither still, go the same way you went;
Whoso would change do covet or repent;
Neither can reach you, great and innocent.

Composed 1608–15?   First published 1633

The First Anniversary:
An Anatomy of the World

WHEREIN, BY OCCASION OF THE
UNTIMELY DEATH OF MISTRESS
ELIZABETH DRURY, THE FRAILTY
AND THE DECAY OF THIS WHOLE
WORLD IS REPRESENTED

When that rich soul which to her heaven is gone,
Whom all they celebrate who know they 've one
(For who is sure he hath a soul, unless
It see, and judge, and follow worthiness,
And by deeds praise it? he who doth not this,
May lodge an inmate soul, but 'tis not his),
When that queen ended here her progress time,
And, as t' her standing house, to heaven did climb,
Where loath to make the saints attend her long,
She's now a part both of the choir and song,   10
This world in that great earthquake languishèd;
For in a common bath of tears it bled,
Which drew the strongest vital spirits out.
But succoured then with a perplexèd doubt,
Whether the world did lose or gain in this
(Because since now no other way there is

But goodness, to see her whom all would see,
All must endeavour to be good as she),
This great consumption to a fever turned,
And so the world had fits; it joyed, it mourned.   20
And as men think that agues physic are,
And, th' ague being spent, give over care,
So thou, sick world, mistak'st thyself to be
Well, when, alas, thou'rt in a lethargy.
Her death did wound and tame thee then, and then
Thou mightst have better spared the sun, or man.
That wound was deep, but 'tis more misery
That thou hast lost thy sense and memory.
'Twas heavy then to hear thy voice of moan,
But this is worse, that thou art speechless grown.   30
Thou hast forgot thy name thou hadst; thou wast
Nothing but she, and her thou hast o'erpast.
For as a child kept from the font until
A prince, expected long, come to fulfil
The ceremonies, thou unnamed hadst laid,
Had not her coming thee her palace made:
Her name defined thee, gave thee form and frame,
And thou forget'st to celebrate thy name.
Some months she hath been dead (but being dead,
Measures of times are all determinèd),   40
But long she hath been away, long, long, yet none
Offers to tell us who it is that's gone.
But as in states doubtful of future heirs,
When sickness without remedy impairs
The present prince, they're loath it should be said
The prince doth languish, or the prince is dead,
So mankind feeling now a general thaw,
A strong example gone, equal to law,
The cement which did faithfully compact
And glue all virtues, now resolved and slacked,   50
Thought it some blasphemy to say she was dead;
Or that our weakness was discoverèd
In that confession; therefore spoke no more

132

Than tongues, the soul being gone, the loss deplore.
But though it be too late to succour thee,
Sick world, yea dead, yea putrefied, since she
Thy intrinsic balm and thy preservative
Can never be renewed, thou never live,
I (since no man can make thee live) will try
What we may gain by thy anatomy.   60
Her death hath taught us dearly that thou art
Corrupt and mortal in thy purest part.
Let no man say, the world itself being dead,
'Tis labour lost to have discoverèd
The world's infirmities, since there is none
Alive to study this dissection;
For there's a kind of world remaining still;
Though she which did inanimate and fill
The world be gone, yet in this last long night
Her ghost doth walk; that is, a glimmering light,   70
A faint weak love of virtue and of good
Reflects from her on them which understood
Her worth; and though she have shut in all day,
The twilight of her memory doth stay;
Which, from the carcass of the old world free,
Creates a new world; and new creatures be
Produced; the matter and the stuff of this,
Her virtue, and the form our practice is.
And though to be thus elemented arm
These creatures from home-born intrinsic harm   80
(For all assumed unto this dignity,
So many weedless paradises be,
Which of themselves produce no venomous sin,
Except some foreign serpent bring it in),
Yet, because outward storms the strongest break,
And strength itself by confidence grows weak,
This new world may be safer, being told
The dangers and diseases of the old:
For with due temper men do then forgo
Or covet things, when they their true worth know.   90

There is no health; physicians say that we
At best enjoy but a neutrality.
And can there be worse sickness than to know
That we are never well, nor can be so?
We are born ruinous: poor mothers cry
That children come not right nor orderly
Except they headlong come, and fall upon
An ominous precipitation.
How witty's ruin! how importunate
Upon mankind! It laboured to frustrate   100
Even God's purpose; and made woman, sent
For man's relief, cause of his languishment.
They were to good ends, and they are so still,
But accessory and principal in ill.
For that first marriage was our funeral:
One woman at one blow then killed us all,
And singly, one by one, they kill us now.
We do delightfully ourselves allow
To that consumption; and, profusely blind,
We kill ourselves, to propagate our kind.   110
And yet we do not that; we are not men:
There is not now that mankind which was then,
Whenas the sun and man did seem to strive
(Joint tenants of the world) who should survive;
When stag, and raven, and the long-lived tree,
Compared with man, died in minority;
When, if a slow-paced star had stol'n away
From the observer's marking, he might stay
Two or three hundred years to see't again,
And then make up his observation plain;   120
When, as the age was long, the size was great;
Man's growth confessed, and recompensed the meat;
So spacious and large that every soul
Did a fair kingdom and large realm control;
And when the very stature, thus erect,
Did that soul a good way towards heaven direct.
Where is this mankind now? Who lives to age

Fit to be made Methusalem his page?
Alas, we scarce live long enough to try
Whether a new-made clock run right or lie. 130
Old grandsires talk of yesterday with sorrow,
And for our children we reserve tomorrow.
So short is life, that every peasant strives
In a torn house or field to have three lives.
And as in lasting, so in length is man
Contracted to an inch, who was a span;
For had a man at first in forests strayed,
Or shipwrecked in the sea, one would have laid
A wager that an elephant or whale
That met him would not hastily assail 140
A thing so equal to him; now, alas,
The fairies and the pygmies well may pass
As credible; mankind decays so soon,
We're scarce our fathers' shadows cast at noon.
Only death adds t' our length: nor are we grown
In stature to be men, till we are none.
But this were light, did our less volume hold
All the old text; or had we changed to gold
Their silver; or disposed into less glass
Spirits of virtue which then scattered was. 150
But 'tis not so: we're not retired, but damped;
And as our bodies, so our minds are cramped;
'Tis shrinking, not close weaving, that hath thus
In mind and body both bedwarfèd us.
We seem ambitious God's whole work t' undo;
Of nothing he made us, and we strive too
To bring ourselves to nothing back; and we
Do what we can, to do't so soon as he.
With new diseases on ourselves we war,
And with new physic, a worse engine far. 160
Thus man, this world's vice-emperor, in whom
All faculties, all graces are at home –
And if in other creatures they appear,
They're but man's ministers and legates there,

135

To work on their rebellions, and reduce
Them to civility and to man's use –
This man, whom God did woo, and loath t' attend
Till man came up, did down to man descend,
This man, so great that all that is is his,
Oh what a trifle and poor thing he is!   170
If man were anything, he's nothing now:
Help, or at least some time to waste, allow
T' his other wants, yet when he did depart
With her whom we lament, he lost his heart.
She of whom th' ancients seemed to prophesy,
When they called virtues by the name of she;
She in whom virtue was so much refined,
That for allay unto so pure a mind
She took the weaker sex; she that could drive
The poisonous tincture and the stain of Eve   180
Out of her thoughts and deeds, and purify
All, by a true religious alchemy;
She, she is dead; she's dead: when thou know'st this,
Thou know'st how poor a trifling thing man is,
And learn'st thus much by our anatomy,
The heart being perished, no part can be free.
And that except thou feed (not banquet) on
The supernatural food, religion,
Thy better growth grows witherèd and scant;
Be more than man, or thou'rt less than an ant.   190
Then, as mankind, so is the world's whole frame
Quite out of joint, almost created lame:
For before God had made up all the rest,
Corruption entered, and depraved the best:
It seized the angels, and then first of all
The world did in her cradle take a fall,
And turned her brains, and took a general maim
Wronging each joint of th' universal frame.
The noblest part, man, felt it first; and then
Both beasts and plants, cursed in the curse of man.   200
So did the world from the first hour decay,

That evening was beginning of the day,
And now the springs and summers which we see
Like sons of women after fifty be.
And new philosophy calls all in doubt;
The element of fire is quite put out;
The sun is lost, and th' earth, and no man's wit
Can well direct him where to look for it.
And freely men confess that this world's spent,
When in the planets and the firmament   210
They seek so many new; they see that this
Is crumbled out again to his atomies.
'Tis all in pieces, all coherence gone,
All just supply, and all relation:
Prince, subject, father, son, are things forgot,
For every man alone thinks he hath got
To be a phoenix, and that there can be
None of that kind of which he is, but he.
This is the world's condition now, and now
She that should all parts to reunion bow,   220
She that had all magnetic force alone
To draw and fasten sundered parts in one;
She whom wise nature had invented then
When she observed that every sort of men
Did in their voyage in this world's sea stray,
And needed a new compass for their way;
She that was best and first original
Of all fair copies; and the general
Steward to Fate; she whose rich eyes, and breast,
Gilt the West Indies, and perfumed the East;   230
Whose having breathed in this world did bestow
Spice on those isles, and bade them still smell so,
And that rich Indy which doth gold inter
Is but as single money coined from her;
She to whom this world must itself refer,
As suburbs, or the microcosm of her,
She, she is dead; she's dead: when thou know'st this,
Thou know'st how lame a cripple this world is,

137

And learn'st thus much by our anatomy,
That this world's general sickness doth not lie   240
In any humour, or one certain part;
But as thou saw'st it rotten at the heart,
Thou seest a hectic fever hath got hold
Of the whole substance, not to be controlled,
And that thou hast but one way not to admit
The world's infection, to be none of it.
For the world's subtlest immaterial parts
Feel this consuming wound, and age's darts.
For the world's beauty is decayed or gone,
Beauty, that's colour and proportion.   250
We think the heavens enjoy their spherical,
Their round proportion embracing all,
But yet their various and perplexèd course,
Observed in diverse ages, doth enforce
Men to find out so many eccentric parts,
Such diverse downright lines, such overthwarts,
As disproportion that pure form. It tears
The firmament in eight-and-forty shares,
And in those constellations there arise
New stars, and old do vanish from our eyes,   260
As though heaven suffered earthquakes, peace or war,
When new towns rise, and old demolished are.
They have impaled within a zodiac
The free-born sun, and keep twelve signs awake
To watch his steps; the goat and crab control,
And fright him back, who else to either pole
(Did not these tropics fetter him) might run:
For his course is not round; nor can the sun
Perfect a circle, or maintain his way
One inch direct; but where he rose today   270
He comes no more, but with a cozening line,
Steals by that point, and so is serpentine:
And seeming weary with his reeling thus,
He means to sleep, being now fall'n nearer us.
So, of the stars which boast that they do run

In circle still, none ends where he begun;
All their proportion's lame, it sinks, it swells,
For of meridians and parallels
Man hath weaved out a net, and this net thrown
Upon the heavens, and now they are his own.   280
Loath to go up the hill, or labour thus
To go to heaven, we make heaven come to us.
We spur, we rein the stars, and in their race
They're diversely content to obey our pace.
But keeps the earth her round proportion still?
Doth not a Tenerife, or higher hill,
Rise so high like a rock, that one might think
The floating moon would shipwreck there, and sink?
Seas are so deep, that whales being struck today,
Perchance tomorrow, scarce at middle way   290
Of their wished journey's end, the bottom, die.
And men, to sound depths, so much line untie
As one might justly think that there would rise
At end thereof one of th' Antipodes:
If under all a vault infernal be
(Which sure is spacious, except that we
Invent another torment, that there must
Millions into a strait hot room be thrust),
Then solidness and roundness have no place.
Are these but warts and pock-holes in the face   300
Of th' earth? Think so: but yet confess, in this
The world's proportion disfigured is,
That those two legs whereon it doth rely,
Reward and punishment, are bent awry.
And, O, it can no more be questionèd,
That beauty's best, proportion, is dead,
Since even grief itself, which now alone
Is left us, is without proportion.
She by whose lines proportion should be
Examined, measure of all symmetry,   310
Whom had that ancient seen, who thought souls made
Of harmony, he would at next have said

That harmony was she, and thence infer
That souls were but resultances from her,
And did from her into our bodies go,
As to our eyes the forms from objects flow:
She, who if those great doctors truly said
That th' Ark to man's proportions was made,
Had been a type for that, as that might be
A type of her in this, that contrary   320
Both elements and passions lived at peace
In her, who caused all civil war to cease.
She, after whom, what form soe'er we see
Is discord and rude incongruity;
She, she is dead; she's dead; when thou know'st this,
Thou know'st how ugly a monster this world is,
And learn'st thus much by our anatomy,
That here is nothing to enamour thee,
And that not only faults in inward parts,
Corruptions in our brains, or in our hearts,   330
Poisoning the fountains whence our actions spring,
Endanger us; but that if everything
Be not done fitly and in proportion,
To satisfy wise and good lookers-on
(Since most men be such as most think they be),
They're loathsome too, by this deformity.
For good and well must in our actions meet;
Wicked is not much worse than indiscreet.
But beauty's other second element,
Colour and lustre, now is as near spent,   340
And had the world his just proportion,
Were it a ring still, yet the stone is gone.
As a compassionate turquoise which doth tell,
By looking pale, the wearer is not well,
As gold falls sick being stung with mercury,
All the world's parts of such complexion be.
When nature was most busy, the first week,
Swaddling the new-born earth, God seemed to like
That she should sport herself sometimes and play,

140

To mingle and vary colours every day: 350
And then, as though she could not make enow,
Himself his various rainbow did allow.
Sight is the noblest sense of any one,
Yet sight hath only colour to feed on,
And colour is decayed: summer's robe grows
Dusky, and like an oft-dyed garment shows.
Our blushing red, which used in cheeks to spread,
Is inward sunk, and only our souls are red.
Perchance the world might have recoverèd,
If she whom we lament had not been dead: 360
But she, in whom all white, and red, and blue
(Beauty's ingredients) voluntary grew,
As in an unvexed paradise; from whom
Did all things' verdure and their lustre come,
Whose composition was miraculous,
Being all colour, all diaphanous
(For air and fire but thick gross bodies were,
And liveliest stones but drowsy and pale to her)
She, she is dead; she's dead: when thou know'st this,
Thou know'st how wan a ghost this our world is,   370
And learn'st thus much by our anatomy,
That it should more affright than pleasure thee;
And that, since all fair colour then did sink,
'Tis now but wicked vanity to think
To colour vicious deeds with good pretence,
Or with bought colours to illude men's sense.
Nor in aught more this world's decay appears,
Than that her influence the heaven forbears,
Or that the elements do not feel this,
The father or the mother barren is.   380
The clouds conceive not rain, or do not pour,
In the due birth-time, down the balmy shower.
Th' air doth not motherly sit on the earth,
To hatch her seasons, and give all things birth.
Spring-times were common cradles, but are tombs;
And false conceptions fill the general wombs.

Th' air shows such meteors, as none can see
Not only what they mean but what they be;
Earth such new worms, as would have troubled much
Th' Egyptian mages to have made more such.   390
What artist now dares boast that he can bring
Heaven hither, or constellate anything,
So as the influence of those stars may be
Imprisoned in an herb, or charm, or tree,
And do by touch all which those stars could do?
The art is lost, and correspondence too.
For heaven gives little, and the earth takes less,
And man least knows their trade and purposes.
If this commerce 'twixt heaven and earth were not
Embarred, and all this traffic quite forgot,   400
She, for whose loss we have lamented thus,
Would work more fully and powerfully on us.
Since herbs and roots by dying lose not all,
But they, yea ashes too, are med'cinal,
Death could not quench her virtue so, but that
It would be (if not followed) wondered at,
And all the world would be one dying swan,
To sing her funeral praise, and vanish then.
But as some serpents' poison hurteth not,
Except it be from the live serpent shot,   410
So doth her virtue need her here, to fit
That unto us; she working more than it.
But she, in whom to such maturity
Virtue was grown, past growth, that it must die;
She, from whose influence all impressions came,
But, by receivers' impotencies, lame;
Who, though she could not transubstantiate
All states to gold, yet gilded every state,
So that some princes have some temperance,
Some counsellors some purpose to advance   420
The common profit, and some people have
Some stay, no more than kings should give to crave,
Some women have some taciturnity,

142

Some nunneries some grains of chastity;
She that did thus much, and much more could do,
But that our age was iron, and rusty too,
She, she is dead; she's dead; when thou know'st this,
Thou know'st how dry a cinder this world is,
And learn'st thus much by our anatomy,
That 'tis in vain to dew or mollify   430
It with thy tears, or sweat, or blood: nothing
Is worth our travail, grief, or perishing,
But those rich joys, which did possess her heart,
Of which she's now partaker, and a part.
But as in cutting up a man that's dead,
The body will not last out to have read
On every part, and therefore men direct
Their speech to parts that are of most effect;
So the world's carcass would not last, if I
Were punctual in this anatomy.   440
Nor smells it well to hearers if one tell
Them their disease, who fain would think they're well.
Here therefore be the end: and blessed maid,
Of whom is meant whatever hath been said,
Or shall be spoken well by any tongue,
Whose name refines coarse lines, and makes prose song,
Accept this tribute, and his first year's rent,
Who till his dark short taper's end be spent,
As oft as thy feast sees this widowed earth,
Will yearly celebrate thy second birth,   450
That is, thy death. For though the soul of man
Be got when man is made, 'tis born but then
When man doth die. Our body's as the womb,
And as a midwife death directs it home.
And you her creatures, whom she works upon,
And have your last and best concoction
From her example and her virtue, if you
In reverence to her do think it due
That no one should her praises thus rehearse
(As matter fit for chronicle, not verse),   460

143

Vouchsafe to call to mind that God did make
A last and lasting'st piece, a song. He spake
To Moses, to deliver unto all
That song, because he knew they would let fall
The Law, the prophets, and the history,
But keep the song still in their memory.
Such an opinion (in due measure) made
Me this great office boldly to invade.
Nor could incomprehensibleness deter
Me from thus trying to imprison her.   470
Which when I saw that a strict grave could do,
I saw not why verse might not do so too.
Verse hath a middle nature: heaven keeps souls,
The grave keeps bodies, verse the fame enrols.

Composed 1611   First published 1611

Religious Poems

HOLY SONNETS

1

Thou hast made me, and shall thy work decay?
Repair me now, for now mine end doth haste;
I run to death, and death meets me as fast,
And all my pleasures are like yesterday;
I dare not move my dim eyes any way,
Despair behind and death before doth cast
Such terror, and my feeble flesh doth waste
By sin in it, which it towards hell doth weigh;
Only thou art above, and when towards thee
By thy leave I can look, I rise again;   10
But our old subtle foe so tempteth me,
That not one hour I can myself sustain;
Thy grace may wing me to prevent his art,
And thou like adamant draw mine iron heart.

Composed 1609?   First published 1633

2

As due by many titles I resign
Myself to thee, O God; first I was made

By thee, and for thee, and when I was decayed
Thy blood bought that, the which before was thine;
I am thy son, made with thyself to shine,
Thy servant, whose pains thou hast still repaid,
Thy sheep, thine image, and, till I betrayed
Myself, a temple of thy Spirit divine;
Why doth the Devil then usurp in me?
Why doth he steal, nay ravish that's thy right?   10
Except thou rise and for thine own work fight,
O, I shall soon despair, when I do see
That thou lov'st mankind well, yet wilt not choose me,
And Satan hates me, yet is loath to lose me.

Composed 1609?   First published 1633

3

O might those sighs and tears return again
Into my breast and eyes, which I have spent,
That I might in this holy discontent
Mourn with some fruit, as I have mourned in vain;
In mine idolatry what showers of rain
Mine eyes did waste! what griefs my heart did rent!
That sufferance was my sin I now repent;
Because I did suffer I must suffer pain.
Th' hydroptic drunkard, and night-scouting thief,
The itchy lecher, and self-tickling proud,   10
Have the remembrance of past joys for relief
Of coming ills. To poor me is allowed
No ease; for long yet vehement grief hath been
Th' effect and cause, the punishment and sin.

Composed 1609?   First published 1635

4

O my black soul! now thou art summonèd
By sickness, death's herald and champion;
Thou 'rt like a pilgrim, which abroad hath done

146

Treason, and durst not turn to whence he is fled,
Or like a thief, which till death's doom be read
Wisheth himself delivered from prison,
But damned and haled to execution,
Wisheth that still he might be imprisonèd;
Yet grace, if thou repent, thou canst not lack;
But who shall give thee that grace to begin? 10
O, make thyself with holy mourning black,
And red with blushing, as thou art with sin;
Or wash thee in Christ's blood, which hath this might,
That, being red, it dyes red souls to white.

Composed 1609?   First published 1633

5

I am a little world made cunningly
Of elements, and an angelic sprite,
But black sin hath betrayed to endless night
My world's both parts, and, O, both parts must die.
You which beyond that heaven which was most high
Have found new spheres, and of new lands can write,
Pour new seas in mine eyes, that so I might
Drown my world with my weeping earnestly,
Or wash it if it must be drowned no more:
But O, it must be burnt; alas, the fire 10
Of lust and envy have burnt it heretofore,
And made it fouler; let their flames retire,
And burn me, O Lord, with a fiery zeal
Of thee and thy house, which doth in eating heal.

Composed 1609?   First published 1635

6

This is my play's last scene, here heavens appoint
My pilgrimage's last mile; and my race,
Idly yet quickly run, hath this last pace,
My span's last inch, my minute's latest point;

And gluttonous death will instantly unjoint
My body and soul, and I shall sleep a space,
But my ever-waking part shall see that face
Whose fear already shakes my every joint:
Then, as my soul t' heaven her first seat takes flight,
And earth-born body in the earth shall dwell,   10
So fall my sins, that all may have their right,
To where they 're bred, and would press me, to hell.
Impute me righteous, thus purged of evil,
For thus I leave the world, the flesh, the Devil.

Composed 1609?   First published 1633

7

At the round earth's imagined corners, blow
Your trumpets, angels, and arise, arise
From death, you numberless infinities
Of souls, and to your scattered bodies go,
All whom the flood did, and fire shall o'erthrow,
All whom war, dearth, age, agues, tyrannies,
Despair, law, chance, hath slain, and you whose eyes
Shall behold God, and never taste death's woe.
But let them sleep, Lord, and me mourn a space,
For if above all these my sins abound,   10
'Tis late to ask abundance of thy grace,
When we are there; here on this lowly ground,
Teach me how to repent; for that's as good
As if thou'dst sealed my pardon with thy blood.

Composed 1609?   First published 1633

9

If poisonous minerals, and if that tree,
Whose fruit threw death on else immortal us,
If lecherous goats, if serpents envious
Cannot be damned, alas, why should I be?
Why should intent or reason, born in me,

Make sins, else equal, in me more heinous?
And mercy being easy and glorious
To God, in his stern wrath why threatens he?
But who am I, that dare dispute with thee,
O God? O, of thine only worthy blood   10
And my tears make a heavenly Lethean flood,
And drown in it my sins' black memory;
That thou remember them some claim as debt;
I think it mercy if thou wilt forget.

Composed 1609?   First published 1633

10

Death, be not proud, though some have callèd thee
Mighty and dreadful, for thou art not so,
For those whom thou think'st thou dost overthrow
Die not, poor Death, nor yet canst thou kill me;
From rest and sleep, which but thy pictures be,
Much pleasure, then from thee much more must flow,
And soonest our best men with thee do go,
Rest of their bones, and souls' delivery.
Thou 'rt slave to fate, chance, kings, and desperate men,
And dost with poison, war, and sickness dwell,   10
And poppy or charms can make us sleep as well,
And better than thy stroke; why swell'st thou then?
One short sleep past, we wake eternally,
And death shall be no more; Death, thou shalt die.

Composed 1609?   First published 1633

11

Spit in my face, ye Jews, and pierce my side,
Buffet, and scoff, scourge and crucify me,
For I have sinned, and sinned, and only he
Who could do no iniquity hath died:
But by my death cannot be satisfied
My sins, which pass the Jews' impiety:

149

They killed once an inglorious man, but I
Crucify him daily, being now glorified.
O, let me then his strange love still admire:
Kings pardon, but he bore our punishment.   10
And Jacob came clothed in vile harsh attire
But to supplant, and with gainful intent:
God clothed himself in vile man's flesh, that so
He might be weak enough to suffer woe.

Composed 1609?   First published 1633

13

What if this present were the world's last night?
Mark in my heart, O soul, where thou dost dwell,
The picture of Christ crucified, and tell
Whether that countenance can thee affright;
Tears in his eyes quench the amazing light,
Blood fills his frowns, which from his pierced head fell,
And can that tongue adjudge thee unto hell,
Which prayed forgiveness for his foes' fierce spite?
No, no; but as in my idolatry
I said to all my profane mistresses,   10
'Beauty, of pity, foulness only is
A sign of rigour', so I say to thee,
'To wicked spirits are horrid shapes assigned;
This beauteous form assures a piteous mind.'

Composed 1609?   First published 1633

14

Batter my heart, three-personed God; for you
As yet but knock, breathe, shine, and seek to mend;
That I may rise and stand, o'erthrow me, and bend
Your force to break, blow, burn, and make me new.
I, like an usurped town, to another due,
Labour to admit you, but O, to no end;
Reason, your viceroy in me, me should defend,

150

But is captived, and proves weak or untrue;
Yet dearly I love you, and would be loved fain,
But am betrothed unto your enemy;   10
Divorce me, untie, or break that knot again,
Take me to you, imprison me, for I,
Except you enthral me, never shall be free,
Nor ever chaste, except you ravish me.

Composed 1609?   First published 1633

17

Since she whom I loved hath paid her last debt
To nature, and to hers and my good is dead,
And her soul early into heaven ravishèd,
Wholly in heavenly things my mind is set.
Here the admiring her my mind did whet
To seek thee, God; so streams do show the head;
But though I 've found thee, and thou my thirst hast fed,
A holy thirsty dropsy melts me yet.
But why should I beg more love, whenas thou
Dost woo my soul, for hers offering all thine: 10
And dost not only fear lest I allow
My love to saints and angels, things divine,
But in thy tender jealousy dost doubt
Lest the world, flesh, yea Devil put thee out?

Composed in or after 1617   First published 1894

18

Show me, dear Christ, thy spouse, so bright and clear.
What, is it she which on the other shore
Goes richly painted? or which robbed and tore
Laments and mourns in Germany and here?
Sleeps she a thousand, then peeps up one year?
Is she self truth and errs? now new, now outwore?
Doth she, and did she, and shall she evermore
On one, on seven, or on no hill appear?

Dwells she with us, or like adventuring knights
First travel we to seek and then make love?   10
Betray, kind husband, thy spouse to our sights,
And let mine amorous soul court thy mild dove,
Who is most true and pleasing to thee, then
When she's embraced and open to most men.

Composed 1620?   First published 1899

19

O, to vex me, contraries meet in one:
Inconstancy unnaturally hath begot
A constant habit; that when I would not
I change in vows and in devotion.
As humorous is my contrition
As my profane love, and as soon forgot:
As riddlingly distempered, cold and hot;
As praying, as mute; as infinite, as none.
I durst not view heaven yesterday; and today
In prayers and flattering speeches I court God: 10
Tomorrow I quake with true fear of his rod.
So my devout fits come and go away
Like a fantastic ague: save that here
Those are my best days, when I shake with fear.

Composed in or after 1615?   First published 1899

THE CROSS

Since Christ embraced the Cross itself, dare I,
His image, th' image of his Cross deny?
Would I have profit by the sacrifice,
And dare the chosen altar to despise?
It bore all other sins, but is it fit
That it should bear the sin of scorning it?
Who from the picture would avert his eye,
How would he fly his pains who there did die!

From me no pulpit nor misgrounded law
Nor scandal taken shall this Cross withdraw;   10
It shall not, for it cannot; for the loss
Of this Cross were to me another cross;
Better were worse, for no affliction,
No cross, is so extreme as to have none.
Who can blot out the Cross which th' instrument
Of God dewed on me in the Sacrament?
Who can deny me power and liberty
To stretch mine arms, and mine own cross to be?
Swim, and, at every stroke, thou art thy cross.
The mast and yard make one, where seas do toss.   20
Look down, thou spy'st out crosses in small things;
Look up, thou seest birds raised on crossèd wings;
All the globe's frame, and sphere's, is nothing else
But the meridians crossing parallels.
Material crosses, then, good physic be,
And yet spiritual have chief dignity.
These for extracted chemic medicine serve,
And cure much better, and as well preserve;
Then are you your own physic, or need none,
When stilled or purged by tribulation.   30
For when that cross, ungrudged, unto you sticks
Then are you to yourself a crucifix.
As, perchance, carvers do not faces make,
But that away, which hid them there, do take,
Let crosses, so, take what hid Christ in thee,
And be his image, or not his, but he.
But, as oft alchemists do coiners prove,
So may a self-despising get self-love.
And then as worst surfeits of best meats be,
So is pride issued from humility,   40
For 'tis no child, but monster; therefore cross
Your joy in crosses, else 'tis double loss;
And cross thy senses, else both they and thou
Must perish soon and to destruction bow.
For if th' eye seek good objects, and will take

No cross from bad, we cannot 'scape a snake.
So with harsh, hard, sour, stinking, cross the rest,
Make them indifferent; call nothing best.
But most the eye needs crossing, that can roam
And move; to th' others th' objects must come home.   50
And cross thy heart: for that in man alone
Points downwards, and hath palpitation.
Cross those dejections when it downward tends,
And when it to forbidden heights pretends.
And as thy brain through bony walls doth vent
By sutures which a cross's form present,
So, when thy brain works, ere thou utter it,
Cross and correct concupiscence of wit.
Be covetous of crosses, let none fall.
Cross no man else, but cross thyself in all.   60
Then doth the Cross of Christ work fruitfully
Within our hearts, when we love harmlessly
That Cross's pictures much, and with more care
That Cross's children, which our crosses are.

Composed 1596–1604?   First published 1633

GOOD FRIDAY, 1613. RIDING
WESTWARD

Let man's soul be a sphere, and then, in this,
The intelligence that moves, devotion is;
And as the other spheres, by being grown
Subject to foreign motions, lose their own,
And being by others hurried every day,
Scarce in a year their natural form obey,
Pleasure or business, so, our souls admit
For their first mover, and are whirled by it.
Hence is't that I am carried towards the west
This day, when my soul's form bends toward the east.   10
There I should see a sun by rising set,
And by that setting endless day beget;

But that Christ on this Cross did rise and fall,
Sin had eternally benighted all.
Yet dare I almost be glad I do not see
That spectacle of too much weight for me.
Who sees God's face, that is self life, must die;
What a death were it then to see God die?
It made his own lieutenant Nature shrink,
It made his footstool crack, and the sun wink.   20
Could I behold those hands which span the poles,
And turn all spheres at once, pierced with those holes?
Could I behold that endless height which is
Zenith to us and t' our antipodes,
Humbled below us? or that blood which is
The seat of all our souls, if not of his,
Make dirt of dust, or that flesh which was worn
By God for his apparel, ragg'd, and torn?
If on these things I durst not look, durst I
Upon his miserable mother cast mine eye,   30
Who was God's partner here, and furnished thus
Half of that sacrifice which ransomed us?
Though these things, as I ride, be from mine eye,
They are present yet unto my memory,
For that looks towards them; and thou look'st towards me,
O Saviour, as thou hang'st upon the tree;
I turn my back to thee but to receive
Corrections, till thy mercies bid thee leave.
O think me worth thine anger, punish me,
Burn off my rusts and my deformity,   40
Restore thine image, so much, by thy grace,
That thou mayst know me, and I'll turn my face.

Composed 1613   First published 1633

A HYMN TO CHRIST, AT THE AUTHOR'S
LAST GOING INTO GERMANY

In what torn ship soever I embark,
That ship shall be my emblem of thy ark;
What sea soever swallow me, that flood
Shall be to me an emblem of thy blood;
Though thou with clouds of anger do disguise
Thy face, yet through that mask I know those eyes
Which, though they turn away sometimes, they never will despise.

I sacrifice this island unto thee,
And all whom I loved there, and who loved me;
When I have put our seas 'twixt them and me,   10
Put thou thy sea betwixt my sins and thee.
As the tree's sap doth seek the root below
In winter, in my winter now I go
Where none but thee, th' eternal root of true love, I may know.

Nor thou nor thy religion dost control
The amorousness of an harmonious soul;
But thou wouldst have that love thyself. As thou
Art jealous, Lord, so I am jealous now.
Thou lov'st not, till from loving more thou free
My soul; whoever gives, takes liberty;   20
O, if thou car'st not whom I love, alas, thou lov'st not me.

Seal then this bill of my divorce to all
On whom those fainter beams of love did fall;
Marry those loves which in youth scattered be
On fame, wit, hopes (false mistresses) to thee.
Churches are best for prayer that have least light:
To see God only, I go out of sight;
And to 'scape stormy days, I choose an everlasting night.

Composed 1619   First published 1633

156

HYMN TO GOD MY GOD, IN MY SICKNESS

Since I am coming to that holy room
    Where, with thy choir of saints for evermore,
I shall be made thy music, as I come
    I tune the instrument here at the door,
    And what I must do then, think now before.

Whilst my physicians by their love are grown
    Cosmographers, and I their map, who lie
Flat on this bed, that by them may be shown
    That this is my south-west discovery
    Per fretum febris, by these straits to die,   10

I joy that in these straits I see my west;
    For though their currents yield return to none,
What shall my west hurt me? As west and east
    In all flat maps (and I am one) are one,
    So death doth touch the resurrection.

Is the Pacific Sea my home? Or are
    The eastern riches? Is Jerusalem?
Anyan, and Magellan, and Gibraltar,
    All straits, and none but straits, are ways to them,
    Whether where Japhet dwelt, or Cham, or Shem.   20

We think that Paradise and Calvary,
    Christ's Cross and Adam's tree, stood in one place;
Look, Lord, and find both Adams met in me;
    As the first Adam's sweat surrounds my face,
    May the last Adam's blood my soul embrace.

So in his purple wrapped receive me, Lord,
    By these his thorns give me his other crown;
And as to others' souls I preached thy word,
    Be this my text, my sermon to mine own:
    'Therefore that he may raise the Lord throws down.'   30

Composed 1623?   *First published 1635*

A HYMN TO GOD THE FATHER

Wilt thou forgive that sin where I begun,
   Which is my sin, though it were done before?
Wilt thou forgive those sins through which I run,
   And do them still, though still I do deplore?
     When thou hast done, thou hast not done,
       For I have more.

Wilt thou forgive that sin by which I 've won
   Others to sin, and made my sin their door?
Wilt thou forgive that sin which I did shun
   A year or two, but wallowed in a score?   10
     When thou hast done, thou hast not done,
       For I have more.

I have a sin of fear that when I 've spun
   My last thread I shall perish on the shore;
Swear by thy self, that at my death thy sun
   Shall shine as it shines now, and heretofore;
     And, having done that, thou hast done,
       I fear no more.

Composed 1623?   *First published 1633*

Devotions

1 The first alteration, the first grudging of the sickness.

Variable, and therefore miserable, condition of man! This minute I was well, and am ill this minute. I am surprised with a sudden change and alteration to worse, and can impute it to no cause, nor call it by any name. We study health, and we deliberate upon our meats, and drink, and air, and exercises, and we hew and we polish every stone that goes to that building; and so our health is a long and a regular work; but in a minute a cannon batters all, overthrows all, demolishes all; a sickness unprevented for all our diligence, unsuspected for all our curiosity, nay, undeserved, if we consider only disorder, 10 summons us, seizes us, possesses us, destroys us in an instant. O miserable condition of man, which was not imprinted by God, who, as he is immortal himself, had put a coal, a beam of immortality into us, which we might have blown into a flame, but blew it out by our first sin; we beggared ourselves by harkening after false riches, and infatuated ourselves by harkening after false knowledge. So that now we do not only die, but die upon the rack, die by the torment of sickness; nor that only, but are pre-afflicted, super-afflicted with these jealousies and suspicions and apprehensions of sickness, before we can call it a 20 sickness; we are not sure we are ill; one hand asks the other by the pulse, and our eye asks our own urine, how we do. O

159

multiplied misery! We die, and cannot enjoy death, because we die in this torment of sickness; we are tormented with sickness, and cannot stay till the torment come, but pre-apprehensions and presages prophesy those torments which induce that death before either come; and our dissolution is conceived in these first changes, quickened in the sickness itself, and born in death, which bears date from these first changes. Is this the honour which man hath by being a little world, that he hath these 30 earthquakes in himself, sudden shakings; these lightnings, sudden flashes; these thunders, sudden noises; these eclipses, sudden offuscations and darkenings of his senses; these blazing stars, sudden fiery exhalations; these rivers of blood, sudden red waters? Is he a world to himself only therefore, that he hath enough in himself not only to destroy and execute himself but to presage that execution upon himself, to assist the sickness, to antedate the sickness, to make the sickness the more irremediable, by sad apprehensions, and as if he would make a fire the more vehement by sprinkling water upon the coals, so to wrap 40 a hot fever in cold melancholy, lest the fever alone should not destroy fast enough without this contribution, nor perfect the work (which is destruction) except we joined an artificial sickness, of our own melancholy, to our natural, our unnatural fever? O perplexed discomposition, O riddling distemper, O miserable condition of man!

6 The physician is afraid.

I observe the physician with the same diligence as he the disease; I see he fears, and I fear with him; I overtake him, I overrun him in his fear, and I go the faster because he makes his pace slow; I fear the more because he disguises his fear, and I see it with the more sharpness because he would not have me see it. He knows that his fear shall not disorder the practice and exercise of his art, but he knows that my fear may disorder the effect and working of his practice. As the ill affections of the spleen complicate and mingle themselves with every infirmity of the body, so doth fear insinuate itself in every action or passion of 10

160

the mind; and as the wind in the body will counterfeit any disease, and seem the stone and seem the gout, so fear will counterfeit any disease of the mind. It shall seem love, a love of having, and it is but a fear, a jealous and suspicious fear of losing; it shall seem valour in despising and undervaluing danger, and it is but fear, in an overvaluing of opinion and estimation, and a fear of losing that. A man that is not afraid of a lion is afraid of a cat; not afraid of starving, and yet is afraid of some joint of meat at the table, presented to feed him; not afraid of the sound of drums and trumpets and shot, and those which   20 they seek to drown, the last cries of men, and is afraid of some particular harmonious instrument; so much afraid as that with any of these the enemy might drive this man, otherwise valiant enough, out of the field. I know not what fear is, nor I know not what it is that I fear now. I fear not the hastening of my death, and yet I do fear the increase of the disease; I should belie nature if I should deny that I feared this, and if I should say that I feared death I should belie God; my weakness is from nature, who hath put her measure; my strength is from God, who possesses and distributes infinitely. As then every cold air is not a   30 damp, every shivering is not a stupefaction, so every fear is not a fearfulness, every declination is not a running away, every debating is not a resolving, every wish that it were not thus is not a murmuring nor a dejection though it be thus; but as my physician's fear puts not him from his practice, neither doth mine put me from receiving from God, and man, and myself, spiritual and civil and moral assistances and consolations.

7 The physician desires to have others joined with him.

There is more fear, therefore more cause. If the physician desire help, the burden grows great. There is a growth of the disease then; but there must be an autumn too; but whether an autumn of the disease or me it is not my part to choose; but if it be of me, it is of both; my disease cannot survive me, I may overlive it. Howsoever, his desiring of others argues his candour and his ingenuity; if the danger be great, he justifies his proceedings

and he disguises nothing that calls in witnesses; and if the
danger be not great, he is not ambitious that is so ready to
divide the thanks and the honour of that work which he begun   10
alone with others. It diminishes not the dignity of a monarch
that he derive part of his care upon others; God hath not made
many suns, but he hath made many bodies that receive and give
light. The Romans began with one king; they came to two
consuls; they returned in extremities to one dictator: whether
in one or many, the sovereignty is the same in all states, and the
danger is not the more, and the providence is the more, where
there are more physicians, as the state is the happier where busi-
nesses are carried by more counsels than can be in one breast
how large soever. Diseases themselves hold consultations, and   20
conspire how they may multiply and join with one another, and
exalt one another's force so; and shall we not call physicians to
consultations? Death is in an old man's door, he appears and
tells him so, and death is at a young man's back and says
nothing; age is a sickness and youth is an ambush; and we need
so many physicians as may make up a watch and spy every
inconvenience. There is scarce anything that hath not killed
somebody; a hair, a feather hath done it; nay, that which is our
best antidote against it hath done it; the best cordial hath been
deadly poison; men have died of joy, and almost forbidden their   30
friends to weep for them when they have seen them die laughing. Even that tyrant Dionysius (I think the same that suffered
so much after), who could not die of that sorrow, of that high
fall from a king to a wretched private man, died of so poor a joy
as to be declared by the people at a theatre that he was a good
poet. We say often that a man may live of a little; but alas, of
how much less may a man die! And therefore the more assist-
ants the better. Who comes to a day of hearing, in a cause of
any importance, with one advocate? In our funerals we ourselves have no interest; there we cannot advise, we cannot   40
direct; and though some nations (the Egyptians in particular)
built themselves better tombs than houses, because they were to
dwell longer in them, yet, amongst ourselves, the greatest man
of style whom we have had, the Conqueror, was left, as soon as

162

his soul left him, not only without persons to assist at his grave, but without a grave. Who will keep us then we know not; as long as we can, let us admit as much help as we can. Another and another physician is not another and another indication and symptom of death, but another and another assistant and proctor of life; nor do they so much feed the imagination with apprehension of danger as the understanding with comfort; let not one bring learning, another diligence, another religion, but every one bring all, and, as many ingredients enter into a receipt, so may many men make the receipt. But why do I exercise my meditation so long upon this, of having plentiful help in time of need? Is not my meditation rather to be inclined another way, to condole and commiserate their distress who have none? How many are sicker, perchance, than I, and laid on their woeful straw at home (if that corner be a home), and have no more hope of help, though they die, than of preferment, though they live, nor do no more expect to see a physician then than to be an officer after; of whom the first that takes knowledge is the sexton that buries them, who buries them in oblivion too! For they do but fill up the number of the dead in the bill, but we shall never hear their names till we read them in the book of life with our own. How many are sicker, perchance, than I, and thrown into hospitals where (as a fish left upon the sand must stay the tide) they must stay the physician's hour of visiting, and then can be but visited! How many are sicker, perchance, than all we, and have not this hospital to cover them, not this straw to lie in, to die in, but have their gravestone under them, and breathe out their souls in the ears and in the eyes of passengers harder than their bed the flint of the street! that taste of no part of our physic but a sparing diet; to whom ordinary porridge would be julep enough, the refuse of our servants bezoar enough, and the off-scouring of our kitchen tables cordial enough! O my soul, when thou art not enough awake to bless thy God enough for his plentiful mercy in affording thee many helpers, remember how many lack them, and help them to them, or to those other things which they lack as much as them.

163

16 From the bells of the church adjoining, I am daily
remembered of my burial in the funerals of others.

We have a convenient author who writ a *Discourse of Bells* when
he was prisoner in Turkey. How would he have enlarged himself if he had been my fellow-prisoner in this sick-bed, so near to
that steeple which never ceases, no more than the harmony of
the spheres, but is more heard? When the Turks took Constan-
tinople they melted the bells into ordnance; I have heard both
bells and ordnance, but never been so much affected with those
as with these bells. I have lain near a steeple in which there are
said to be more than thirty bells, and near another where there
is one so big as that the clapper is said to weigh more than six   10
hundred pound, yet never so affected as here. Here the bells can
scarce solemnize the funeral of any person but that I knew him,
or knew that he was my neighbour: we dwelt in houses near to
one another before, but now he is gone into that house into
which I must follow him. There is a way of correcting the
children of great persons, that other children are corrected in
their behalf, and in their names, and this works upon them,
who indeed had more deserved it. And when these bells tell me
that now one and now another is buried, must not I acknowledge that they have the correction due to me, and paid the debt   20
that I owe? There is a story of a bell in a monastery which,
when any of the house was sick to death, rung always voluntarily, and they knew the inevitableness of the danger by that.
It rung once when no man was sick; but the next day one of the
house fell from the steeple and died, and the bell held the reputation of a prophet still. If these bells that warn to a funeral now
were appropriated to none, may not I, by the hour of the
funeral, supply? How many men that stand at an execution, if
they would ask 'For what dies that man?', should hear their
own faults condemned, and see themselves executed by   30
attorney! We scarce hear of any man preferred but we think of
ourselves that we might very well have been that man; why
might not I have been that man that is carried to his grave now?
Could I fit myself to stand or sit in any man's place, and not to

lie in any man's grave? I may lack much of the good parts of the
meanest, but I lack nothing of the mortality of the weakest;
they may have acquired better abilities than I, but I was born to
as many infirmities as they. To be an incumbent by lying down
in a grave, to be a doctor by teaching mortification by example,
by dying, though I may have seniors, others may be elder than   40
I, yet I have proceeded apace in a good university, and gone a
great way in a little time, by the furtherance of a vehement
fever; and whomsoever these bells bring to the ground today, if
he and I had been compared yesterday, perchance I should have
been thought likelier to come to this preferment then than he.
God hath kept the power of death in his own hands, lest any
man should bribe death. If man knew the gain of death, the ease
of death, he would solicit, he would provoke death to assist him
by any hand which he might use. But as when men see many of
their own professions preferred it ministers a hope that that   50
may light upon them, so when these hourly bells tell me of so
many funerals of men like me, it presents, if not a desire that it
may, yet a comfort whensoever mine shall come.

17 Now this bell tolling softly for another says to me, 'Thou
must die.'

Perchance he for whom this bell tolls may be so ill as that he
knows not it tolls for him; and perchance I may think myself so
much better than I am as that they who are about me, and see
my state, may have caused it to toll for me, and I know not
that. The church is catholic, universal, so are all her actions: all
that she does belongs to all. When she baptizes a child, that
action concerns me; for that child is thereby connected to that
head which is my head too, and engraffed into that body
whereof I am a member. And when she buries a man, that
action concerns me: all mankind is of one author, and is one   10
volume; when one man dies, one chapter is not torn out of the
book but translated into a better language; and every chapter
must be so translated; God employs several translators; some
pieces are translated by age, some by sickness, some by war,

165

some by justice; but God's hand is in every translation; and his hand shall bind up all our scattered leaves again, for that library where every book shall lie open to one another. As therefore the bell that rings to a sermon calls not upon the preacher only, but upon the congregation, to come, so this bell calls us all; but how much more me, who am brought so near the door by this 20 sickness. There was a contention as far as a suit (in which both piety and dignity, religion and estimation, were mingled) which of the religious orders should ring to prayers first in the morning; and it was determined that they should ring first that rose earliest. If we understand aright the dignity of this bell that tolls for our evening prayer, we would be glad to make it ours by rising early, in that application that it might be ours as well as his whose indeed it is. The bell doth toll for him that thinks it doth; and though it intermit again, yet from that minute that that occasion wrought upon him he is united to God. Who 30 casts not up his eye to the sun when it rises? But who takes off his eye from a comet when that breaks out? Who bends not his ear to any bell which upon any occasion rings? But who can remove it from that bell which is passing a piece of himself out of this world? No man is an island entire of itself; every man is a piece of the continent, a part of the main; if a clod be washed away by the sea, Europe is the less, as well as if a promontory were, as well as if a manor of thy friends' or of thine own were; any man's death diminishes me, because I am involved in mankind; and therefore never send to know for whom the bell tolls; 40 it tolls for thee. Neither can we call this a begging of misery or a borrowing of misery, as though we were not miserable enough of ourselves, but must fetch in more from the next house in taking upon us the misery of our neighbours. Truly it were an excusable covetousness if we did; for affliction is a treasure, and scarce any man hath enough of it. No man hath affliction enough that is not matured and ripened by it, and made fit for God by that affliction. If a man carry treasure in bullion, or in a wedge of gold, and have none coined into current moneys, his treasure will not defray him as he travels. Tribulation is treasure 50 in the nature of it, but it is not current money in the use of it

166

except we get nearer and nearer our home, heaven, by it. Another man may be sick too, and sick to death, and this affliction may lie in his bowels as gold in a mine, and be of no use to him; but this bell, that tells me of his affliction, digs out and applies that gold to me, if by this consideration of another's danger I take mine own into contemplation, and so secure myself by making my recourse to my God, who is our only security.

23 The physicians warn me of the fearful danger of relapsing.

It is not in man's body as it is in the city, that when the bell hath rung to cover your fire and rake up the embers you may lie down and sleep without fear. Though you have by physic and diet raked up the embers of your disease, still there is a fear of a relapse; and the greater danger is in that. Even in pleasures and in pains there is a propriety, a *meum* and *tuum*; and a man is most affected with that pleasure which is his, his by former enjoying and experience, and most intimidated with those pains which are his, his by a woeful sense of them in former afflictions. A covetous person, who hath preoccupated all his senses, 10 filled all his capacities, with the delight of gathering, wonders how any man can have any taste of any pleasure in any openness or liberality. So also in bodily pains, in a fit of the stone, the patient wonders why any man should call the gout a pain; and he that hath felt neither, but the toothache, is as much afraid of a fit of that as either of the other of either of the other. Diseases which we never felt in ourselves come but to a compassion of others that have endured them; nay, compassion itself comes to no great degree if we have not felt in some proportion in ourselves that which we lament and condole in another. But when 20 we have had those torments in their exaltation ourselves, we tremble at a relapse. When we must pant through all those fiery heats, and sail through all those overflowing sweats, when we must watch through all those long nights, and mourn through all those long days (days and nights so long, as that nature herself shall seem to be perverted, and to have put the longest day

167

and the longest night, which should be six months asunder, into one natural unnatural day), when we must stand at the same bar, expect the return of physicians from their consultations, and not be sure of the same verdict in any good indications, when we must go the same way over again, and not see the same issue, this is a state, a condition, a calamity, in respect of which any other sickness were a convalescence, and any greater less. It adds to the affliction that relapses are (and for the most part justly) imputed to ourselves, as occasioned by some disorder in us; and so we are not only passive but active in our own ruin; we do not only stand under a falling house but pull it down upon us; and we are not only executed (that implies guiltiness), but we are executioners (that implies dishonour), and executioners of ourselves (and that implies impiety). And we fall from that comfort which we might have in our first sickness, from that meditation, 'Alas, how generally miserable is man, and how subject to diseases' (for in that it is some degree of comfort that we are but in the state common to all), we fall, I say, to this discomfort, and self-accusing, and self-condemning: 'Alas, how unprovident, and in that how unthankful to God and his instruments am I, in making so ill use of so great benefits, in destroying so soon so long a work, in relapsing by my disorder to that from which they had delivered me'; and so my meditation is fearfully transferred from the body to the mind, and from the consideration of the sickness to that sin, that sinful carelessness, by which I have occasioned my relapse. And amongst the many weights that aggravate a relapse this also is one, that a relapse proceeds with a more violent dispatch, and more irremediably, because it finds the country weakened and depopulated before. Upon a sickness which as yet appears not we can scarce fix a fear, because we know not what to fear; but as fear is the busiest and irksomest affection, so is a relapse (which is still ready to come) into that which is but newly gone, the nearest object, the most immediate exercise of that affection of fear.

Composed 1624   First published 1624

Sermons

1 From a sermon preached at Lincoln's Inn. Easter Term,
   1620 (?). Text: Job 19: 26. 'And though after my skin
   worms destroy this body, yet in my flesh shall I see God.'

I am not all here: I am here now preaching upon this text, and I
am at home in my library considering whether Saint Gregory or
Saint Jerome have said best of this text before. I am here speaking to you, and yet I consider by the way, in the same instant,
what it is likely you will say to one another when I have done.
You are not all here neither: you are here now, hearing me, and
yet you are thinking that you have heard a better sermon somewhere else of this text before; you are here, and yet you think
you could have heard some other doctrine of downright predestination and reprobation roundly delivered somewhere else   10
with more edification to you; you are here, and you remember
yourselves that, now ye think of it, this had been the fittest
time, now, when everybody else is at church, to have made
such and such a private visit; and because you would be there,
you are there.

Composed 1620?   First published 1649

2 From a sermon preached to the Lords upon Easter Day at
the Communion, the King being then dangerously sick at
Newmarket. 28 March 1619. Text: Psalm 89: 48. 'What
man is he that liveth, and shall not see death?'

We are all conceived in close prison; in our mothers' womb we
are close prisoners all; when we are born, we are born but to the
liberty of the house, prisoners still, though within larger walls;
and then all our life is but a going out to the place of execution,
to death. Now was there ever any man seen to sleep in the cart
between Newgate and Tyburn? Between the prison and the
place of execution does any man sleep? And we sleep all the
way; from the womb to the grave we are never thoroughly
awake, but pass on with such dreams and imaginations as these,
'I may live, as well as another' and 'Why should I die, rather   10
than another?' 'But awake and tell me,' says this text, '*Quis
homo?* Who is that other that thou talkest of? What man is he
that liveth, and shall not see death?'

Composed 1619   First published 1640

3 From a sermon preached at Whitehall, the first Friday in
Lent. 8 March 1622. Text: 1 Corinthians 15: 26. 'The last
enemy that shall be destroyed is death.'

Doth not man die even in his birth? The breaking of prison is
death, and what is our birth but a breaking of prison? As soon
as we were clothed by God, our very apparel was an emblem of
death. In the skins of dead beasts he covered the skins of dying
men. As soon as God set us on work, our very occupation was
an emblem of death. It was to dig the earth; not to dig pitfalls
for other men, but graves for ourselves. Hath any man here
forgot, today, that yesterday is dead? And the bell tolls for
today, and will ring out anon, and for as much of every one of
us as appertains to this day. '*Quotidie morimur, et tamen nos esse   10
aeternos putamus,*' says Saint Jerome. We die every day, and we
die all the day long; and because we are not absolutely dead, we

170

call that an eternity, an eternity of dying. And is there comfort in that state? Why, that is the state of hell itself, eternal dying, and not dead.

But for this there is enough said by the moral man (that we may respite divine proofs for divine points anon, for our several resurrections): for this death is merely natural, and it is enough that the moral man says, '*Mors lex, tributum, officium mortalium*.' First it is *lex*; you were born under that law, upon that con-   20
dition, to die; so it is a rebellious thing not to be content to die; it opposes the law. Then it is *tributum*, an imposition which nature the queen of this world lays upon us, and which she will take when and where she list; here a young man, there an old man, here a happy, there a miserable man; and so it is a seditious thing not to be content to die; it opposes the prerogative. And lastly it is *officium*; men are to have their turns, to take their time, and then to give way by death to successors; and so it is *incivile, inofficiosum*, not to be content to die; it opposes the frame and form of government. It comes equally to us all, and   30
makes us all equal when it comes. The ashes of an oak in the chimney are no epitaph of that oak, to tell me how high or how large that was; it tells me not what flocks it sheltered while it stood, nor what men it hurt when it fell. The dust of great persons' graves is speechless too, it says nothing, it distinguishes nothing; as soon the dust of a wretch whom thou wouldst not, as of a prince whom thou couldst not look upon, will trouble thine eyes if the wind blow it thither; and when a whirlwind hath blown the dust of the churchyard into the church, and the man sweeps out the dust of the church into the churchyard,   40
who will undertake to sift those dusts again, and to pronounce, 'This is the patrician, this is the noble flour, and this the yeomanly, this the plebeian bran'?

Composed 1622   First published 1640

4 From a sermon preached to the Earl of Carlisle and his
company, at Syon House. Autumn 1622 (?). Text: Mark
16: 16. 'He that believeth not shall be damned.'

When all is done, the hell of hells, the torment of torments, is
the everlasting absence of God, and the everlasting impossibility of returning to his presence; '*Horrendum est*,' says the
apostle, 'It is a fearful thing to fall into the hands of the living
God.' Yet there was a case in which David found an ease to fall
into the hands of God to scape the hands of men. *Horrendum est*,
when God's hand is bent to strike, it is a fearful thing to fall
into the hands of the living God; but to fall out of the hands of
the living God is a horror beyond our expression, beyond our
imagination.   10

That God should let my soul fall out of his hand into a
bottomless pit, and roll an unremovable stone upon it, and
leave it to that which it finds there (and it shall find that there
which it never imagined till it came thither), and never think
more of that soul, never have more to do with it; that of that
providence of God that studies the life and preservation of every
weed, and worm, and ant, and spider, and toad, and viper,
there should never, never any beam flow out upon me; that that
God who looked upon me when I was nothing, and called me
when I was not, as though I had been, out of the womb and   20
depth of darkness, will not look upon me now, when, though a
miserable, and a banished, and a damned creature, yet I am his
creature still, and contribute something to his glory even in my
damnation; that that God who hath often looked upon me in
my foulest uncleanness, and when I had shut out the eye of the
day, the sun, and the eye of the night, the taper, and the eyes of
all the world with curtains and windows and doors, did yet see
me, and see me in mercy, by making me see that he saw me, and
sometimes brought me to a present remorse and (for that time)
to a forbearing of that sin, should so turn himself from me, to   30
his glorious saints and angels, as that no saint nor angel, nor
Christ Jesus himself, should ever pray him to look towards me,
never remember him that such a soul there is; that that God

172

who hath so often said to my soul, '*Quare morieris?* Why wilt
thou die?', and so often sworn to my soul, '*Vivit Dominus*, as
the Lord liveth, I would not have thee die but live', will neither
let me die nor let me live, but die an everlasting life and live an
everlasting death; that that God who, when he could not get
into me by standing and knocking, by his ordinary means of
entering, by his word, his mercies, hath applied his judge-   40
ments, and hath shaked the house, this body, with agues and
palsies, and hath set this house on fire with fevers and calentures, and frighted the master of the house, my soul, with
horrors and heavy apprehensions, and so made an entrance into
me; that that God should lose and frustrate all his own purposes
and practices upon me, and leave me, and cast me away as
though I had cost him nothing, that this God at last should let
this soul go away as a smoke, as a vapour, as a bubble, and that
then this soul cannot be a smoke, nor a vapour, nor a bubble,
but must lie in darkness as long as the Lord of light is light   50
itself, and never a spark of that light reach to my soul; what
Tophet is not paradise, what brimstone is not amber, what
gnashing is not a comfort, what gnawing of the worm is not a
tickling, what torment is not a marriage bed to this damnation,
to be secluded eternally, eternally, eternally, from the sight of
God? Especially to us, for as the perpetual loss of that is most
heavy with which we have been best acquainted and to which
we have been most accustomed, so shall this damnation which
consists in the loss of the sight and presence of God be heavier to
us than others, because God hath so graciously, and so evi-   60
dently, and so diversely appeared to us, in his pillar of fire, in
the light of prosperity, and in the pillar of the cloud, in hiding
himself for a while from us; we that have seen him in the
execution of all the parts of this commission, in his word, in his
sacraments, and in good example, and not believed, shall be
further removed from his sight in the next world than they to
whom he never appeared in this. But *vincenti et credenti*, to him
that believes aright and overcomes all temptations to a wrong
belief, God shall give the accomplishment of fullness, and fullness of joy, and joy rooted in glory, and glory established in   70

173

eternity, and this eternity is God; to him that believes and over-comes, God shall give himself in an everlasting presence and fruition. Amen.

Composed 1622?   First published 1640

5 From a sermon preached at St Paul's, upon Christmas Day, in the evening, 1624. Text: Isaiah 7: 14. 'Therefore the Lord himself shall give you a sign; behold, a virgin shall conceive, and bear a son, and shall call his name Immanuel.'

We begin with that which is elder than our beginning, and shall overlive our end, the mercy of God. 'I will sing of thy mercy and judgement,' says David; when we fix ourselves upon the meditation and modulation of the mercy of God, even his judgements cannot put us out of tune, but we shall sing and be cheerful even in them. As God made grass for beasts before he made beasts, and beasts for man before he made man; as in that first generation, the creation, so in the regeneration, our re-creating, he begins with that which was necessary for that which follows, mercy before judgement. Nay, to say that   10
mercy was first is but to postdate mercy; to prefer mercy but so is to diminish mercy; the names of first or last derogate from it, for first and last are but rags of time, and his mercy hath no relation to time, no limitation in time, it is not first nor last but eternal, everlasting; let the Devil make me so far desperate as to conceive a time when there was no mercy and he hath made me so far an atheist as to conceive a time when there was no God; if I despoil him of his mercy any one minute, and say, 'Now God hath no mercy', for that minute I discontinue his very godhead and his being. Later grammarians have wrung the name of   20
mercy out of misery: '*Misericordia praesumit miseriam*,' say these; 'there could be no subsequent mercy if there were no precedent misery.' But the true root of the word mercy, through all the prophets, is *racham*, and *racham* is *diligere*, to love; as long as there hath been love (and God is love) there hath been mercy;

and mercy considered externally, and in the practice and in the
effect, began not at the helping of man when man was fallen
and become miserable, but at the making of man when man was
nothing. So, then, here we consider not mercy as it is radically
in God and an essential attribute of his, but productively in us,   30
as it is an action, a working upon us, and that more especially as
God takes all occasions to exercise that action and to shed that
mercy upon us; for particular mercies are feathers of his wings,
and that prayer 'Lord, let thy mercy lighten upon us, as our
trust is in thee' is our bird-lime; particular mercies are that
cloud of quails which hovered over the host of Israel, and that
prayer 'Lord, let thy mercy lighten upon us', is our net to
catch, our gomer to fill of those quails. The air is not so full of
motes, of atoms, as the church is of mercies; and as we can suck
in no part of air but we take in those motes, those atoms, so   40
here in the congregation we cannot suck in a word from the
preacher, we cannot speak, we cannot sigh a prayer to God, but
that that whole breath and air is made of mercy. But we call not
upon you from this text to consider God's ordinary mercy, that
which he exhibits to all in the ministry of his church, nor his
miraculous mercy, his extraordinary deliverances of states and
churches, but we call upon particular consciences, by occasion
of this text, to call to mind God's occasional mercies to them,
such mercies as a regenerate man will call mercies, though a
natural man would call them accidents or occurrences or   50
contingencies. A man wakes at midnight full of unclean
thoughts, and he hears a passing-bell; this is an occasional
mercy, if he call that his own knell, and consider how unfit he
was to be called out of the world then, how unready to receive
that voice, 'Fool, this night they shall fetch away thy soul.' The
adulterer, whose eye waits for the twilight, goes forth and casts
his eyes upon forbidden houses, and would enter, and sees a
'Lord, have mercy upon us' upon the door; this is an occasional
mercy, if this bring him to know that they who lie sick of the
plague within pass through a furnace, but by God's grace to   60
heaven, and he without carries his own furnace to hell, his lustful loins to everlasting perdition. What an occasional mercy had

175

Balaam when his ass catechized him! What an occasional mercy
had one thief when the other catechized him so, 'Art not thou
afraid, being under the same condemnation?'! What an
occasional mercy had all they that saw that, when the Devil
himself fought for the name of Jesus, and wounded the sons of
Sceva for exorcizing in the name of Jesus, with that indignation, with that increpation, 'Jesus we know, and Paul we
know, but who are ye?'! If I should declare what God hath   70
done (done occasionally) for my soul, where he instructed me
for fear of falling, where he raised me when I was fallen,
perchance you would rather fix your thoughts upon my illness,
and wonder at that, than at God's goodness, and glorify him in
that; rather wonder at my sins than at his mercies; rather
consider how ill a man I was than how good a God he is. If I
should enquire upon what occasion God elected me and writ
my name in the book of life, I should sooner be afraid that it
were not so than find a reason why it should be so. God made
sun and moon to distinguish seasons, and day and night, and we   80
cannot have the fruits of the earth but in their seasons; but God
hath made no decree to distinguish the seasons of his mercies; in
paradise the fruits were ripe the first minute, and in heaven it is
always autumn, his mercies are ever in their maturity. We ask
panem quotidianum, our daily bread, and God never says 'You
should have come yesterday', he never says 'You must again
tomorrow', but today if you will hear his voice, today he will
hear you. If some king of the earth have so large an extent of
dominion in north and south as that he hath winter and
summer together in his dominions, so large an extent east and   90
west as that he hath day and night together in his dominions,
much more hath God mercy and judgement together. He
brought light out of darkness, not out of a lesser light; he can
bring thy summer out of winter, though thou have no spring;
though in the ways of fortune, or understanding, or conscience,
thou have been benighted till now, wintered and frozen,
clouded and eclipsed, damped and benumbed, smothered and
stupefied till now, now God comes to thee, not as in the
dawning of the day, not as in the bud of the spring, but as the

176

sun at noon to illustrate all shadows, as the sheaves in harvest to 100
fill all penuries; all occasions invite his mercies, and all times are
his seasons.

Composed 1624   First published 1640

6 From a sermon preached at St Paul's. 29 January 1626.
Text: Psalm 63: 7. 'Because thou hast been my help,
therefore in the shadow of thy wings will I rejoice.'

Let me wither and wear out mine age in a discomfortable, in an
unwholesome, in a penurious prison, and so pay my debts with
my bones, and recompense the wastefulness of my youth with
the beggary of mine age; let me wither in a spital under sharp
and foul and infamous diseases, and recompense the wantonness
of my youth with that loathsomeness in mine age; yet, if God
withdraw not his spiritual blessings, his grace, his patience, if I
can call my suffering his doing, my passion his action, all this
that is temporal is but a caterpillar got into one corner of my
garden, but a mildew fallen upon one acre of my corn; the body 10
of all, the substance of all, is safe, as long as the soul is safe. But
when I shall trust to that which we call a good spirit, and God
shall deject and impoverish and evacuate that spirit; when I
shall rely upon a moral constancy, and God shall shake and
enfeeble and enervate, destroy and demolish that constancy;
when I shall think to refresh myself in the serenity and sweet air
of a good conscience, and God shall call up the damps and
vapours of hell itself, and spread a cloud of diffidence and an
impenetrable crust of desperation upon my conscience; when
health shall fly from me, and I shall lay hold upon riches to 20
succour me and comfort me in my sickness, and riches shall fly
from me, and I shall snatch after favour and good opinion to
comfort me in my poverty; when even this good opinion shall
leave me, and calumnies and misinformations shall prevail
against me; when I shall need peace, because there is none but
thou, O Lord, that should stand for me, and then shall find that
all the wounds that I have come from thy hand, all the arrows

177

that stick in me, from thy quiver; when I shall see that because I
have given myself to my corrupt nature thou hast changed
thine, and because I am all evil towards thee therefore thou hast   30
given over being good towards me; when it comes to this
height, that the fever is not in the humours but in the spirits,
that mine enemy is not an imaginary enemy, fortune, nor a
transitory enemy, malice in great persons, but a real and an
irresistible and an inexorable and an everlasting enemy, the
Lord of Hosts himself, the Almighty God himself, the Almighty
God himself only knows the weight of this affliction, and
except he put in that *pondus gloriae*, that exceeding weight of an
eternal glory, with his own hand into the other scale, we are
weighed down, we are swallowed up, irreparably, irrevocably,   40
irrecoverably, irremediably.

Composed 1626   First published 1640

7 From a sermon preached at the funerals of Sir William
   Cokayne. 12 December 1626. Text: John 11: 21. 'Then said
   Martha unto Jesus, Lord, if thou hadst been here, my
   brother had not died.'

But when we consider with a religious seriousness the manifold
weaknesses of the strongest devotions in time of prayer, it is a
sad consideration. I throw myself down in my chamber, and I
call in and invite God and his angels thither, and when they are
there I neglect God and his angels for the noise of a fly, for the
rattling of a coach, for the whining of a door. I talk on, in the
same posture of praying, eyes lifted up, knees bowed down, as
though I prayed to God; and if God or his angels should ask me
when I thought last of God in that prayer, I cannot tell. Sometimes I find that I had forgot what I was about, but when I   10
began to forget it I cannot tell. A memory of yesterday's
pleasures, a fear of tomorrow's dangers, a straw under my knee,
a noise in mine ear, a light in mine eye, an anything, a nothing,

a fancy, a chimera in my brain, troubles me in my prayer. So certainly is there nothing, nothing in spiritual things, perfect in this world.

Composed 1626   First published 1640

8 From a sermon preached at Whitehall to the king upon the occasion of the fast. 5 April 1628. Text: Psalm 6: 6–7. 'I am weary with my groaning; all the night make I my bed to swim; I water my couch with my tears. Mine eye is consumed because of grief; it waxeth old because of all mine enemies.'

Now *Stipendium peccati mors est*, there is the punishment for sin, the reward of sin is death. If there remain no death, there remains no punishment: for the reward of sin is death, and death complicated in itself, death wrapped in death; and what is so intricate, so entangling, as death? Who ever got out of a winding sheet? It is death aggravated by itself, death weighed down by death; and what is so heavy as death? Who ever threw off his gravestone? It is death multiplied by itself; and what is so infinite as death? Who ever told over the days of death? It is *morte morieris*, a double death, eternal and temporary, temporal and spiritual death. Now the temporary, the natural death, God never takes away from us, he never pardons that punishment, because he never takes away that sin that occasioned it, which is original sin; to what sanctification soever a man comes, original sin lives to his last breath. And therefore *statutum est*, that decree stands, *semel mori*, that every man must die once; but for any *bis mori*, for twice dying, for eternal death upon any man, as man, if God consider him not as an impotent sinner, there is no such invariable decree; for, that death being also the punishment for actual sin, if he take away the cause, the sin, he takes away that effect, that death also; for this death itself, eternal death, we all agree that it is taken away with the sin; and then for other calamities in this life, which we call *morticulas*, little deaths, the children, the issue, the offspring, the propagation of death, if we would speak properly, no affliction, no judgement of God in this life hath in it exactly the nature of a punishment; not only not the nature of satisfaction, but not the nature of a punishment. We call not coin base coin till the allay be more than the pure metal: God's judgements are not punishments except there be more anger than love, more justice than mercy, in them; and that is never; for *miserationes eius super omnia opera*, his mercies are above all his works. In his first work, in the creation, his spirit the Holy Ghost moved upon the face of the waters; and still upon the face of all our waters (as waters are emblems of tribulation in all the scriptures) his spirit, the spirit of comfort, moves too; and as the waters produced the first creatures in the creation, so tribulations offer us the first comforts, sooner than prosperity does. God executes no judgement upon man in this life but in mercy; either in mercy to that person, in his sense thereof, if he be sensible, or at least in mercy to his church, in the example thereof, if he be not. There is no person to whom we can say that God's corrections are punishments any otherwise than medicinal, and such as he may receive amendment by that receives them; neither does it become us in any case to say God lays this upon him because he is so ill, but because he may be better.

Composed 1628   First published 1640

9 From a sermon preached at St Paul's. Easter Day, 13 April 1628. Text: 1 Corinthians 13: 12. 'For now we see through a glass, darkly; but then face to face: now I know in part; but then shall I know even as also I am known.'

He that asks me what heaven is means not to hear me but to silence me: he knows I cannot tell him. When I meet him there, I shall be able to tell him, and then he will be as able to tell me; yet then we shall be but able to tell one another, 'This, this that we enjoy is heaven'; but the tongues of angels, the tongues of glorified saints, shall not be able to express what that heaven is;

for even in heaven our faculties shall be finite. Heaven is not a
place that was created; for all place that was created shall be dissolved. God did not plant a paradise for himself and remove to
that, as he planted a paradise for Adam and removed him to   10
that; but God is still where he was before the world was made.
And in that place, where there are more suns than there are stars
in the firmament (for all the saints are suns), and more light in
another sun, the Son of righteousness, the Son of glory, the Son
of God, than in all them, in that illustration, that emanation,
that effusion of beams of glory, which began not to shine 6000
years ago, but 6000 millions of millions ago had been 6000
millions of millions before that, in those eternal, in those
uncreated heavens shall we see God.

Composed 1628   First published 1640

10 From a sermon preached to the king at court in April 1629.
    Text: Genesis 1: 26. 'And God said, Let us make man in our
    image, after our likeness.'

Never such a frame so soon set up as this in this chapter. For, for
the thing itself, there is no other thing to compare it with; for it
is all, it is the whole world. And for the time, there was no
other time to compare it with; for this was the beginning of
time, 'In the beginning God created heaven and earth.' That
earth which in some thousands of years men could not look
over, nor discern what form it had (for neither Lactantius,
almost three hundred years after Christ, nor Saint Augustine,
more than one hundred years after him, would believe the earth
to be round); that earth which no man in his person is ever said   10
to have compassed till our age; that earth which is too much for
man yet (for as yet a very great part of the earth is unpeopled);
that earth which, if we will cast it all but into a map, costs many
months' labour to grave it; nay, if we will cast but a piece of an
acre of it into a garden, costs many years' labour to fashion and
furnish it; all that earth; and then that heaven which spreads so
far as that subtle men have, with some appearance of

probability, imagined that in that heaven, in those manifold
spheres of the planets and the stars, there are many earths, many
worlds, as big as this which we inhabit; that earth and that   20
heaven which spent God himself, Almighty God, six days in
furnishing, Moses sets up in a few syllables, in one line, '*In
principio*, In the beginning God created heaven and earth.' If a
Livy or a Guicciardini or such extensive and voluminous
authors had had this story in hand, God must have made
another world to have made them a library to hold their books
of the making of this world. Into what wire would they have
drawn out this earth! Into what leaf-gold would they have beat
out these heavens! It may assist our conjecture herein to
consider that amongst those men who proceed with a sober   30
modesty and limitation in their writing, and make a conscience
not to clog the world with unnecessary books, yet the volumes
which are written by them upon this beginning of Genesis are
scarce less than infinite. God did no more but say 'Let this and
this be done'; and Moses does no more but say that upon God's
saying it was done. God required not nature to help him to do
it; Moses required not reason to help him to be believed. The
Holy Ghost hovered upon the waters, and so God wrought; the
Holy Ghost hovered upon Moses too, and so he wrote; and we
believe these things to be so by the same Spirit in Moses' mouth   40
by which they were made so in God's hand. Only, beloved,
remember that a frame may be thrown down in much less time
than it was set up. A child, an ape can give fire to a cannon; and
a vapour can shake the earth; and these fires and these vapours
can throw down cities in minutes. When Christ said, 'Throw
down this temple, and in three days I will raise it', they never
stopped upon the consideration of throwing it down: they
knew that might be soon done; but they wondered at the
speedy raising of it. Now if all this earth were made in that
minute, may not all come to the general dissolution in this   50
minute? Or may not thy acres, thy miles, thy shires shrink into
feet, and so few feet as shall but make up thy grave? When he
who was a great lord must be but a cottager, and not so well;
for a cottager must have so many acres to his cottage; but in this

182

case a little piece of an acre, five foot, is become the house itself;
the house and the land; the grave is all; lower than that, the
grave is the land and the tenement and the tenant too. He that
lies in it becomes the same earth that he lies in; they all make
but one earth, and but a little of it. But then raise thyself to a
higher hope again. God hath made better land, the land of   60
promise; a stronger city, the new Jerusalem; and inhabitants for
that everlasting city, us; whom he made, not by saying 'Let
there be men', but by consultation, by deliberation; God said,
'Let us make man in our image, after our likeness.'

Composed 1629   First published 1649

Critical commentary

In poetry, as in the other arts, a great artist is by definition unique, producing works that cannot be mistaken for anyone else's. This generalization applies with particular force to Donne, whose individuality continually stares us in the face as we read. To some readers – indeed, in the eighteenth and nineteenth centuries, to most readers – he has appeared rather a brilliant eccentric wit than a great imaginative poet. In the present century, by contrast, he has been regarded as standing in the main tradition of English poetry: it has been pointed out that, though Pope defined 'true wit' as 'What oft was thought, but ne'er so well expressed' (*An Essay on Criticism*, l. 298), the wit that he practised often involved the bringing together of ideas and images into unlikely but striking association in the manner of Donne and his followers; and several of the other qualities most evident in twentieth-century poetry and most admired by twentieth-century criticism – irony, a colloquial idiom, the sound of a speaking voice reflected in the movement of the verse – are as conspicuous in Donne's poetry as they are in Eliot's or Auden's, or as they were in Chaucer's.

Whether in fashion or out of fashion, Donne's poetry has always had admirers. The exhilaration of reading it is largely due to the way in which it seems to enlarge our own powers of seeing, thinking, feeling and expressing. It is impossible to read it without being conscious of the satisfaction which Donne must have felt in achieving his arresting comparisons, his audacious hyperboles, his ingenious twists of argument and turns of emotion, his intricate yet fluent stanzas. Not every reader will vicariously experience that satisfaction. Some readers will react to it with hostility, seeing Donne as an egoist and an exhibitionist. The prominence, or apparent prominence, of Donne himself in his poems is an additional factor in the reader's response. The majority include the pronoun 'I', and only a very few of them, such as 'Break of day', are put into the mouth of a speaker who is evidently not Donne. To note this is not to allege that most of the poems are therefore autobiographical, dealing with actual experiences of Donne's, or expressing actual sentiments of his: he was quite capable of writing dramatically, of imagining a situation or a mood and then giving it appropriate expression. But it is surely significant that he found it necessary to use the pronoun 'I' so often, though what this fact signifies is a matter of opinion.

From first to last – the *Devotions* and *Sermons* included – Donne is a great self-dramatizer. The first of the *Satires*, written when he was about 21 and still a student at Lincoln's Inn, opens in the middle of a dialogue, like some Elizabethan play. Here is Shakespeare (*The Two Gentlemen of Verona*):

VALENTINE: Cease to persuade, my loving Proteus:
　　　　　　 Home-keeping youth have ever homely wits.

Here is Jonson (*The Alchemist*):

FACE:　　 Believe't, I will.
SUBTLE:　　　　　　 Thy worst. I fart at thee.

And here is Donne (the scene: his study at Lincoln's Inn):

Away, thou fondling motley humorist,
Leave me, and in this standing wooden chest,
Consorted with these few books, let me lie
In prison, and here be coffined, when I die;
Here are God's conduits, grave divines; and here
Nature's secretary, the philosopher;
And jolly statesmen, which teach how to tie
The sinews of a city's mystic body;
Here gathering chroniclers, and by them stand

Giddy fantastic poets of each land.
Shall I leave all this constant company,
And follow, headlong, wild uncertain thee?

This opening is not only dramatic, it is explosive. The abrupt imperatives ('Away', 'Leave me') and heaped-up epithets ('thou fondling motley humorist', 'wild uncertain thee') put a world of distance between the speaker and his visitor; so do the swift precise gestures towards the different shelves of books ('Here . . . and here . . . Here . . . and by them . . .'), and the comprehensive wave of the arm that has taken in the whole study and its furnishings. Everything expresses annoyance at interruption. To show the speaker's superiority further, he is not plodding in Plowden, grinding away at his law studies; not one shelf contains law books (or, if it does, they are not mentioned); he is a young 'complete man' of the Renaissance, surrounded by the symbols of his completeness. And he is not too annoyed to be witty, contrasting the constancy of his authors (even the giddy fantastic poets) with the flightiness of his visitor, and likening his study to a prison and a coffin. Of course there is some self-contradiction in wanting to be left undisturbed in his coffin and his prison, but the self-contradiction is not accidental, unintentionally revealing that Donne (which, rather than 'the speaker', we may as well call him in this and most of his other poems) really wants to be out in the London street; it is deliberate, emphasizing the strength of will with which he rejects the invitation. Having already shown us his all-round culture, he can afford to be the cynic philosopher Diogenes in his tub, dressed in 'coarse attire' in contrast with the captains, courtiers and justices whose notice his visitor habitually solicits.

Presently the invitation is accepted, all the same, because only thus can the visitor, who has been well pulverized in the meantime, be given the chance to show his folly to its height. 'Now we are in the street', and Donne begins to speak of his companion in the third person, so that the poem moves from drama to narrative, and the reader is brought in, by implication, as a sensible person who shares Donne's views, even while, at the same time, he or she continues to identify with Donne as the sardonic hero of the story, always ready with a crushing retort or an ironical question. Some parts of the dialogue are still wholly dramatic, without any 'he cries' or 'said I'. The narrative is vivid, with its similes of prentices, schoolboys, fiddlers and performing animals, and with its active verbs ('grins, smacks, shrugs') in the present tense. It is not until 'said I' (l. 85) that we are given any hint that the action is in the past, and this is only because the neat ending of the story will require it: the companion, wounded in a quarrel over a woman,

> Directly came to me hanging the head,
> And constantly a while must keep his bed

– where the wit lies in the adverb 'constantly'. In spirit the whole poem takes place in the present, this being one of the many changes Donne made in adapting the satire of Horace (Book I, satire ix) which was probably its source.

Another change is that, whereas in Horace's satire the joke is partly on the poet (when a friend meets him and his wearisome companion, and refuses to take a hint and rescue him), in Donne's the poet, though irritated both before and during the excursion, never loses control of the situation. In this the first Satire is like the *Elegies*, which, although they vary in type between Ovidian narratives of romance or intrigue on the one hand and Italianate wittily argued propositions on the other, are all written with wit and spirit, and radiate self-confidence; sometimes this self-confidence swells into the brash insolence of a clever young man glorying in his cleverness and masculinity, while at other times, notably in 'His picture' and 'On his mistress', there is a foretaste of the romantic valedictory poems of the *Songs and Sonnets*.

Unlike Ovid's elegies, the *Amores*, Donne's *Elegies* are unrelated to each other except in mood and style: there is no narrative continuity, and no sign that any two of them have any two of their dramatis personae in common, as Ovid's have himself, his mistress Corinna, Corinna's husband and Corinna's maidservant. In 'Jealousy' Donne is addressing a mistress who is married to a jealous husband; in 'Nature's lay idiot' he is addressing a former mistress whom he initiated into sexual experience and who has now married another man; in 'The perfume' he is addressing an unmarried mistress who is jealously guarded by her parents, and the woman addressed in 'On his mistress' seems to be in a similar situation, since she is threatened with her parents' wrath, though she differs in sharing a bedroom with her nurse; hardly anything can be even guessed about the circumstances of the mistresses addressed in 'Change', 'Love's war' and 'To his mistress going to bed' – though it has been suggested that in the last-named poem the mistress's finery shows her to be a rich citizen's wife (against which it might be argued that the finery, necessary if her undressing is to include enough items to sustain the wit, is an end in itself rather than a means to revealing her social status). The argumentative *Elegies* show no more continuity or mutual consistency. In 'The anagram' and 'The comparison' Donne writes two poems about ugly women; in each case the woman is the mistress of the man addressed; but in 'The anagram' he recommends the man to marry her, and in 'The comparison' he recommends him to leave her. The different advice springs entirely from the wit of the argument: the last twenty lines of 'The anagram' maintain that an ugly woman can give no grounds for jealousy and therefore will afford married happiness; the final couplet of 'The comparison' is a perfunctory conclusion after the item-by-item comparison of the poet's mistress with the other man's has exhausted Donne's invention:

> Leave her, and I will leave comparing thus;
> She and comparisons are odious.

In a third argumentative poem, 'The autumnal', Donne employs a subtler tone than either the gross irony of 'The anagram' or the gross vituperation of 'The comparison'; writing about an older woman who has kept her attractiveness, he is both genuinely complimentary and playfully ironical; only the lines on 'winter-faces' give vent to the brilliant but brutal ridicule that fills the other two poems.

What unites the *Elegies* as a group is their energy and inventiveness: the ideas and the images crowd upon each other. 'The grim eight-foot-high iron-bound serving-man' (what an inimitable trio of epithets!) in 'The perfume' is brought into the poem simply as one of a series of examples showing how well the lovers hid their intrigue, but, having brought him in, Donne spontaneously interjects three remarks about him before completing the sentence. In 'On his mistress' the Frenchmen and Italians who, from their different perspectives on sex, will converge on the pretended page are introduced in a knowing and witty tone which the poem's romantic spirit can only just accommodate: it is as if Donne is not only Romeo but Mercutio too.

But it is Marlowe rather than Shakespeare whom Donne's *Elegies* recall. Donne may have known Marlowe's translation of Ovid's *Amores*; he may have known his erotic narrative poem *Hero and Leander*; he certainly knew *Tamburlaine*, as a reference in 'The calm' shows. The self-assurance and irresistible sex-appeal of Tamburlaine have something like a counterpart in the hero of the *Elegies*, and though Leander is a novice in love he is a quick learner:

> At last, like to a bold sharp sophister,
> With cheerful hope thus he accosted her.
>
> *(Hero and Leander, I, 197–8)*

Leander's arguments anticipate Donne's in their use of sophistry:

> One is no number; maids are nothing, then,
> Without the sweet society of men . . .
> Base bullion for the stamp's sake we allow,
> Even so for men's impression do we you.
>
> *(Hero and Leander, I, 255–6, 265–6)*

His exposure of Hero's illogical position as a virgin priestess of Venus is, if not quite in Donne's style, very much in his tone:

> Thee as a holy idiot doth she scorn,
> For thou in vowing chastity hast sworn
> To rob her name and honour, and thereby
> Committ'st a sin far worse than perjury,
> Even sacrilege against her deity,
> Through regular and formal purity.
>
> *(Hero and Leander, I, 303–8)*

When, after swimming the Hellespont, Leander persuades Hero to let him warm himself in her bed and then begins trying to embrace her, image follows upon image with a diversity within continuity which is already in the *Elegies* a feature of Donne's style:

> Yet ever as he greedily assayed
> To touch those dainties, she the harpy played,
> And every limb did as a soldier stout
> Defend the fort, and keep the foeman out.
> For though the rising ivory mount he scaled,
> Which is with azure circling lines empaled
> Much like a globe (a globe may I term this,
> By which love sails to regions full of bliss),
> Yet there with Sisyphus he toiled in vain,
> Till gentle parley did the truce obtain.
>
> *(Hero and Leander*, II, 269–78)

In this passage the veins visible on Hero's breast resemble the lines of latitude on a globe, which brings in the parenthetical image of sea-discoverers, after which the breast returns to being a hill, but now it is the mythological hill up which Sisyphus for ever tried to roll the huge round stone. The images of Donne's 'Love's progress' and 'To his mistress going to bed' may be compared.

Hero and Leander, though it contains plenty of dialogue, is a narrative poem. Donne's *Elegies*, like Ovid's, are dramatic monologues, some of them addressed to an imagined reader or hearer ('The autumnal', 'Love's progress'), others to another man ('The anagram', 'The comparison'), and the majority to a mistress. Two of this last group, 'His picture' and 'To his mistress going to bed', are like Satire 1 in involving physical action. In the former, the miniature portrait is presented in the first line and indicated in the thirteenth: 'This shall say what I was'. In the latter, the opening couplets imply that Donne is already, restlessly, in bed:

> Come, Madam, come, all rest my powers defy;
> Until I labour, I in labour lie.
> The foe oft-times, having the foe in sight,
> Is tired with standing though he never fight.

After his mistress has taken off everything but her smock, she comes to join him there. He embraces her with his 'roving hands'. Finally he urges her to be in a state of 'full nakedness' like him.

In dramatizing a progressive action, this poem is like two of the *Songs and Sonnets*. In 'The dream' the first two stanzas are concerned with the initial situation. Donne has been dreaming (whether in bed or elsewhere is not evident) of his mistress, who has now come and interrupted his dream; he appeals to her to come to his arms and realize the part of the dream that he has not yet reached. Thus far the first stanza. The second reinforces the appeal by a high-flown compliment verging upon blasphemy. Between its end and the beginning of the third the appeal has failed, and she has risen to go:

> Coming and staying showed thee thee,
> But rising makes me doubt that now
> Thou art not thou.

All he can do is expostulate with her, and then console himself by speculating that she is only going away temporarily in order to arouse him the more in readiness for her return. What – if anything – went on while she stayed is left for the reader to imagine: the last stanza makes it clear that it was not sexual union, and the probability is that she did no more than sit down and listen. Whether she will be persuaded to return by his last words is also an open question. 'The flea' is another poem of attempted seduction. Again the physical circumstances (where are the lovers, and how fully clothed are they?) are not indicated: Donne could possibly have told us, but the fact that he did not suggests either that he thought it obvious or that he thought it unimportant (perhaps the more likely of the two). What matters is the argumentative sequence and the way in which it reflects the implied sequence of action (flea bites man; flea bites woman; woman catches flea; woman kills flea). At the end of the action, and of the argument, Donne predictably has the last word. Whereas in 'The dream' he resorted to pathos ('but else would die'), in 'The flea' he relies on presumption: 'when thou yield'st to me' (not 'if').

All the poetry that has been discussed so far can be called a young man's poetry (irrespective of the actual dates, which are a matter of conjecture; for instance, some critics date 'The dream' after 1602 –

when, in any case, Donne was still only 30). It is predominantly clever, exuberant and confident. Donne is usually triumphant, and when he finds himself defeated in a situation ('The perfume', 'Nature's lay idiot', 'The dream') he is not abashed or perturbed. The other kind of young man's poetry, that of the romantically idealizing lover

> Sighing like furnace, with a woeful ballad
> Made to his mistress' eyebrow

(as Shakespeare expresses it in *As You Like It*), he did not write. Not all these poems, as we have seen, are love-poems. There are satires and satiric elegies. Before we come to the rest of the *Songs and Sonnets* (all of which are poems on various aspects of love) there are a few more poems from Donne's early period to consider: the 'Epithalamion made at Lincoln's Inn', the third Satire, the two verse letters 'The storm' and 'The calm', and *The Progress of the Soul*.

The 'Epithalamion made at Lincoln's Inn' is so like, and so unlike, Spenser's 'Epithalamion' that it has sometimes been thought a parody. The resemblance is chiefly one of structure: both Spenser and Donne describe in order the events of the wedding day, from the rising of the bride to the bedding of the married couple, by way of the wedding procession, the ceremony and the feast. There is also, at the end of each stanza in both poems, a refrain, variable according to context, in alexandrine metre; and Donne has one Spenserian archaism ('nill' in l. 57: not accepted by all editors, though it gives much better sense than 'will'). The differences are profound: Spenser's poem is set in Ireland, in the country, while Donne's is set in the City of London; Spenser is the bridegroom, while Donne is (at most) a wedding guest; and Spenser's poetic sensibility is poles apart from Donne's. That Donne's poem is an imitation of Spenser's, in the same way as painters will sometimes use another painter's composition for a picture of their own and will expect spectators to recognize the fact, seems evident. But if parody involves burlesque, and is to any degree written in derision of the original, then Donne does not seem to be parodying Spenser. The differences-within-resemblance are less particular than parody in this sense would require.

Donne's creation of the London setting, as contrasted with Spenser's idealized countryside peopled with nymphs, brings out in him the poet of the *Elegies* and *Satires*: the rich merchants' daughters and sons, the courtiers, the farmers up from the country, the Inns of Court students, are all described with worldly wit; the musicians and dancers, at the end of the evening, are gratuitously compared to other 'toiled beasts'. But he does not exercise his worldly wit at the expense of the bride and bridegroom, and he treats the wedding ceremony and the wedding night with seriousness and refinement:

> This bed is only to virginity
> A grave, but to a better state a cradle.

Being Donne, he can never keep extravagance out of his style for long. His notorious comparison of the bride to a sacrificial lamb, and of the bridegroom to the sacrificing priest, is discussed in the notes. The lines in which he addresses the temple have also caused comment. The Oxford editor, W. Milgate, while allowing that the primary sense of 'hunger-starvèd womb' is the church's vault or crypt which will later receive the couple's dead parents and much later their dead selves, glosses it as 'a phrase coarsely relevant to the bride (carrying on the bawdy sense of "Temple" and "two-leaved")'. What the bawdy sense of 'temple' may be he does not explain. In 'two-leaved gates' there could be a sexual innuendo: Milgate might have cited Nashe's *Unfortunate Traveller*, where a ruffian raping a woman 'used his knee as an iron ram to beat ope the two-leaved gate of her chastity.' Yet the sequence 'two-leaved gates . . . bosom . . . womb' (where 'womb', of course, does not mean the uterus but the stomach, as the context makes clear and as Romeo's address to the Capulets' vault as 'Thou detestable maw, thou womb of death' confirms) positively discourages any such innuendo, and, as Milgate also allows, 'two-leaved' is the Latin *biforis* (double-doored) and harmonizes with the Latin diction of 'patricians' and 'senators'. It is possible to argue that 'two-leaved gates' and 'hunger-starvèd womb' can still make a bawdy effect in defiance of their immediate context, but that they should also do it in defiance of their total context, the poem, seems improbable. It is just conceivable that Donne put them in to catch some of his prurient contemporaries out.

Compared with Spenser's 'Epithalamion', which was actually his wedding present to his bride, Donne's is a literary exercise. 'The storm' and 'The calm', on the contrary, were products of his own experience: he must have been as seasick and terrified, as sweltering and frustrated, as the rest of his shipmates. 'The storm' can hardly have been written at the time, though 'The calm' may have been; all the verbs in 'The calm' are in the present tense, but those in 'The storm' move into the present tense for the last thirty lines for the sake of greater immediacy and to justify the final couplet. The couplet form is particularly suited to the stream of impressions, many of them in the form of similes (in a dozen lines of 'The storm' there are as many as seven), though other figures, notably hyperbole, are introduced to vary the method:

> Lightning was all our light, and it rained more
> Than if the sun had drunk the sea before.

Sometimes a plain statement is the most effective method of all, as in the couplet that Ben Jonson quoted with admiration:

> No use of lanterns; and in one place lay
> Feathers and dust, today and yesterday.

At other times Donne rises to hauntingly macabre fantasies:

> Only the calenture together draws
> Dear friends, which meet dead in great fishes' jaws

– where the consecutive stresses on 'meet dead' bring out the paradox of such a meeting.

The third Satire, with its reference to 'ships' wooden sepulchres' and 'fires of Spain', seems to belong (perhaps in anticipation) to the Cadiz and Islands period of Donne's life, the period of the two verse letters just discussed, and of the elegy 'His picture' where he visualizes his return marked by the hardships of an overseas campaign. In its opening harangue it recalls the first Satire, but it has a much more serious tone. There was no suggestion that the 'fondling motley humorist' was courting damnation, and though Donne accused him of hating unadorned virtue it was really his imbecility that was his fault. But the man addressed here sounds like a tough adventurer, and Donne pays him the compliment of reasoning with him. If it were not for the opening, in which Donne decides that he must be neither a laughing nor a weeping philosopher but a railing one, one might be tempted to guess that the 'thou' was himself. (To weep for his own sins would be proper, but to weep for others' sins is futile.) This satire is structurally strong, and is in three sections. The first two, of almost equal length, are respectively an exposure of irreligious courage as spiritual cowardice and an exhortation to 'seek true religion'; the third is another exhortation, to 'Keep the truth which thou hast found'. Each section is powerfully argued, with plenty of illustration and analogy: the image of truth's huge hill is deservedly one of Donne's most famous passages. The couplets, instead of moving forward one at a time with the sense, are fused into paragraphs, and the sense runs on at many line-endings: the word 'blind-/ness' is even divided in the middle. A very strong impression of urgent speaking is created. Although Donne himself was probably in a state of doctrinal uncertainty, debating whether to retain or renounce his Catholicism, at about this time, it is possible to foresee in this Satire the preacher of the *Sermons*.

By contrast, *The Progress of the Soul*, dated by Donne 1601, creates an impression of irresponsibility and waywardness: if Donne is serious at all, his seriousness is well hidden by the mock-seriousness of the prefatory epistle and of the first six stanzas of the poem, where he dwells on its magnitude and begs for the time and strength to complete it. Then comes the mysterious seventh stanza, in which he obscurely hints at a deep political-topical theme in prospect. But from here onwards the poem becomes a free-wheeling story of the soul's transmigrations from Eve's apple through a mandrake, a sparrow, a fish, a second fish, a whale, a mouse, a wolf, a cross-bred wolf-dog and an ape, until stanza 51 finds it in Cain's sister Themech. The different creatures are brilliantly described – though 'described' is too limited a word for the empathy that Donne evokes for the thrusting mandrake and for the sparrow which kicks and pecks its way out of the shell and feels its 'stiff feathers' coming through its skin 'as children's teeth through gums'. The sequence of transmigrations is governed by no obvious logic – which would deaden the interest – but some of the transitions are notably apt:

from a hot sparrow the soul goes into a cold fish, and from the 'great castle' of the whale into the 'strait cloister' of the mouse. Though Donne calls it a satiric poem, it might be better defined as a fantastic one. Satirical elements – serious reflections on heresy, cynical remarks about women and officers of state – are present, but are present rather as part of the play of Donne's mind than as the thematic substance of the poem. It comes as something of a disappointment when the soul arrives within a human body. This looks like a point of no return: no more mandrakes, sparrows and other non-human creatures in which we can imagine what it would be like to live. If Donne really did intend to bring in Luther and Mahomet, and to conduct the soul through 'every great change' in history, then we may feel that in its incompleteness the poem is of just the right length. What he intended, and whether stanza 52 is merely the end of the 'First Song' or a patched-up conclusion to the whole poem when Donne decided that he was not going to write any more of it, can only be guessed. *The Progress of the Soul* is a puzzle; but it is as a poem, not as a puzzle, that it repays reading, and it ought to be better known.

The *Songs and Sonnets* are Donne's best-known and most admired poems. They are as remarkable for their variety of mood and tone as for their uniqueness of style: cynical dismissal of love, promiscuous love, unrequited love, mutual love, all find a place, and the situations range from the height of sensuous satisfaction to the depth of gloom in bereavement. Something of this variety, as well as some of the distinctive features of Donne's style, may be suggested by considering a few of them here, though not in all the detail in which they are capable of being analysed.

'The broken heart' begins with one of Donne's dogmatic statements:

> He is stark mad, whoever says
> That he hath been in love an hour.

This is ambiguous (the more obvious meaning is the wrong one), and in clarifying it Donne gives weight to the right meaning:

> Yet not that love so soon decays,
> But that it can ten in less space devour.

The longer fourth line, besides adding metrical interest to the quatrain, shifts the emphasis to make it fall heavily on 'ten'. Now follow couplets, again of different lengths, the longer one rounding off the stanza. They provide a parallel pair of extravagant analogies. In the second stanza the 'heart' of the title is introduced, but with a general reference to lovers; love itself now becomes personified as Love, and the figurative 'devour' reappears in terrifyingly literal form: 'He swallows us, and never chaws.' Two more analogies – both packed into a single couplet this time – reinforce the impression of mass destruction. (Incidentally, no useful purpose would be served by observing that a pike is also an implement of war, since obviously no word-play is intended.) In the third stanza the point is proved by particular experience, and the heart is '*my* heart': the metre provides the stress. At first the reader is allowed to think that the heart has been lost, so that the revelation that Love has shattered it at a blow comes with maximum force, and is reserved for the final couplet.

The end of this stanza might have been the end of the poem; but with the very characteristic conjunction 'yet' Donne develops it a stage further. In the third stanza, 'glass', as a type of fragility, is almost a cliché, though as applied to a human heart it has a deliberate and shocking incongruity. Now it becomes the reflecting glass of a mirror. This image is brought into conjunction with the scientific observations that matter cannot be wholly destroyed and that a vacuum cannot naturally exist. Donne is thus able to end his poem with a brilliant compliment: to like, to wish, even to adore, are all far short of the love he has felt.

'Community' is in every way a simpler poem: simpler in attitude, simpler in idea and image, simpler in versification. This is not to its disadvantage, for it has an attractive self-consistency, and its outrageous argument is expressed without a shadow of misgiving. It begins dogmatically and it carries on dogmatically. Its ifs and buts are not those of the doubter but those of the logical disputant. Its imagery, dictated by the reference to 'wise Nature' in the second stanza, is of greenery, of fruits and of nuts, and it reduces love to a matter of taste and appetite. It fittingly ends with a carefree gesture ('Who doth not fling away the shell?') and a rhetorical question which assumes the reader's agreement.

'The anniversary' has a quite different movement from either of the other two poems, though it is like them in embodying an argument. From the first sentence onwards Donne is addressing his mistress. It should perhaps be made clear that this term is used, as it was by Donne and his contemporaries, to mean the woman beloved, without any reference to her married or unmarried status or to her physical relationship – or lack of it – with the poet. This is an intimate and tender poem. It is also a grand and expansive one. The opening lines are a comprehensive review of all that is great, set against the passing of time. With the line 'All other things to their destruction draw' Donne implies, as he often does, the uniqueness of the lovers and their love. The rhyme-scheme of the stanza is remarkable. With 'Only our love hath no decay' and the three following lines, rhyme (and with it time) stands still. Donne is fond of ending a stanza with triple rhyme, but quadruple rhyme is evidently used with special intention here. So is the variation in the length of the four lines: first a line of four stresses, then two lines of five, finally one of six. Nothing could seem more final, and at the same time infinite.

That is why the blunt statement of fact with which the second stanza opens comes as such a blow. It is not a denial of what went before (Donne did not assert that they were immortal, only that their love was), but it is a recognition that death has its own finality, and, as such, it prompts the exclamation 'Alas'. Donne's literary tact – not his most celebrated quality – can be easily overlooked when he mentions what they will have to leave. In 'A valediction: forbidding mourning' he says that, compared with wholly sensual lovers, they 'Care less eyes, lips, and hands to miss.' Here he mentions only eyes and ears, and evokes the poignant beauty of love, not its sensuous rapture. From here it is a short step to 'souls where nothing dwells but love' as he reasserts his confidence that their love can survive even death.

This might be the end if the poem were not by Donne. The third stanza gives the argument a characteristic twist: since everyone who goes to heaven will be perfectly happy, it is here on earth that he and his mistress are unique. The imagery of kings, announced in the poem's opening line and briefly returned to in the second stanza, permeates the final one, and 'this is the second of our reign' rings out triumphantly.

In 'A lecture upon the shadow' Donne takes as his argument's starting-point an observed fact, as he takes the acts and the fate of the flea in the poem of that name. Shadows, he points out to his mistress, are at their shortest at noon, when the sun is at its height. He then ('So') draws an analogy between the diminishing shadows that they have been casting between 9 a.m. and noon and their diminishing concern to hide their love from others as it gathered strength. The second of the two stanzas pursues the argument by drawing a further analogy between the increasing shadows after noon and their increasing concern to hide their disloyal actions from each other if their mutual love should decline.

These analogies are not altogether satisfactory. The objection is not that the natural course of the actual sun gives the poem a fatalistic and pessimistic character. Donne is quite capable of making the figurative sun ('our loves') stand still for ever at noon, an image that would be in his high hyperbolical manner. It is that the correspondence between the actual and the figurative shadows, while presented as close, is not close enough. There is no optical reason why the actual shadows cast from east to west should 'blind' others, and why those cast from west to east should 'blind' the lovers. Donne has to resort to emphatic assertions that they would do so. He even has to fudge the language, in the line 'Disguises did, and shadows, flow', where he implies that figurative shadows are synonymous with figurative disguises, which they are not and were not in his time (the verb 'to shadow' did mean to conceal, but the noun 'a shadow' was always used of an insubstantial or illusory imitation of something real). Nevertheless, the poem's two-stanza structure helps us to accept the analogies, and the two aphoristic couplets reinforce that structure, the mildness of the first serving as a foil to the truly blinding hyperbole of the second. In one of his *Sermons* (not included in this selection) Donne writes that, in composition, 'the whole frame of the poem is a beating out of a piece of gold, but the last clause is as the impression of the stamp, and that is it that makes it current.' That is certainly true of 'A lecture upon the shadow'. Could the final couplet have come to Donne first, and the rest of the poem been written to lead up to it?

'The funeral' does not suffer from imagery in which imperfect analogies, offered as perfect ones, disturb the reader. Its central stanza, in which Donne asserts that his mistress's lock of hair, wound about his arm as he lies in the grave, will hold his body together in death better than his spinal cord and nervous system could do in life, has all the poetic force of unreason. Unreason does not imply absurdity, but to avoid absurdity it has to be thoroughly in tune with the poem. The opening words, 'Whoever comes to shroud me' (that he is dying of love does not yet need to be stated), make the image of his corpse very positive, and the tone of fanatical exaltation with which he speaks of the lock of hair prepares us for his extraordinary claims on its behalf. The poem's concern with substance assists, rather than hinders, our imaginative acceptance of these claims. The lock is a 'subtle wreath', fine hairs intricately woven, yet it is stronger than the 'sinewy thread' which can 'tie' the parts of his body together ('thread', in the context, suggesting amazing slightness, like that of the newly hatched sparrow's bones in *The Progress of the Soul*, and also, coupled with 'sinewy' and 'tie', amazing strength like that of packthread). Donne's argument –

> These hairs which upward grew, and strength and art
>> Have from a better brain,
> Can better do't

– emphasizes the threefold parallelism with 'the sinewy thread my brain lets fall'. Though we cannot take this seriously as argument, we must respond to its ingenuity. This is a poem which makes us ask ourselves what we mean when we talk of seriousness. There is conscious extravagance in Donne's argument, and in his attitude ('I am / Love's martyr'); and in the last four lines, where he addresses his mistress in the second person, after speaking of her in the third, there is a detectable perking-up. But though he may be only playing at dying, and producing a gallant compliment, his imagination has been deeply engaged in the game, and in that sense 'The funeral' is serious.

None of Donne's *Songs and Sonnets* is more difficult than 'The ecstasy'. The ideas and images that he uses here are unusually complex, and most of them are unfamiliar to a modern reader. Beyond these difficulties (which are briefly dealt with in the notes) is the difficulty, which has divided the critics, of deciding exactly what the poem is about. That it is about two lovers, Donne and his mistress, who together enter a state of mystical rapture in which their souls leave their bodies, is clear enough. It is clear that their souls, speaking and feeling as one, recognize that love has united, strengthened and enlightened them; they recognize also that they must not remain indefinitely separate from their bodies. But what is the conclusion to be drawn from the souls' reflections and decision, and what does the last quatrain mean?

> And if some lover such as we
>   Have heard this dialogue of one,
> Let him still mark us, he shall see
>   Small change when we're to bodies gone.

Some critics take this to mean that when the souls have returned to their bodies they will retain the benefits that they have gained from their ecstatic union outside them. Others take it to mean that when the lovers' bodies are joined in sexual union their love will be no less spiritual than when their souls mingled in ecstasy.

Neither interpretation is free from problems. The first interpretation makes the poem end very tamely; Donne's usual technique is to produce and play an ace as his final card, as 'the impression of the stamp' that 'makes [the poem] current'. The second interpretation, on the other hand, may make it end too strongly – even, perhaps, given the presence of the observer, indecently. The matter is complicated by the ambiguity of the pronoun 'we', and by uncertainty as to when the souls' dialogue ends. Donne has not consistently distinguished between the lovers and their souls, nor has he consistently made them identical. At lines 17–20 'we' means the lovers and not the souls; at line 30 'we said' must mean 'our souls said' (for 'we said nothing all the day'), and all the following pronouns refer to the souls until at line 61 we are pulled up by 'our blood' (which cannot be souls' blood) and 'That subtle knot which makes us man' in the same sentence. It could be argued that the souls' dialogue ends at line 60 and that what follow are Donne's observations, with line 69 as his exhortation to his mistress; but this is probably too drastic a shift from the well-established past tense of all that has happened in the poem so far. Yet why should the souls be so emphatic about the importance of the bodies if the bodies are to do nothing when they return to them? Is there an implication, however cautiously we interpret the literal meaning of the poem's lines, that sexual union is an indispensable element of human love? The reader is invited to examine some of the critical discussions of the poem, especially those by Helen Gardner and by Theodore Redpath, before deciding.

Donne's writings continually show how he could use his large stock of information and observation to supply analogies and imagery, how he could weld these together from the furnace of his imagination, and how he could control diction and rhythm to make his utterance natural and forceful. *The First Anniversary* (*An Anatomy of the World*) makes little appeal as a personal elegy for Elizabeth Drury, especially since she is celebrated in such extravagant terms as the unique embodiment of virtue and beauty; it is like a monstrous inflation of the stanza in 'A fever':

Or if, when thou, the world's soul, go'st,
　It stay, 'tis but thy carcass then,
The fairest woman but thy ghost,
　But corrupt worms the worthiest men.

But as an elegiac rhapsody on the world's decay the poem is, in spite of its melancholy thesis, full of invention and exuberant wit: the passage (lines 91–170) on the physical deterioration of humankind, or that (lines 285–99) on the irregularity of the earth's surface, serves as an example of fantastic vision pointedly expressed:

But keeps the earth her round proportion still?
Doth not a Tenerife, or higher hill,
Rise so high like a rock, that one might think
The floating moon would shipwreck there, and sink?

The controlling idea, that of the dissection of the dead world, gives

203

form to the poem, and the recurring device of anaphora (the repetition of one or more words at the beginning of two or more lines or phrases), always a favourite of Donne's both in verse and prose, signals the approaching end of each section: 'She of whom . . . She in whom . . . She, she is dead; she's dead', etc.

Among the specifically religious poems, 'Good Friday, 1613. Riding westward' stands out for its original idea and for the combined intellectual and emotional power with which Donne handles this idea. In travelling westward he is turning his back upon his crucified Saviour. East and west were always more important points of the compass to him than north and south, and, given his interest in languages (see, for example, his discussion of the word 'mercy' in the fifth extract from his *Sermons*), he must have noticed that the English language was unusual in not deriving the word 'Easter', like many European ones, from the Greek and Latin *pascha*. Hence the stupendous paradox of

> There I should see a sun by rising set,
> And by that setting endless day beget.

This, like the whole poem, is both brilliantly clever and deeply moving. Donne does not allow his ingenuity to run away with him. In *An Anatomy of the World* (just after the passage where the moon is in danger of being shipwrecked on a mountain peak) he had fancied a sounding-line sinking so far into the ocean deeps that it goes right through the world and comes up with an Antipodean (holding on by his feet?) at the end of it. That was fine in a poem which was wholly based on exaggeration, but anything of the kind would have been fatal to 'Good Friday, 1613'. When, in the latter poem, he writes

> Could I behold that endless height which is
> Zenith to us and t' our antipodes,
> Humbled below us?

he is not writing hyperbolically at all, which makes his statement the more amazing to contemplate.

That Donne combines thought and feeling to a very high degree is by now a truism, but since it is also a truth it will stand repetition. It applies to his prose as well as to his poetry. The young man who ingeniously analysed his hardships at sea in 'The storm' and 'The calm' can still be recognized in the middle-aged man who ingeniously analyses the progress of his illness in the *Devotions*. Wit is always ready to burst through the sobering reflections on human mortality, as it does in the sixteenth Devotion, where Donne – who had coveted 'preferment' long enough and painfully enough in his time – treats dying as promotion, and, with analogies and puns, reviews his qualifications for it; and, as so often in Donne and his successors, the wit intensifies the seriousness. When, in some parts of the *Sermons*, Donne's subject calls for great solemnity, he can be serious in a different way, with a deep impassioned tone. His picture of the horror of damnation (extract 4) might be set beside the closing soliloquy of Doctor Faustus in Marlowe's tragedy. What Donne gains by speaking of damnation in the first person can hardly be measured, it is so great. We must never forget that his sermons, as the Latin root of the word means, are speeches. Imagine the effect of Donne's voice and presence, in the pulpit, the sounding-board above his head, his looks, his gestures. This is oratory bordering upon drama. Take account also of the piquant incongruity between the damned sinner and the gowned and surpliced figure in the pulpit, an incongruity which can hardly have escaped Donne: Faustus, too, was a doctor of divinity. As Donne well knew, no one could presume his own spiritual security: death and judgement faced him as well as the most open sinner in his congregation.

Donne's individuality, it was said at the beginning of this critical commentary on his work, continually stares us in the face as we read. All the works are so obviously the product of a single mind that whether we are trying to interpret a particular phrase or trying to form a critical opinion of Donne as a writer it is reasonable to take into account as much as possible of what he wrote. The more we know of Donne – not only what he wrote but what he did and what happened to him – the better. It is unfortunate that we do not know more: for example, we do not know whether he wrote all his *Holy Sonnets* after he was ordained or only some of them; we do not know the date of any of the *Songs and Sonnets* or the order of their composition; we do not know which of them – if any – were addressed to his wife; we do not even know how far he believed half of the things he said. But all this ignorance of ours need not prevent our trying to get together as complete and as faithful a mental picture of him and his writings as we can.

Select bibliography

no shawcross!

TEXT

Donne's work, particularly the poetry, presents two kinds of difficulty: that of deciding which of two or more variant readings to follow (for example, 'The canonization', l. 40, 'contract' or 'extract'); and that of interpreting the meaning. The editions listed below (collected poems first, groups of poems second, prose third) will be found useful in both respects. All have an introduction and a commentary.

Poems, ed. Herbert J. C. Grierson, 2 vols, Oxford, 1912. An old-spelling edition.

Complete English Poems, ed. C. A. Patrides, London, 1985. An old-spelling edition with footnotes. Contains a comprehensive bibliography of criticism.

Complete English Poems, ed. A. J. Smith, Harmondsworth, 1971, rev. 1973. A modern-spelling edition with extensive commentary.

The Divine Poems, ed. Helen Gardner, Oxford, 1952, rev. 1978. An old-spelling edition.

The Elegies and the Songs and Sonnets, ed. Helen Gardner, Oxford, 1965. An old-spelling edition.

The Epithalamions, Anniversaries, and Epicedes, ed. W. Milgate, Oxford, 1978. An old-spelling edition.

The Satires, Epigrams, and Verse Letters, ed. W. Milgate, Oxford, 1967. An old-spelling edition.

The Songs and Sonnets, ed. Theodore Redpath, London, 1956, extensively revised 1983. A modern-spelling edition, with the most detailed editorial commentary available.

Devotions upon Emergent Occasions, ed. Anthony Raspa, Montreal, 1975. An old-spelling edition.

Sermons, ed. George R. Potter and Evelyn M. Simpson, 10 vols, Berkeley, Cal., 1953–62. An old-spelling edition.

SECONDARY WORKS

1 Biography and criticism

Bald, R. C., *John Donne: A Life*, ed. W. Milgate, Oxford, 1970. The standard biography.

Carey, John, *John Donne: Life, Mind, and Art*, London, 1981. A biographical/critical study, emphasizing the relationship between his life and work, with particular reference to his change of religion and to his ambition.

Fiore, Peter A. (ed.), *Just So Much Honor*, University Park, Pa., 1972. A collection of critical essays written for the volume.

Gardner, Helen (ed.), *John Donne: A Collection of Critical Essays*, Englewood Cliffs, NJ, 1962.

Lovelock, Julian (ed.), *Donne: 'Songs and Sonnets': A Casebook*, London, 1973. A collection of critical essays, including extracts from writers earlier than the modern period.

Smith, A. J. (ed.), *Donne and the Metaphysical Poets: The Critical Heritage*, London, 1968. A comprehensive collection of the most important critical comments from Donne's contemporaries onwards.

—— (ed.), *John Donne: Essays in Celebration*, London, 1972. A collection of critical essays written for the volume.

2 Background

Briggs, Julia, *This Stage-Play World: English Literature and its Back-*

ground, 1580–1625, Oxford, 1983. Chapters on views of nature, social life, religion, education, court life, and the theatre.

Lewis, C. S., *The Discarded Image: An Introduction to Medieval and Renaissance Literature*, Cambridge, 1964. The medieval concept or 'image' of the universe, with discussion of, for example, the heavens and their inhabitants, the earth, beasts, the human soul, other kinds of soul, and the human body.

3 Reference

The Oxford English Dictionary (abbreviated in the notes as *OED*). The reissued form (1933) of J. Murray, H. Bradley, W. A. Craigie and C. T. Onions (eds), *A New English Dictionary on Historical Principles*, 20 vols (1888–1928). An indispensable guide to the changing meanings of words.

Notes

Songs and Sonnets

1–6   The first few times I met you, I loved you, but was aware of nothing but your wondrous presence. 7–14 But just as the soul has to operate through the body, love has to have an object, and so I directed my love to your body. 15–22 But I found your beauties so distractingly numerous that my love remained without a suitable object. 23–8 Let me, then, have *your* love as the dwelling-place of *mine*.

6   The paradox of *seeing* a *nothing* which is *lovely* and *glorious* (compare l. 3, *shapeless flame*) conveys the lover's confused adoration.

7–8   (Compare 'The ecstasy', ll. 65–8.) The proposed analogy between this and love's taking the body of the beloved is witty because illogical.

19   *Every thy hair* every single hair of yours.

20   *some fitter* some fitter object.

22   *Extreme and scatt'ring bright* so extremely bright as to distract (*scatter*) the viewer's thoughts.

23–4   *Angels* (being wholly spiritual) were thought to assume bodies made of condensed *air* (the purest material element) in order to become visible.

| 25 | The universe was supposed to consist of nine concentric *spheres*, each ruled by an angel called an intelligence. Compare 'The ecstasy', l. 52, and 'Good Friday, 1613', ll. 1–2. |
| 26–8 | This emphatic conclusion – that men's love is purer than women's – is left to the reader to interpret and judge. |

THE ANNIVERSARY

2	*honours* high-ranking people.
3	The sun, by measuring time, *makes* years, seasons, months, etc.
4	The verb *is* applies to the sun, but the sense includes everything listed in ll. 1–2. Compare l. 6.
7–10	The idea of continuation to eternity is reflected in the persistent rhyme and the final alexandrine.
11–12	The lovers require *two graves*, either because they are not married and their love is secret, or because their souls would otherwise not wish to leave their bodies, or because it is not to be expected that they will die on the same day.
17–18	The words *dwells* and *inmates* distinguish the householder from the temporary lodgers.
19	*This . . . increasèd* this love or a greater love.
	there above up there (in heaven).
20	The souls' *graves* are the bodies.
24	*nor . . . be* This could be punctuated 'nor, of such, subjects be', but the verse suggests that the meaning is 'nor can be kings of such subjects'.
27	The *true fear* is of death (which will happen); the *false fear* is of mutual treason (which will not).

THE APPARITION

5	*feigned vestal* pretended virgin. The priestesses of the Roman goddess Vesta were virgins.
7	The implication is that *he* is just one of a series of lovers.
11	The leaves of an *aspen* tree tremble in the wind.

12   The drops of sweat will gather in large globules like
        quicksilver.
13   pale like a *ghost*, and more dead than alive with fear.
15   *preserve*   from this apparition, and from the misconduct
        that will have led to it (compare ll. 16–17).

THE BAIT

Written in imitation of Christopher Marlowe's 'The passionate
shepherd to his love', which begins: 'Come live with me, and be my
love, / And we will all the pleasures prove / That valleys, groves,
hills and fields, / Woods, or steepy mountain yields.' Sir Walter
Ralegh also wrote an imitation, 'The nymph's reply'.

9   *that live bath*   the water of the running river.
13   *to be so seen*   to be seen naked.
23   *sleavesilk flies*   artificial flies made from sleaved (unravelled)
        silk.

THE BLOSSOM

10   *to nestle thee*   to build yourself a nest.
12   A *forbidden* tree may imply that the woman is married;
        alternatively, it may be used (with its Garden of Eden
        association) simply to emphasize *forbidding* ('a forbidden, or
        rather a forbidding, tree'), thus blaming her coldness.
15–16   The lady is *that sun*, the actual sun *this sun*.
27   *makes no show*   cannot be seen.
31   *some other part*   by implication, another part (besides a
        heart) that women do not have.
35   in better spirits and physical condition by being in
        company.
38   *I would*   I wish to.
39   *another friend*   a different woman.

BREAK OF DAY

The speaker is a woman (ll. 11–18).

8   I saw a flask of gunpowder take a whole day to burn.

15   *chained shot*   cannon-balls chained together to kill soldiers
         marching abreast in *ranks*.

16   The *pike* is the most savage freshwater fish, preying here on
         the *fry* (young or very small fish), and therefore called a
         tyrant: 'The mighty pike is the tyrant of the fresh water'
         (Izaak Walton, *The Complete Angler*, 1653).

25–6   Matter can neither be created nor (as here) destroyed, and
         nature abhors a vacuum.

THE CANONIZATION

The opening line, besides arresting the attention, provides the
rhyme-word for the first and last line of every stanza, both allowing
ingenious rhyming and making 'love' the most important word in
the poem. The title is explained in l. 36.

2–3   various disabilities (not necessarily self-inflicted) of which
         blame would be more tolerable.

5   *Take you a course*   get busy.

6   pay court to some lord (*his Honour*) or archbishop (*his Grace:*
         this could also mean a duke, but would lose the secular/
         clerical contrast).

7–8   *Or . . . Contemplate*   look upon either the king's *real* face (at
         court) or his *stamped* one (on coins).

9   *So*   so long as; provided that.

11   *drowned*   sunk (as by a gale).

13   When did my cold fits, like late frosts, spoil a well-advanced
         spring? The *colds, heats, sighs* and *tears* are all conventional
         symptoms of Petrarchan love.

14–15   When did my fevers make anyone die of plague? A *bill* of
         mortality was a weekly list of the numbers of deaths, and
         their causes, in all London parishes.

17   litigious men who start aggressive legal actions. (The
         lawyers do not start these, any more than the soldiers start
         the wars.)

20   Flies are often seen copulating, and are a common image for shortness of life.

21   A lighted candle is self-consuming. There is also word-play on 'die' ((1) perish; (2) experience orgasm), especially as it was thought that frequent sexual activity reduced expectation of life.

22   *we ... dove*   The eagle (strength, masculinity) and the dove (gentleness, feminity) are both combined in both of us.

23–5 We give more meaning to the puzzling legend of the phoenix (see l. 26) because *we two* (one of either *sex*) combine into *it* (a unique creature which, being self-renewing, needs neither to be male nor female).

26   *We die and rise the same*   After achieving orgasm (see ll. 21, 28) we are still physically unimpaired and as much in love as before – thus resembling the phoenix, which periodically sacrifices itself and is reborn from its own ashes.

26–7 *prove / Mysterious*   become beyond ordinary comprehension, like the mysteries of religion.

29–30 *Tombs* of the period usually have a panel inscribed with the achievements of the person commemorated. The *hearse* was a temple-shaped structure of wood placed over the coffin of noble persons during the funeral service, decorated with candles, banners and heraldic devices, and having epitaphs pinned to it.

30   *legend*   (1) that which is read; (2) saint's life.

32   *sonnets*   love lyrics, the *hymns* of l. 35; contrasted with bulky historical *chronicles*. There may be word-play in *rooms*: the Italian for 'room' is 'stanza'.

33–4 The contrast between *a well-wrought urn* and *half-acre tombs* is reinforced by word-play (*greatest*: (1) highest in rank; (2) largest in size).

38–9 The mutual *hermitage* of the now *canonized* lovers embodied the *peace* which, after their deaths, is replaced by the *rage* (frenzy) of conventionally suffering lovers.

40–4 *Who ... courts*   The curved eyeballs are metaphorically called *mirrors* (convex ones had been made in southern Germany for more than a hundred years); they can *contract*

215

within the vision the contents of a whole room (in reduced, or *epitomized*, form). But the idea is the mutual self-sufficiency of the lovers. Compare 'The good-morrow', stanzas 2 and 3. Some texts have *extract* for *contract*, thus making the metaphor an alchemical one.

44–5   *beg . . . love*   pray to God to send us down a love modelled on yours. The god in question may be *reverend love* (Cupid: l. 37), but the poem draws also upon Roman Catholicism's creation of saints by *canonization*.

COMMUNITY

3   *indifferent*   neither good nor bad.

8   made some women good and others bad.

12   only this conclusion remains, that all men may use all women. Compare *Othello*, V. ii. 73: 'That he hath used thee' (sexually).

14   The commonest colour in nature is green.

16–17   The implied image is perhaps of a rotten apple rotting others. Compare the *fruits* of ll. 19–21.

THE COMPUTATION

The 24 hours of the lovers' separation are calculated as 2400 years (20 + 40 + 40 + 100 + 200 + 1000 + 1000).

4   *wouldst*   wouldst that (i.e. I hoped you wished that you could continue your past favours to me).

7   *Or not divide*   The double negative (after *neither . . . nor . . .*, l. 6) is not an affirmative but is emphatic (i.e. I took no account whatever of the thousand years that made up this period).

8   *forgot that too*   lapsed into complete insensibility.

10   *by being dead*   having died the moment they parted.

3–4   may his only purse, and nothing but his purse, dispose some unfeeling woman to love him. For the syntax, compare l. 20 (*which none of his may be*).

6   *one*   the woman of ll. 4, 6, 10, 13.

7–8   deny, on oath, to others the promises that he has sworn to her, being torn between the fear of losing her and the shame of winning her.

9–10   may he increase his sorrow to madness, and his cramps to gout, by merely remembering who has given him them.

11–13   and may he feel no pang of conscience, only one of reputation (*fame*), and suffer not because of having committed fornication but because of having done so with her.

14–16   may he decay in early and long-lasting poverty, for the lack of land which he would have inherited if he had not incestuously begotten his kinsman's heir.

22–4   or may he have maintained parasites for so long that he would gladly be *their* parasite, and may he finally turn Jew, in order to subsist.

29   *Prophets*   such as Ezekiel 5: 7–17.

           poets   Virgil and Ovid were both traditionally (but doubtfully) regarded as the authors of 'curse' poems, the *Dirae* and *Ibis*.

29–30   *and all . . . by me*   a legal formula allowing for additional bequests; here comically incongruous because the bequests have been curses and have been comprehensive.

32   because to be a woman is, by definition, to be thoroughly accursed; a final satirical surprise.

THE DAMP

5   *damp*   loss of consciousness or vitality (*OED*, 4), rather than a noxious vapour (*OED*, 1).

7–8   *prefer . . . massacre*   promote your murder (of me) to the degree of a massacre (of me and the doctors).

11–12   *Disdain* and *Honour* are personifications of feminine reluctance to love (as are *Constancy* and *Secretness* of masculine persuasiveness) in the tradition of medieval allegorical love poetry such as *The Romance of the Rose*. Disdain is thus portrayed as a giant in Spenser's *Faerie Queene*, VI. vii. 41–4.

13–15   The Goths and Vandals, northern barbarians, overthrew the Roman Empire and destroyed its monuments of greatness. The woman is urged to forgo her fame as a conqueror of hearts.

20   but I neither require their aid nor make a great show of having them.

21–4   All the implications are sexual: to *kill* is to give an orgasm, to *die* to experience one; woman's *passive valour* is her courage to endure the assault of man. There is word-play in *naked*: (1) unarmed; (2) unclothed.

24   *odds . . . of* superiority over.

THE DISSOLUTION

1–8   Because my beloved and I were one, her death has left all her bodily elements in my body. 9–15 These elements – fire, air, water and earth, embodied in love's emotions and symptoms – would prolong my wretched life, but for the fact that the fire (passion) burns the others up. 16–24 This process is so rapid that when I die my soul will fly so fast that it will overtake hers.

12   but which had almost run out, because of the confidence (*security*) which our love had given me.

18   *break*   become bankrupt.

THE DREAM

3–4   The subject of the dream (that she came to his bed) was suited to fact, not to imagination.

7   *so true*   so thoroughly real. Some texts have 'so truth' (so absolutely truth itself).

14	*For thou lov'st truth* equivalent to 'to tell you the truth' – when he is in fact about to pay an extravagant compliment.
16	To be able to read thoughts directly, an attribute of God alone, is here attributed to the woman, who is accordingly deified (compare ll. 7, 19–20).
19	*it could not choose but be* it could not fail to be.
21	*showed thee thee* showed you to be yourself.
29	*goest to come* a paradoxical way of saying 'You go now to return later'.

THE ECSTASY

3	*violet* traditionally emblematic of truth.
6	*fast balm* adhesive warm moisture, suggesting amorousness.
7	*twisted* were twined together.
9–10	To graft is to insert a small piece of a plant into another so that they grow together (such as a rose grafted on the rootstock of a briar). Here each lover's hand is grafted into the other's.
11–12	Each lover's picture is reflected in the other's eyes. This was known as 'looking babies' (hence *get*, beget; *propagation*).
15	*advance their state* improve their condition by *negotiating* (l. 17).
18	Effigies on late sixteenth- and early seventeenth-century tombs often lay on one side, resting on one elbow; see, for example, the tomb of Elizabeth Drury (d. 1610), the subject of Donne's *The First Anniversary*, illustrated in R. C. Bald, *Donne and the Drurys* (Cambridge, 1959), plate III. This would be consistent with the lovers' holding hands, mingling looks and sitting (rather than lying) on the bank.
27	*concoction* purification (as of metals in alchemy). Compare *refined* (l. 21).
29–32	This ecstasy explains to the lovers what it is that they love: it is not just sexual attraction, and they were not moved to love simply by what they saw (each other's appearance).

219

29	*ecstasy* the state of spiritual rapture in which the soul is free of the body.
33–6	Their two souls (each of which is a mixture) are mixed together by love, so that both become one, and each is itself and the other.
37–40	More gardening imagery (compare ll. 9–10), employing the *violet* of l. 3.
37	*A single violet transplant* If you transplant a single violet.
41–4	When love thus combines the life of two souls (see ll. 33–6), the resulting superior soul overpowers (*controls*) the limitations of the single souls (*defects of loneliness*).
45–8	The assertion that their single and combined souls are made of immortal atoms (*atomies*) prepares for the mention of their bodies in ll. 49–72.
52	See note on 'Air and angels', l. 25. The singular *sphere* is required by the rhyme, though the sense is plural.
56	In refining metals, the *dross* is the impurity which is discarded; an *allay* (modern 'alloy') is a baser metal purposely combined with a finer one, usually to strengthen it.
57–60	This analogy uses the belief that the stars' influence on human beings was transmitted by the air.
61–8	This analogy uses the belief that what linked the physical body and the spiritual soul were vapours, called *spirits*, produced by the *blood*.
63	*need* are needed.
66–7	to emotions (*affections*) and physical powers (*faculties*) which the senses can reach and grasp.
68	The *great prince* is the *abler soul* (l. 43), *in prison* until he can reach their bodies.
69–70	Human beings cannot see that love which is spiritual until it takes physical form.
74	*this dialogue of one* the reflections stated in ll. 29–72. The paradoxical language (it might equally have been 'this monologue of two') expresses the union of souls.
75–6	When the lovers consummate their love physically, it will retain its spiritual character. Alternatively, when the souls

return to the bodies, they will appear just as united as they did when outside them.

THE EXPIRATION

Title   *Expiration* word-play: (1) death; (2) breathing out (l. 2).

2   Compare Marlowe, *Doctor Faustus*, V. i. 97: 'Her lips suck forth my soul, see where it flies.'

5–6   We asked no one's permission to begin loving; nor will we allow anyone the easy act of killing us by ordering us to part.

12   being killed twice over, by parting from you and by ordering you to part from me.

A FEVER

5–8   *This world* (l. 6) and *the whole world* (l. 8) refer to the actual world; *this world* (l. 7), by contrast, is her body. The idea is varied in ll. 9–12, in which, since she is the *soul* that sustains the actual *world*, it will be figuratively, after her death, her *carcass*.

12   *corrupt worms*   maggots bred in a corrupting corpse.

13–16   Scholastic philosophers speculated on whether the world would be finally burned, and, if so, by what fire.

17–24   Two ideas are combined: that fever, like a fire, can burn only as long as there is *corrupt* matter to serve as its *fuel*; and that everything below the moon's sphere is corruptible (*meteors*, for example), while everything above it (the *firmament* or heavens) is incorruptible and therefore *unchangeable*.

25   *seizing*   word-play: (1) grasping; (2) taking legal possession of (compare *owner*, l. 27).

4   This statement, literally true, plays on the idea that in coition the bloods of the couple were intermingled.

7   *this* this flea. The pronoun *this* also means 'in observing this flea' (l. 1), 'this event' (l. 5), 'to drink each other's blood' (l. 9), 'this flea' (l. 12), 'this murder' (l. 17).

14   *Though ... you* though your parents, and you yourself, oppose our sexual union.

15   *cloistered* enclosed; with a paradoxical suggestion of chastity.

       jet a shiny black mineral; appropriate both to the flea's colour and to its figurative role as a *temple* (compare *living walls*).

16   Though your habit of killing me with your refusals may make you ready to kill me again.

18   *sacrilege* i.e. in destroying a *temple* (l. 13).

25–7   The admission that everything argued in stanzas 1 and 2 was false leads to the use of a quite different argument.

THE FUNERAL

5–8   The real soul, having gone to heaven, will have left the lock of hair to preserve the body, as a departing queen leaves a deputy to maintain her kingdom.

9–11   The whole body is described as held together by the spinal cord and nervous system.

12–13   The woman's lock of hair is more effective against the man's bodily dissolution (even after death) than his *sinewy thread* (l. 9) was in life.

15   *pain* penalty, sentence (of death).

19   *Love's martyr* one who has died for Love (from unrequited love).

20   *these relics* the *hairs* (l. 12).

21, 23 Devotion (*humility*) is balanced against defiance (*bravery*).

22   to attribute the powers of a soul to a lock of hair.

24   *save* keep alive. The woman has refused to return the

man's love. The lock of hair that she gave him was perhaps (l. 17) in consolation, though in l. 3 *wreath* and *crowns* deliberately mislead the reader into expecting it to be a symbol of his triumph. The poem may be compared and contrasted with 'The relic'.

THE GOOD-MORROW

3   *sucked on country pleasures, childishly?*   Did we, like children sent to be suckled in the country, know only the simplest satisfactions?

4   The *seven sleepers* of Ephesus were Christian youths who took refuge in a cave (*den*) from persecution in 249. They were discovered and walled up, but miraculously slept for nearly 200 years.

5   *but this . . . fancies be*   apart from love, all pleasures are mere illusions.

8   This line, which explains the title, carries on the idea in *snorted* (snored, l. 4) and *dream* (l. 7).

9–10   Love (which overcomes all desire to see anything or anyone else), not fear, causes our souls to look earnestly at each other.

12, 13   *Let*   what though.

13   what though maps (of the heavens) have revealed innumerable worlds (of stars and planets) to other discoverers.

14   Let us, each having and being the other's world, possess one self-sufficient world between us. Some texts have 'our world'.

15–18   The *hemispheres* – each lover's face reflected in the other's curved eyeball – make up the lovers' world, which has neither coldness (*sharp north*) nor sunset (*declining west:* compare 'A lecture upon the shadow', l. 19).

19–20   Only things which are perfectly constituted are imperishable. Our loves are either one love or they are so alike that neither can decline from the other; therefore they are imperishable.

2	the rich woman and the poor one.
3	*masques and plays* loves going to masques and plays.
5	the woman who trusts (her lover), and the woman who tests (him).
10	*no other vice* i.e. than being true.
15	*know* make sexual love to.
16	The implied metaphor is of highway robbery (compare *1 Henry IV*, II. ii. 90: 'The thieves have bound the true men'), with the sexual innuendo of emptying a purse.
17–18	The 'travel' metaphor now becomes political, again with a sexual innuendo in *thorough* (through).
20	The identification of *love's sweetest part* as *variety* is not, of course, what the reader was encouraged to expect.
25	*dangerous constancy* the dangerous doctrine of constancy.
26	*will be* are determined to be.
27	*shall be* will have to be.

A LECTURE UPON THE SHADOW

1–2	Stand still, my love, and I will deliver you a lecture in love's natural science (that is, in optics).
4	*here* probably in a garden.
10	*shadows* concealments (from others; compare ll. 13, 16–17).
17	*behind* later.
24	A comment on the phrase *all the day* in l. 23. This idea is then violently emphasized in the final epigrammatic couplet, ll. 25–6.

THE LEGACY

7	*which* who (relating to the first *I* in the line). The mind reels when trying to write a paraphrase of this poem – as Donne meant it should – though it is easy to follow the ingenious variations on 'I' and 'me', and on the tenses of the verbs, in reading it.
	I should be I was to be.

8	the executor of my own will, and also the thing I had bequeathed (to you; see l. 12).
10	In love-poetry, the lover's mistress is often referred to as his other self.
18	but it was variously coloured (symbolizing inconstancy) and it had angularities (unlike curves, which approach to the perfect form of a circle).
20	no one lover possessed it wholly, and few had any part of it.
21	*made by art* artificially manufactured.
22	*for our losses sad* saddened by our losses (both having lost the missing heart).
24	*no man . . . 'twas thine* being yours, it was too flighty for anyone (or, more particularly, any *man*) to hold.

LOVERS' INFINITENESS

Title	Printed in 1633 and retained in the five other seventeenth-century editions, it is appropriate to the subject, which is not that love is infinite but that lovers can enjoy an infinity of love. One manuscript has the title 'A lovers infiniteness'; the remainder have no title or 'Mon tout' (French: 'My all').
21–2	Legally a buyer of land acquired the right to any crops it might produce.
29–30	This may be intended to recall Sir Philip Sidney's love-lyric 'My true love hath my heart, and I have his', since ll. 31–3 refer to 'changing hearts'. Yet ll. 27–8 suggest that ll. 29–30 mean that in some miraculous or riddling way she *can* every day give him her heart. There is also an echo of Jesus's words to the disciples (Matthew 16: 25): 'For whosoever will save his life shall lose it: and whosoever will lose his life for my sake shall find it.'

LOVE'S ALCHEMY

2	*his centric happiness* the essential happiness of love; the *hidden mystery* of l. 5.

7–10	And as no alchemist has ever discovered the elixir of life, but praises his fruitful chemical equipment if he accidentally comes across some by-product useful in perfumery or medicine.
7	*elixir* This supposedly discoverable substance, of surpassing purity, was thought capable of turning base metals into gold, healing all diseases, and infinitely prolonging life.
12	but get a night as short as a summer one and as cold as a winter one.
13	*day* life.
15	*any man* Most texts have 'my man' (my servant), which is metrically inferior, and which expresses the idea that physical love admits no social distinctions, whereas 'any man' means that it admits no distinctions of any kind.
17	go through the brief humiliating action of a bridegroom.
22	*that day's* the wedding day's.
	the spheres the concentric globes supposed to rotate about the earth and to produce heavenly music inaudible to mortals.
23–4	Women cannot be expected to have minds; at their best they may rise to sweetness and cleverness, but once you have possessed them they are merely mummy.
24	*mummy* dead (mindless) flesh. The preservative, and the flesh, of Egyptian mummies were used in medicine.

LOVE'S DEITY

5–7	The *destiny* ordained for male lovers by Cupid, and confirmed by custom, which is nature's substitute, is to love a woman who scorns one.
9	*in his young godhead* in his early days as a god.
10–13	*But when . . . subject was* But when lovers loved equally, his function was good-naturedly to join males to females. He was concerned only with reciprocal love.
15–16	But now every ordinary god wants to make his power as great as that of the king of gods.

18	all these activities are within Cupid's area of authority.
22	*Rebel and atheist too* i.e. in defying Cupid, his king and his god.
26	*she loves before* She has a lover (perhaps a husband) already. Therefore it is better for her to hate me than be false to him.

LOVE'S DIET

2	*had grown* would have grown.
8	and even part of that was allotted to lamenting my misfortune and my faults.
12	it was neither truly wholesome nor caused by thinking of me.
13	*brined* salted.
17	*meat* food (the *she-sigh* of l. 10).
21	*And that* and when.
22–4	*Title*, *conveyed*, and *entail* are legal terms: the right of possession transferred to him by her letter amounts to no more than being fortieth in succession to an estate.
25	*my buzzard love* Buzzards (being sluggish and greedy) were not used for hawking by falconers, who used peregrines, goshawks and sparrowhawks. To train the *buzzard love* for the chase was thus a real achievement.
27, 28	*Now . . . / And now* sometimes . . . / at other times.
29	*spring a mistress* i.e. as a falconer starts up a bird for his hawk to pursue.

LOVE'S EXCHANGE

1–2	Love, any *other* devil would give something in exchange for the gift of a soul (as Marlowe's Doctor Faustus received twenty-four years of magic power for his).
3–5	Your fellow devils, at court, give fashionable skills in exchange for those souls (those of the courtiers) which they are already sure of getting.
8–14	A *dispensation* and a *non obstante* (Latin: notwithstanding) are both concessions allowing someone to act contrary to some

particular law; *nature's law* is being naturally truthful (compare *falsify, forswear*). Such special powers (*prerogatives*) belong only to Love, the ruler, and his favourites (*minions*).

15–16 Love (Cupid) is literally blind, his followers metaphorically blind.

21 a painful self-consciousness should make me my own fresh cause of suffering.

24–5 small towns which hold out until compelled by cannon fire to yield are not allowed by the conventions of war to make conditions.

28–9 The first *face* is the warlike face he has *put* (compelled) Love to show. The second *face* is that of the woman he loves – which is, by an implied metaphor, Love's artillery.

30 *idolatry* religion; but, in love-poetry, usually woman-worship (compare Holy Sonnet 13, l.9).

34–5 *make ... before* make mines of precious metals and jewels more numerous than stone-quarries.

36 *this* this rebellion of mine.

37–9 *If I must ... torn* Two ideas (*kill* and *dissect*, l. 40) are combined: his death will be a warning against rebellion, and his dissection will contribute to future knowledge.

40–2 *for this ... anatomies* for this torture is contrary to your purpose: bodies dislocated by the rack are unsuitable as anatomical subjects.

LOVE'S GROWTH

3–4 because it is subject to change and times, like the grass (which starts growing again in spring; compare ll. 5–6).

7–10 but if love, this homoeopathic medicine, far from being the elixir of life (see 'Love's alchemy', l. 7), is a mixture of everything that can hurt the soul or the senses, and responds to the sun's heat and light (compare ll. 3–6).

13–14 but, being a compound of elements, like everything else, therefore has periods of inactivity and activity.

15 *not ... eminent* not bigger, only more conspicuous.

17–18 The sense and application of the analogy are obscure. As applied to ll. 15–16 it seems to mean 'the sun does not enlarge stars but only *makes them more conspicuous*'; as applied to ll. 19–20, 'the sun does not *create* stars but only shows them'; in either case the italicized words strain the sense of the corresponding words in l. 18, and in the first case it is not clear to what phenomenon Donne is referring.

21–4   These new signs of love are like multiplying ripples in water, or the concentric spheres that make up heaven (see 'Love's alchemy', l. 22): they are all related, and all centre upon you.

LOVE'S USURY

1–3   Love is considered as a money-lender: the *bargain* (l. 17) is for a present loan of love-free hours, to be repaid in later life at 20.per cent (twice the maximum authorized interest rate at the time), in love-enslaved hours.

4   ambiguous: (1) in middle age (when I have as many grey hairs as brown ones); (2) in old age (when I have as many grey hairs as I have brown ones now).

5   *let my body reign*   let me be ruled by my physical senses.

6   *sojourn*   make only brief stays.

    snatch   seize sexual opportunities.

7–8   take up again with the woman I had and left last year; forget that we had met before.

9–12   These are examples of casual behaviour: if he intercepts a letter from the woman to another admirer, he will be as little disturbed as if it were written to him; if he makes an assignation for midnight, he will turn up next morning at nine; if he goes to keep an assignation he will seduce the maidservant first – and tell the mistress why he is late.

13   *no, not the sport*   no, not even the physical pleasure. He will enjoy it but will not be obsessed by it.

14–16   The three classes of women are metaphorically classed as food: grass (fit for beasts to eat), sweetmeats (*comfitures*) and fancy dishes (*quelque-choses*: often anglicized to 'kickshawses').

15–16   *let . . . transport*   let my fancy be led by any news I hear (i.e.
        of suitable women to enjoy).
21–2   Do thy will when that time comes; and when it comes I
        leave (*submit*) to thee the decision as to whom I shall love
        (*subject*), how much I shall love (*degree*), and what the result
        (*fruit*) of my love shall be.
23   *it*   being in love.
23–4   *though . . . me*   even if I am compelled to love a woman who
        is in love with me – the ultimate enslavement, from the
        libertine's point of view.

THE MESSAGE

4–5   such affected behaviour and false emotions.
8   *Fit . . . sight*   incapable of seeing well.
12–13   to treat its own solemn declarations as mere jests.
14   *cross*   cancel.
23   that will have nothing to do with you.

NEGATIVE LOVE

5–6   for what they love is able to be felt by the senses and under-
        stood by the mind.
7   *silly*   simple.
        more brave   finer.
8   *may . . . crave*   may I fail to obtain what I want when I
        come to ask for it; an asseveration, like 'May I be damned if
        I know what I want'.
9   *would have*   desire.
10–12   alluding to the theologians' defining God's purity and per-
        fection by means of negatives (immortal, invisible, etc.).
13   I refuse everything that all other people love (i.e. both the
        sensual and the platonic, ll. 1–4).
14–16   *If any . . . nothing*   If anyone who can best explain what we
        do not understand, our own selves, knows what that
        nothing is, let him teach it me.

18   *speed*   succeed.
        miss   fail.

Title   A *nocturnal* is both (1) a night-piece (like this poem) and (2) a
        nocturn or night-service of the Roman Catholic Church
        held at midnight. The time is the *midnight* (l. 1) at which St
        Lucy's Day (13 December) begins. This, according to the
        old calendar, was the winter solstice when the sun reached
        the Tropic of Capricorn (now about 21 December); there-
        after the days lengthen again. St Lucy (her name is related to
        Latin *lux*, light) is the patron saint of sight. Lucy was the
        name of Donne's patroness the Countess of Bedford, and
        the poem may have been occasioned by her serious illness
        (22 November 1612) or by her death (1627), though
        ll. 22–4 are highly emotional, perhaps too much so for the
        relationship of the poet and patroness. The poem may
        alternatively refer to the death of Donne's wife (1617) or to
        his fear (letter of mid-April 1612) that she might have died
        in childbirth while he was abroad. Or the bereavement may
        be wholly fictitious.

3   *flasks*   gunpowder flasks.
4   *light squibs*   trifling firecrackers (fitful gleams as contrasted
        with *constant rays*).
5–6   The *general balm* is the vital substance in all living things,
        here metaphorically *drunk* by the *hydroptic* (dropsical, water-
        accumulating) earth as the sap sinks in the vegetation.
7–9   All life has sunk down to the earth (as a dying person slips
        down in bed) till it is dead and buried; yet everything seems
        cheerful compared with me, the last word in deadness.
        Compare l. 12, *every dead thing*.
13–16   Love's *alchemy* was *new* because it distilled (*did express*) from
        the lover's deadness a negative, not a positive, *quintessence*
        (see 'Love's alchemy', l. 7, *elixir*).

17	*ruined* broke down into the constituent elements (*absence, darkness, death*, l. 18).
21	*limbeck* alembic, an early form of retort (in chemical experiments).
24	*the ... two* Compare 'A valediction: of weeping', ll. 14–20, and 'The good-morrow', l. 14.
24–6	*oft ... aught else* Since lovers wish only to be conscious of each other (compare 'The good-morrow', l. 10), they become *chaoses* (states in which nothing is in order) when obliged to attend to other things.
26–7	*absences ... carcasses* i.e. because each lover's soul had gone with the absent lover.
28	*which ... her* i.e. because only her body has died.
29	become the quintessence (see l. 15) of the original nothingness before God created anything.
30–4	Human beings, beasts, plants and stones are on a descending scale: human beings understand what they are, beasts do what they wish, plants extract their food, even stones (the magnetic lodestone) may be attracted or repelled. Some qualities reside in them all.
35–6	Shadows (traditionally contrasted with substances) at least have a sort of being, since they are cast by light shining on objects.
37	*none* no 'ordinary nothing' (not even a shadow).
	my sun i.e. she who has died (l. 28).
38–41	See note on title. Capricorn is the sign of the *Goat*, traditionally lecherous (compare Holy Sonnet 9, l. 3).
44	*vigil* a religious service, or private prayer, on the *eve* of a holy day.

THE PARADOX

Title	The *paradox* is that no lover can be said to be a lover.
1–6	No one can say he loves (because love kills instantly, ll. 5–6, 17), and no lover will admit that anyone else but himself can be in love.

7–8	Love kills more young people with too much heat than death kills old people with too much cold.
9	*who loved last did die* whoever has most recently fallen in love is thereby dead.
10	whoever says that we die twice is lying. Therefore whoever says that one struck dead by love can later die by natural causes is lying.
12	it deceives our eyes.
14	*the light's life* the sun.
19	*Here* in epitaphs upon tombs.
20	*lie* probably not a pun (any more than *lie*, l. 10, is in the other direction).

THE PRIMROSE

Title	In the edition of 1635 it is subtitled 'being at Montgomery Castle, upon the hill, on which it is situate'. Donne stayed at Montgomery Castle (the seat of the Herbert family) in the spring of 1613, and may have written the poem then.
4	*manna* honeydew, a sugary secretion from aphides or plants (see *OED*, honeydew, 1, first quotation (1577): 'our common people call it manna'). For the biblical manna, see Exodus 16: 14–35.
8	*to find a true-love* to find a four-petalled primrose (popularly called a true-love because of its resemblance to a double-bowed lovers' knot) or a six-petalled one; and thereby to foretell his future beloved.
18	*were monsters* would be freaks.
19–20	*I could . . . falsified* I would prefer her to practise women's artifice rather than be a freak of nature.
24	*mysterious* significant (for reasons explained in the following lines).
25–30	*Ten* being the highest number, and *five* (women's number) being half ten, each woman may take half the men as sexual partners; or (if this will not satisfy them), since *all numbers* are odd or even, and the first to combine both sorts is *five* (three plus two: one was not regarded as a *number*), then *five*

may be said to contain *all numbers*, and therefore each woman may take all the men. Both *serve their turn* and *take* are used in a sexual sense.

3–6   not because I shall recover breath and blood (which I have prodigally spent) from your sighs and tears by being then your object of love as you have been the object of mine, but because the sudden joy of having my love returned may kill me.

11–12   not because I shall take the law into my own hands and revenge myself by hating you.

13–14   A *conqueror* used to lead his captives in his triumphal procession.

19   Compare stanza 1; also with word-play on *die* (experience sexual orgasm).

20   Compare stanza 1.

21   or let your love and hate destroy each other, not me.

22   *stay* support; (in the context) champion (*OED*, stay, *sb.*², 1.b). Some texts have 'stage'.
       triumph subject of triumph (*OED*, triumph, *sb.*, 2.b, citing Milton, *Samson Agonistes*, l. 426: 'their captive and their triumph').

THE RELIC

1–4   In churchyards, bones were often removed to a charnel house so that the earth could be used for new burials.

3   *that womanhead* that behaviour of women.

6   Compare 'The funeral', l. 3.

10   *busy* i.e. because, at the resurrection, souls will rejoin – and reassemble – their bodies. Compare Elegy 9, ll. 41–2.

13   *mis-devotion* here, the worship of saints, credited with the power of performing *miracles* (l. 20).

17–18   *Mary Magdalen*, whom Jesus healed of demonic possession (Luke 8: 2) and to whom he appeared after rising from the

tomb (John 20), was traditionally identified with the
repentant woman who anointed Jesus's feet (Luke 7: 37)
and with the sister of Martha and Lazarus; as a saint she was
credited with performing miracles. *A something else* has been
variously interpreted as 'a Jesus Christ' and 'a lover of
Mary's in her wicked days'; it may mean no more than
'anything you like to imagine.'

21   *this paper*   this poem.

24   *what*   what in each other.

25–6   This was a spiritual love without physical consummation.
        (Angels were thought to have no sexual nature.)

27–8   The kisses we exchanged when meeting or parting were the
        only ones our love needed to feed upon.

29–30   The metaphorical *seals* prevent access to the sexual organs;
        they have been placed there by *late law* (the seventh of the
        Ten Commandments); this has injured *nature* (the natural
        inclination of the human animal). Donne is echoing, in
        Which nature . . . sets free, Ovid's *quod natura remittit* (*Meta-
        morphoses*, x. 330, where Myrrha is justifying incestuous
        passion).

32   I should go beyond anything that can be measured or
        expressed.

33   *was*   in emphatic antithesis to *did* (l. 31).

SONG ('Go and catch a falling star')

2   The root of the mandrake (*atropa mandragora*) bears some
        resemblance to the human body; see *The Progress of the Soul*,
        ll. 131–60.

4   The Devil was supposed to have a cloven hoof like a goat's.

8   *wind*   favourable wind (metaphor from sailing).

9   *an honest mind*   a truthful male lover (in the context of this
        poem).

10   *borne to*   inclined to.

18   *true and fair*   i.e. because beauty invites temptation to
        inconstancy.

7–8   to accustom myself to death by undergoing pretended ones (absences).

21–4   But if misfortune should come, we help to prolong its power over us.

25–32   Since the two lovers are one, the sorrow that injures her life injures his.

27   *unkindly kind*   the figure of speech called oxymoron; also word-play on *kind* ((1) natural; (2) affectionate) in both words.

34   foresee any misfortune for me.

THE SUN RISING

1   The sun is *busy* (officious) and *unruly* (ill behaved: with word-play, because the sun rises according to rule).

3   *curtains*   i.e. those of a four-poster bed.

6   *sour prentices*   The apprentices are bad-tempered at having to open their masters' shops.

7   James I had a passion for stag-hunting. The *court-huntsmen* are either professionals or courtiers (compare 'Love's exchange', l. 4).

8   summon countrymen to the tasks of harvesting.

9   *all alike*   always the same.

10   *rags*   fragments (*OED*, rag, sb.¹, 2.b, citing a sermon of Donne's (*Sermons*, extract 5 in this edition): 'First and last are but rags of time').

13   *with a wink*   by simply shutting my eyes.

17   The East Indies (Malay archipelago) produce spices and perfumes, the West (Central and South America) gold, silver and precious stones.

24   *mimic*   make-believe (as in a theatre; compare *play*, l. 23). *alchemy*   imposture (compare 'Love's alchemy', l. 6), hence figuratively meaning 'glittering dross' (*OED*, 4).

26   *contracted thus*   shrunk so (into the lovers' 'one world', 'The good-morrow', l. 14).

30   The bed is the world, the *centre* of the sun's universe; the
            walls of the room are the *sphere*, the limit of its orbit.

Title   Twickenham Park was acquired in 1607 by Donne's
          patroness Lucy, Countess of Bedford, as her principal
          residence, and the poem was probably written during the
          next few years, assuming (as is likely) that it is a compli-
          ment to her.

1   The sighing and weeping lover is like a plant *blasted*
          (blighted) with injurious winds and *surrounded* (overflowed,
          waterlogged: the original meaning) with heavy rains.

4   *balms* fragrant and medicinal oils (here figurative).

5   *self-traitor* traitor to myself.

6–7   The spider (in opposition to the bee, which makes honey)
          was said to turn everything to poison.

6   *transubstantiates* changes the substance of (with an allusion
          to the theological doctrine of transubstantiation, namely
          that the bread and wine of the eucharist become the body
          and blood of Christ).

7   *manna* honeydew (see 'The primrose', l. 4). The biblical
          manna (Exodus 16: 14–35) was a type (symbolic fore-
          shadowing) of the bread of the eucharist.

          gall a substance bitter and poisonous (*OED*, gall, *sb.*[1], 5).

9   *the serpent* alluding both to Genesis 3 and to the poisonous
          bite of the serpent.

12   *grave* word-play: (1) heavy; (2) serious.

15   *nor yet leave loving* Some texts have 'nor leave this garden'.

17   The mandrake was said not only to shriek when pulled out
          of the ground but to groan while rooted there (compare
          Jonson's *Masque of Queens* (1609), ll. 163–6). Some texts
          have 'grow' for *groan*.

19   *crystal vials* bottles of the purest quartz (here suggesting
          transparent honesty).

21   *try* test.

27   who is true (to her husband) in order to kill me (with unrequited love) – and therefore, like the rest of her sex, *perverse*.

THE UNDERTAKING

1   *braver* finer.
2   *Worthies* the nine most celebrated warriors from Hector
to Godfrey of Bouillon (the list varied), often shown in
pageants (as in *Love's Labour's Lost*, V. ii, where they boast
their deeds).
5–8   By *specular* (transparent) *stone* Donne wrongly understood a
hard translucent kind of marble which had become un-
obtainable. His source was a book about ancient lost arts
and new invented ones published in 1599. (In fact specular
stone is selenite, a translucent kind of gypsum, formerly
used for glazing.) Compare 'To the Countess of Bedford',
l. 29.
9–12   Just as there is no more specular stone, there is no woman
left who can be loved in the idealistic manner to be described, ll. 13–20.
14   *all outward* everything that is on the outside.
16   *her* those of *loveliness within*.
19   *say so* i.e. to the beloved.
20   Compare 'The relic', ll. 25–6.
22   *profane* incapable of spiritual understanding.

A VALEDICTION: FORBIDDING MOURNING

7–8   It would be a desecration of our love if we let those outside
its mysterious joys know of it.
9–12   Earthquakes do damage and are considered ominous; but
the oscillations of the spheres, though far greater than earth
tremors, are harmless. See 'Love's alchemy', l. 22.
13   *sublunary* beneath the moon; that is, below the lowest of
the spheres, and therefore (unlike what was higher) subject
to corruption and change.

14	*Whose soul is sense* whose being is merely sensual. A paradox, because *soul* is usually contrasted with *sense*.
15, 16	The first *it* is *absence*; the second *it* is the *love* of l. 13.
17–20	But we, being pledged to each other's mind by a love so pure that we cannot define it, feel less grief at physical parting.
22	*yet* nevertheless (reinforces *though*).
24	like gold beaten to the finest gold leaf (with connotations of value, purity and refinement).
25–36	The famous *compasses* (dividers) image is twofold: (1) when the points are at a distance the legs form a wide angle; (2) when a circle is made, the point at the centre ensures that the other describes a perfect circumference.

A VALEDICTION: OF WEEPING

2	*whilst I stay here* before I embark (see ll. 9, 21–5).
6	*Pregnant* compare *bore*, l. 8; with a suggestion of weight, and so of value.
7	*emblems* symbols (as explained in ll. 8–9).
10–13	By pasting a map on to a blank globe (which, being round, looks like a nought) a workman converts it into the whole world.
15	which bears your image.
16	It is more than a representation of the world (a *globe*), it is the *world* itself.
17–18	His tear-world (ll. 14–16) is overflowed by her tears, as was the earth by the 'flood of waters' when 'the windows of heaven were opened' (Genesis 6: 17; 7: 11).
18	*dissolvèd* melted into tears (related to *thee, my heaven*).
19	more beautiful and more powerful than the moon.
20	*in thy sphere* that is, *in thine arms* (l. 21).
26–7	Compare 'Song' ('Sweetest love, I do not go'), ll. 25–32.

THE WILL

3	*Argus* the hundred-eyed giant of Greek mythology.

4	Love (Cupid) is conventionally portrayed as blind.

4   Love (Cupid) is conventionally portrayed as blind.

5   *Fame* rumour, conventionally portrayed in a costume covered with tongues (as in the Induction to *2 Henry IV*).

8   *twenty more* twenty other lovers.

10   *planets* They change their position relative to the fixed stars (Greek *planetes*, a wanderer).

13   *Jesuits* They became notorious for equivocation through the trial (1606) of one of them, Father Garnett, for complicity in the Gunpowder Plot. Shakespeare is thought to refer to Garnett's equivocation in *Macbeth*, II. iii. 9–12.

14   Travellers were notorious bores.

15   The Capuchins were friars vowed to absolute poverty.

18   *have an incapacity* are unable by law to inherit.

19–21   Anglicans regarded *faith* and *good works* as both necessary to salvation, and thought that Roman Catholics over-emphasized the latter and that extreme Protestants over-emphasized the former.

20–1   *the schismatics / Of Amsterdam* an independent sect of extreme Protestants. Two of them appear in Jonson's *The Alchemist*.

21–2   *civility / And courtship* politeness and courtly manner. Scholars were thought to be deficient in both.

26   *disparity* a thing unequal to her.

30   *schoolmen* medieval scholastic philosophers, whose confident pronouncements arouse *doubtfulness* (scepticism).

37   See *Devotions*, 17.

39   *Bedlam* Bethlehem Hospital, the London asylum for lunatics.

40   *brazen medals* Roman bronze coins.

45   *disproportion* mismatch.

48, 50   *your* not particular (Love is addressed as 'thou', and the beloved called 'her') but idiomatic: 'those well-known'.

54   *this one way* See ll. 46–7.

WOMAN'S CONSTANCY

5   Compare Montaigne's *Essays* (Florio's translation, 1603),

II, 12: 'Epicarmus avoucheth, that who erewhile borrowed any money, doth not now owe it; and that he who yester-night was bidden to dinner this day, cometh today un-bidden; since they are no more themselves, but are become others.'

13   *true*   true to your purpose.
14   *lunatic*   word-play: (1) madwoman; (2) woman changeable as the moon.
      'scapes   evasions.
17   *think so too*   also hold the views that I now attribute to you.

Elegies

ELEGY 1 JEALOUSY

4   *sere-bark*   bark-like coating of dry scabs; compare the effects of poison in *Hamlet*, I. v. 71–3.
6   *crotcheting*   ornamenting a tune by breaking up each sus-tained note into a number of short ones.
8   *one hell* is his body, *a new* is hell itself.
31   *his household policies*   his stratagems (*policies*), applied not to high statesmanship but to a trivial domestic (*household*) end.
33–4 The district of Southwark, on the south (*right*) bank of the Thames, was nominally under the Lord Mayor's authority but in practice defied it. The Protestant states of Germany defied the Pope.

ELEGY 2 THE ANAGRAM

4, 5 *they*   her eyes. They are called *ivory* because they are pale, whereas a black (*jet*) eye was admired, especially with golden (*yellow*, l. 7) hair; compare Sidney, *Astrophil and Stella*, sonnet 9, and *Arcadia* (1590), Book 1, chapter 13.
5   *light*   wanton, unchaste.
6   *rough*   hairy.
8   *thine*   your virginity (*maidenhead*), by marrying her (l. 1).

The innuendo is that she has lost her own virginity (being *light*, l. 5).

19   *gamut*   the notes of the musical scale.

22   Things good in themselves cannot fail to be good when combined.

24   *singular*   unique.

28   *changed ... deformities*   beyond the power of ugliness to change.

30   *those ... worse*   the rebel angels who became Satan and the devils.

35   *husbands*   word-play: (1) husbandmen, farmers; (2) married men.

36   The best farmland is found where the roads are muddiest.

37   *sovereign plaster*   supreme remedy (as applied on a plaster).

40   *marmoset*   monkey (traditionally lecherous: compare *Othello*, III. iii. 407).

41   When the cities of the Netherlands flood the surrounding districts.

42   *foulness*   stagnant water. Here and in l. 36 there is word-play on *foul* (ugly).

43   *and so, for thee*   The sentence's main clause is completed in l. 55.

46   To wash a Negro white is a proverbial impossibility; the whole sea cannot do it.

47   *she ... laid*   she had dwelt in the brothel district of the city.

50   *tympany*   illness causing swelling of the belly.

53   *dildoes ... glass*   all instruments of female masturbation. A *dildo* is an artificial penis; a *bedstaff* a staff used for smoothing the sheets and for keeping them in place; and a *velvet glass* a hand-mirror covered in velvet.

54   Joseph refused to commit adultery with Potiphar's wife (Genesis 39).

56   *wear*   word-play: (1) dress in; (2) damage by friction. Compare Satire 1, l. 54.

ELEGY 3   CHANGE

1–2   *hand* and *seal* are legal, *faith* and *good works* religious imagery.

3	*fall back* word-play: (1) commit *apostasy*; (2) lie down. Hence the paradox of *confirm* (l. 4).
9	*these things* birds.
14	*Idly* to no purpose.
15	*clogs* heavy objects to which animals or prisoners were tethered.
17–20	The analogies argue that each woman needs more than one man.
17	*a plough-land* a single piece of land.
23	*if so thou do* if you change lovers.
24	*like* word-play: (1) alike; (2) love (*like and love* is a common idiom).
26	*Allow her change* assent to her changeable behaviour.
27–8	and, by such changing of mine, to compel rather than persuade myself to love neither one woman nor all women (as women by nature are allowed to love more than one man, though not all men, as the two following analogies argue).
30	*roguery* Persons of no fixed abode were counted as rogues.
32	*worse putrefied* i.e. because, being salt, they become undrinkable.

ELEGY 4   THE PERFUME

2	*escapes* misdeeds.
7	*glazèd* word-play: (1) watery (he being old); (2) spectacled.
8	The fabulous lizard-like basilisk (with which the fabulous serpent-like *cockatrice* was usually confused) could kill by its glare. Here the father (1) outglares it, (2) turns its own glare upon itself by his spectacles.
10–11	*Thy beauty's ... his goods* The father supposes that what makes his daughter attractive to her lover is her expected inheritance.
21	mentions exotic foods to test whether you have a pregnant woman's longing for them. The metre is defective, but the 'And' of some texts looks like patching; either 'dost long' or 'if that' (not in any text) may be the lost original.

34   *Rhodian Colossus*   the Colossus of Rhodes, a bronze statue of Apollo which stood astride the harbour entrance.

49   *The precious unicorns*   Whether Donne means unicorns proper or rhinoceroses is debatable: both were called 'unicorns' and their horns thought precious as medicine.

52   *oppressed*   word-play: (1) pressed down in walking; (2) subjected to the torture of pressing with weights (to compel prisoners to plead guilty or not guilty).

57–8   *confound ... sound*   hinder the sense of smell from distinguishing a sick person from a healthy one.

59   *silly amorous*   simple lover.

64   (1) at court there are more seemingly real things than actually real ones; and/or (2) at court they value appearances above realities.

67   The separate ingredients of all perfumes are loathsome.

70   *rare*   thin (and therefore fugitive).

ELEGY 5   HIS PICTURE

1   *picture*   miniature-portrait. Compare Marlowe, *Edward II*, I. iv. 127: 'Here, take my picture, and let me wear thine.'

3–4   The speaker's picture and his ghost will both be *shadows* (whereas now his picture is the shadow of his body's substance) if he literally dies (in warfare), or when he figuratively dies (through absence).

6   *oars*   i.e. having suffered shipwreck, or captivity in the Spanish galleys. The situation in this poem is appropriate to both Donne's expeditions, to Cadiz (1596) and to the Azores (1597).

13   *This*   this picture.

19   *who*   the woman's love (personified).

ELEGY 7

1   *Nature's lay idiot*   ignorant, uninstructed, in a state of nature, as you were.

7   *water*   word-play: (1) (literally) tears; (2) (figuratively)

urine. Physicians diagnosed a patient's *malady* by inspecting the urine.

15   *husband*   husband-to-be.

16   *love-tricks*   love-sports (as contrasted with sexual ones; compare 'Epithalamion made at Lincoln's Inn', l. 53).

19   in incoherent (*broken, torn*) trite sayings (*proverbs, sentences*).

21–2   The marriage imagery is of a landowner who has enclosed (*severed, inlaid*) part of the *common* land.

24   *Refined*   transmuted (imagery from alchemy).

25   I created your graces and good works (religious terms, here applied to sexual charms and skills; compare Elegy 3, l. 1). Some texts have 'words' for *works*.

26   biblical imagery with a sexual application: 'the tree of life also in the midst of the garden, and the tree of knowledge of good and evil' (Genesis 2: 9). Here *knowledge* is carnal knowledge, and *life's tree* the penis.

27–8   *Must I . . . glass?*   Must I make goblets for others from gold or silver plate decorated with enamel, and drink out of ordinary glasses myself?

29   *Chafe . . . seals?*   heat and soften wax for others to set their seals on?

30   *ready*   fit for riding.

ELEGY 8   THE COMPARISON

1   like the perfumed oil distilled from roses.

2   Perfume is obtained from the secretions of the musk-deer and of the civet-cat. The confusion of the two is not peculiar to Donne (see *OED*, musk-cat).

3   Morning dew was thought good for the complexion.

9–12   The siege of Sancerre (1573) caused the inhabitants to extract food from leather articles; 'necessity has no law' is a proverb.

13   and like cheap imitation jewels set in gilded tin.

15   *her head*   my mistress's head. So at ll. 24, 28, 38.

16   The *ball* is the golden apple of discord ('for the fairest') thrown among the guests at the wedding of Peleus and Thetis on Mount Ida (*Ide*); it was *fatal* because it led to the Judgement of Paris and hence to the Trojan War.

17–18   See Genesis 2–3.

19   *Thy head* your mistress's head. So at ll. 25, 32, 34, 39.

21   *the first Chaos* See Genesis 1: 1–2, and compare 'the first nothing', 'A nocturnal upon St Lucy's Day', l. 29.

21–2   *or ... embrace* or the flat-looking face of the moon in eclipse.

23   In the myth of Cupid and Psyche, Psyche was given the task of fetching from Hades the ivory box in which Proserpine kept her ointment of beauty.

24   In Homer's *Iliad*, **XXIV**, 526–7, the ruler of the gods keeps the good and bad fortunes of men in two urns.

30   *for madness* Whipping was part of the medical treatment of lunacy.

31   *quarters* the quartered bodies of traitors, impaled on the roofs of gatehouses at London Bridge and Temple Bar.

35–8   The imagery is of an alchemist (*chemic*) applying an even heat (*equal fire*) to base metal (*th' earth's worthless dirt*) in a spherical retort (*the limbeck's warm womb*) to make gold. Sexual imagery of this kind was frequent in alchemy.

41   *Etna* an active volcano in Sicily.

54   *comparisons are odious* proverbial; compare *Much Ado About Nothing*, III. v. 16.

ELEGY 9   THE AUTUMNAL

7   *the Golden Age* the age of innocence.

13   *graves* used in two related senses: (1) trenches; (2) burial graves.

16   *anachorit* anchorite, a hermit self-confined to a particular place (often a cave).

18   A *grave* is below ground, a *tomb* a raised monument.

19–20   Like a king making a *progress* (ceremonial journey among his subjects), Love may lodge (*sojourn*) in many places, but has his proper mansion (*standing house*) here.

21 *still*   tranquil.

24 *Revels* and *council* continue the royal imagery.

25 *Timber*   burns long, brushwood (*underwood*) briefly.

26 *There*   in youth.

27 *Which*   relates to *wine*.

29–32 The Persian king *Xerxes* is said by Herodotus to have greatly admired a plane (*platane*) tree which he found in *Lydia*; Virgil (*Georgics*, II, 69–70) and others state, wrongly, that the plane tree is barren.

35 *If*   if we love.

36 i.e. because it will then be about to vanish.

37 *winter-faces*   contrasted with *autumnal* ones (l. 2), and modifying the claim in ll. 35–6.

38 *but a soul's sack*   merely a loose sack around the soul.

39 *here*   outside.

41–2 See 'The relic', l. 10.

43 *death's-heads*   skulls, considered as reminders of mortality.

44 *antics*   grotesques.

47 *lation*   the movement of a heavenly body from one place to another (astrological).

ELEGY 16   ON HIS MISTRESS

1 *strange and fatal interview*   remarkable and destined meeting.

3 *remorse*   pity.

8 *want and divorcement*   lack of each other by separation.

11 *overswear them*   swear them over again.

19 *move*   remove.

21–3 Donne appears to have invented this version of the myth in order to show that even as a friend Boreas (god of the north wind) is dangerous. The standard version relates that Boreas carried off Orithea, against her father's wishes, to a mountain where she lived with him and bore his children.

24–5	*proved / Dangers unurged* undergone dangers without being compelled to do so.
27	*Dissemble nothing* assume no disguise.
28–9	*be ... only* do not be disguised only in your own eyes.
31	*Richly ... called apes* apes are apes though clad in scarlet (proverbial).
31–2	*as soon ... bright* equally when eclipsed and when shining.
33	As the chameleon can actually change its colour, the Frenchman can change his mind.
34	*Spitals* hospitals, especially for venereal diseases.
35	*fuellers* stokers.
37	*know* used in two different senses: (1) recognize (as a woman); (2) have sexual intercourse with.
38	*indifferent* not caring whether the object of his lust is female or male.
41	*Lot's fair guests* the two angels whom the men of Sodom wished to abuse sexually (see Genesis 19).
42	*spongy hydroptic* soaked and swollen (dropsical) with drinking.
44	England is the only worthy antechamber.
46	*King* God.

ELEGY 18 LOVE'S PROGRESS

4	*bear-whelp* bear-cub, traditionally born a mere *lump* (l. 6) and licked into shape (ll. 4–5) by the she-bear.
8	*though ... own* though a man's face is better than a calf's.
12–14	the ductility (capacity of being drawn out into threads), the applicability (as gold leaf), the contribution to health (in medicines), the integrity (being unaffected by rust, tarnishing, or exposure to fire).
16	*our ... use* our second nature, custom. Compare 'Love's deity', l. 6.
18	*but one* only one of *these* (l. 17) qualities of *hers* (l. 26).
23	*barren angels* Compare 'The relic', ll. 25–6.
28	*not there* i.e. because no planet is named after him.

36   *centric part*   deliberately ambiguous: (1) the earth, as centre of the universe; (2) woman (as distinct from her attributes); (3) woman's centric part (in a sexual sense). By l. 38 (*this*), the meaning has narrowed to the third.

47   *the first meridian*   the first circle of longitude (0°), now running through the Canary Isles.

48   *two suns*   her eyes.

51   *Islands Fortunate*   Canary Isles.

52   *Canaries* (1) the Canary Isles; (2) their light sweet wine (the plural was commonly used).
        Ambrosial (1) the Ambrosial Isles (Donne's complimentary invention); (2) fragrant with ambrosia (the drink – originally the food – of the gods).

55–6   *there sirens' songs . . . ear*   Pursuing his 'islands' metaphor, Donne refers to the island of the alluring sirens (Homer, *Odyssey*, XII) and to Delos in the Aegean, known in his time as Delphos and (being sacred to Apollo) credited with a wise oracle (like Delphi on the mainland); compare *The Winter's Tale*, III. i.

57   *pearls*   her teeth.

58   *remora*   the sucking-fish, supposed to stop ships by *cleaving* (clinging) to them.
        cleaving   word-play: (1) clinging; (2) dividing (the man's lips).

62   *two lovers*   Hero and Leander (see Marlowe's poem of that name), who lived at Sestos and Abydos.
        two Loves   two Cupids.

65   *India*   the merchant venturer's destination.

67   though from there onwards it is plain sailing.

68   *embayed*   in harbour.

74   *symmetry*   correspondence.

78   *his*   his cloven hoof.

79   *emblem*   symbol (as in such *figurative* expressions as 'to stand *firm*').

81–4   Politeness (*civility*) has *refined* the kiss to progressive degrees of subservience.

85   *nearer*   word-play: (1) more effective; (2) literally nearer.

86	*Rise from the foot* get power by enlisting the Pope's power-ful support.
89	*ethereal* unimpeded except by the most rarefied air.
92	*Two purses* the mouth and the genital opening.
	aversely in opposite directions.
96	*by clyster* with an anal injection.

ELEGY 19   TO HIS MISTRESS GOING TO BED

2	*I in labour lie* I am in an agony of expectation.
4	*standing* word-play: (1) standing by for action (of a soldier); (2) standing erect (of a penis; compare l. 12).
5	*heaven's zone* the furthest circle of the universe around the earth (l. 6), set with the fixed stars.
7	*spangled breastplate* stomacher (a covering for the chest, worn under the lacing of the bodice of the gown) with spangles stitched upon it.
9	*that harmonious chime* i.e. produced by the spangles as the 'breastplate' is removed. Some critics interpret as a chiming watch worn by her.
11	*busk* inner bodice, closely fitting, stiffened and laced.
15	*wiry coronet* headband made of gold or silver wire.
16	*hairy diadem* crown of (golden) hair.
17	*safely* i.e. because the bed is *Love's hallowed temple* (l. 18); compare Exodus 3: 5: 'put off thy shoes from off thy feet, for the place whereon thou standest is holy ground.'
19	*white robes* She has now removed all her clothing but her smock (*this white linen*, l. 45).
21	*Mahomet's paradise* the Mohammedan heaven of sensual delights (pronounced 'Mawmet's').
22	*Ill spirits walk in white* Ghosts (which frighten the beholder, l. 24) conventionally appear in white sheets. There may also be an allusion to Satan's disguise as 'an angel of light' (2 Corinthians 11: 14).
23	*these angels* such angels as you.
24	*our flesh* the penis.

27   Compare the title of Thomas Hariot's *A Brief and True Report of the New Found Land of Virginia* (1588).

28   *manned* word-play: (1) garrisoned (a paradox); (2) sexually supplied.

30   *this discovering thee* word-play: (1) my finding you (as an explorer); (2) your uncovering yourself.

31   *bonds* word-play: (1) fetters (her arms); (2) legal obligations (compare *hand* and *seal*, l. 32, which has a sexual innuendo).

36   *Atlanta's balls* the three golden apples, by successively dropping which Atalanta's suitor Hippomenes (who had to outrun her in order to win her) diverted her attention from the race.

40   *laymen* those unable to understand *mystic books* (l. 41).

42   *imputed grace* the undeserved righteousness (*grace*) which God, in Calvinist theology, attributes (*imputes*) to those he has chosen for salvation. In ll. 41–3 women are both deity and scripture.

43   *know* word-play: (1) have spiritual knowledge; (2) have sexual knowledge.

46   A white sheet was traditionally worn by a person condemned by the church to do penance for sins (usually sexual ones), but this sexual act is innocent and deserves no penance. Some texts have 'Here is no penance, much less innocence', others (the majority) 'There is no penance, much less innocence'.

48   *than a man* word-play: (1) than a man has; (2) than a man is.

ELEGY 20   LOVE'S WAR

1   *war other men* let other men wage war.

3   *scrupulous* matters of principle.

4   *free city* city-state, independent of national rule, such as Geneva and Fribourg.

5–6   *In Flanders ... rebel?* In the Netherlands, who can tell

251

whether Philip II of Spain (*the master*) oppresses the inhabitants (*the men*) or whether they unlawfully rebel?

7   *Only we know*   We know only.

7–8   *that which ... the fray* The common proverb of the unlearned (*idiots*) applies to the English troops which were from time to time involved in the wars there.

9–10   French policy, changeable as the moon, has been consistent in distrusting England, and now (1593) Henry of Navarre, the new king, has changed from a Protestant to a Roman Catholic.

11–12   The gold coins (*angels*) sent to Henry of Navarre will no more return to England than the fallen angels will to heaven.

13–14   Irish rebellion against English rule broke out again in 1594.

16   This uses medical metaphors for political action: *purged* (1) literally, (2) cleared of sedition; *her head-vein let blood* (1) by phlebotomy, (2) by cutting off the heads of the leading rebels.

17–18   King *Midas* in Greek mythology received the gift of turning everything he touched (including his intended food) to gold. The allusion is to the hardships of the raids on Spanish treasure-ships.

24   *swaggering* quarrelling.

26   *carts* Condemned persons were transported in carts from Newgate prison to the gallows at Tyburn.

36   *under* commanded by superior officers.

38   *bullets* by innuendo, testicles. Compare 'I will discharge upon her, Sir John, with two bullets' (Pistol in *2 Henry IV*, II. iv. 108).

39   *lies are wrongs* i.e. because 'for one to say a soldier lies is stabbing' (*Othello*, III. iv.5).
       uprightly lie word-play: (1) straightforwardly (*OED* 1.b) give the lie; (2) honestly (*OED*, 1) tell a lie (paradoxical); (3) lie down on your back (*OED*, upright, *adj.*, 2).

44   This line is metrically defective in all but two versions: one ('To wars, but stay, swords, weapons, arms and shot') looks like weak patching-up; the other ('To wars, but stay

at home, swords, guns and shot / To make for others')
probably preserves the form of this line but modifies the
following one because Donne had accidentally included 'at
home' twice in the sentence.

Epithalamions, or Marriage Songs

EPITHALAMION MADE AT LINCOLN'S INN

Title   Donne was enrolled as a student at Lincoln's Inn between
1592 and 1594, and was probably still a member of it in
1595 when Spenser's 'Epithalamion' was published.
Donne's poem was probably inspired by Spenser's. It is
unlikely that it was written for any special occasion, either
for a real wedding or for a mock one.

7   *balm-breathing* fragrantly scented.

12   A maid achieves full womanhood by marriage (see
ll. 79–83). For the use of a refrain, compare Spenser,
'Epithalamion'.

16   *angels* gold coins (stamped with the figure of an angel on
the reverse).

22   *Flora* the Roman goddess of flowers.
Ind India.

25   *frolic patricians* high-spirited young men of position.

26   *these senators* prosperous city aldermen; *these* indicates a
whole class (compare *Hamlet*, II. ii. 218: 'These tedious old
fools!').
wealth's deep oceans deep oceans of wealth (applied to
senators). It is also possible to read the line (with extended
word-play) as 'Suns of these senators' wealth's deep oceans'
('The suns which drink up the deep oceans of these
senators' wealth').

27   *painted* ostentatiously dressed.

29   *those fellowships* the Inns of Court, such as Lincoln's Inn:
colleges training young men in the law.
he the bridegroom.

30   *hermaphrodits*   hermaphrodites, combing both sexes; here (figuratively) combining both qualities, *study and play*.

31   *the temple*   perhaps particular (the Temple Church in Fleet Street), perhaps general (as in Spenser's 'Epithalamion').

37   *two-leaved gates*   double door.

43   *elder claims*   earlier loves (compare 'forsaking all other' in the marriage service).

55   The wedding is taking place in summer (as in Spenser's 'Epithalamion').

61   *amorous*   i.e. because the *evening star* is Venus.

62   *our amorous star*   the bride.

85–6   like a pious man ready to give up his life in this world for a better life in heaven.

90   *embowel*   disembowel. The simile, which shocks many readers, stresses the bride's passiveness (though '*wished* approach' (l. 88) shows that she is not an unwilling victim). Milgate (*Epithalamions*, p. 113) says that the bridegroom 'embowels' her in the sense (*OED*, 3) of putting himself within her, but *OED* gives no such example: the phrase would have to be 'embowels himself in her'.

91   *watch*   stay awake.

93   *This sun*   the bride.

95–6   This is a paradox (*wonders are wrought*), because she who was previously faultless has become perfect.

AN EPITHALAMION, OR MARRIAGE SONG,
ON THE LADY ELIZABETH AND COUNT PALATINE
BEING MARRIED ON ST VALENTINE'S DAY

Title   James I's eldest daughter Elizabeth (1596–1662) married Frederick V, the Elector Palatine (1596–1632), on 14 February 1613. The Palatinate is in south-west Germany between the Rhine and Alsace-Lorraine. Frederick's career was unfortunate. A strong Protestant, he accepted the crown of Bohemia in 1619, an act which started the Thirty Years War, in which he not only lost Bohemia but was driven from his own Palatinate, which he never regained.

1   *Bishop Valentine*   a bishop martyred in the reign of the emperor Claudius. Birds were traditionally said to choose their mates on his day.

7   The sparrow was proverbially lecherous, and lechery was thought to shorten life.

8   the robin redbreast. (For *stomacher*, see Elegy 19, l. 7 note.)

9   *speed*   prosper, find a mate in spite of blackness (which was thought to be ugly, not only in Negroes but in brunettes).

10   *halcyon*   kingfisher.

18   *two phoenixes*   See 'The canonization', ll. 23–6 and notes.

19   *taper*   bedroom candle (compare l. 22, *one bed*).

20   *the Ark*   See Genesis 6: 19–20; 7: 8–9.

27, 97 *courage*   sexual desire and vigour.

37–8 Comets and meteors were called *blazing* stars and thought to *signify* the death of princes. The princess Elizabeth, herself a star, *falls* (lies down in the marriage bed) but does not *die* (either literally or like a spent meteor).

40   *Ends*   consequences. Note the ingenious echo-effect of *portends / Ends*, and the final placing of the second *ends* in the couplet and the sentence.

42   It was usual to *date records* from the beginning of a reign.

47–50 Their greatness and their unity make them for both reasons inseparable.

51–6 They must be *made one* by joining hearts (already, by St Valentine's agency), hands (in church, by the bishop's) and bodies (in bed, by their own).

81   *sphere after sphere*   imagery from the concentric spheres of the Ptolemaic universe.

85   Male and female, by uniting, become each other.

89–91 In paying their sexual debt to each other, both are so *just* that neither *would* (wishes to) *forbear*, and so *rich* that neither *needs* to *stay* (pause).

95–6 *let fall … liberal*   lose no opportunity to be generous.

97–8 *Turtles* (turtle doves) exemplify *truth*, as *sparrows* do *courage* (see l. 27).

99–102 Compare 'The canonization', l. 24. (Since the phoenix does not really exist in *nature* but is fabulous, the compliment is witty as well as graceful.)

104   *satyrs*   mountain spirits with feet and horns like those of the goats they kept. They are here primitive sun-worshippers.

105–6   *your*   The couple are one, so the sunrise will be made by either's opening eyes (compare ll. 108–10).

110   *a curtain*   i.e. of the four-poster bed. This stanza does not mean that the bedroom will be literally full of people all night. The couple will summon their attendants next morning, and afterwards receive visitors.

Satires

SATIRE 1

This satire was probably written in 1593, the second year of Donne's residence in Lincoln's Inn (see l. 2): the allusions in ll. 79–82 are consistent with this date, which is attached to the poem in one of the manuscripts.

1   *fondling motley humorist*   fool (noun used adjectivally) changeable man of fads and fancies.

2   *this standing wooden chest*   literally, this up-ended wooden box; figuratively, this wood-panelled study. At Lincoln's Inn Donne shared a chamber which was divided into two bedrooms and two studies.

6   Either Aristotle specifically or any natural philosopher (scientist acquainted with nature's secrets).

8   *mystic body*   body politic.

9   *gathering*   accumulating factual detail.

10   *Giddy fantastic*   wild imaginative. Even the poets are *constant* (l. 11) in contrast to his visitor (l. 12).

15   *in the middle street*   in the midst of the street.

18   shining in gold or silver lace bought with the pay of forty dead men whose names he fraudulently keeps on the payroll.

22	*blue coats* liveried servants.
25–6	a humorous application of the words of the marriage service.
27–8	a paradoxical allusion to the fact that Puritans professed (spiritual) refinement and abhorred (church) ceremony.
32	*raise thy formal hat* raise your hat according to due form.
45–6	See Genesis 2: 25, 3: 21.
55	*musk-colour* a dark shade of brown. Black feathers were much affected by gallants about 1593.
58	(figurative) the wealthiest heiress in London. An *infanta* is a Spanish princess, the West *India* Spain's source of treasure.
59	*gulling weather-spy* cheating weather-prophet, pretending to foretell by examining a diagram (*scheme*) of the *heaven*.
62	*subtle-witted* fine-witted (with word-play: (1) ingenious; (2) thin).
68	To 'take the *wall*' (and avoid the dirty middle of the street) implied one's social superiority; ll. 69–70 explain *improvidently*.
74	*smacks* smacks his lips impatiently.
77	Viols were held upright on the lap or between the knees.
79–82	The allusion is to performing animals trained to acknowledge only certain commands (for details, see Milgate, *Satires*, pp. 124–5).
88	*drinking* smoking (then the usual word).
95–8	The last-encounted man is reputed to have the best judgement (*conceit*) of any courtier in his inventiveness (*device*) as to lace, decorative holes (*pink*), strips (*panes*), ruff-crimpings (*print*), slashes (*cut*) and pleats, by way of beautifying (*handsoming*) an outfit (*suit*).
99	*Our ... him* Our actors need him to brighten up their wardrobe.
100	Donne ironically pretends to think that his companion is doubled up with pain.
102	*Which understand none* The companion's naïve parenthesis unconsciously proclaims his inability to judge. Some critics take the parenthesis to be the satirical narrator's.
104	*pox* syphilis, known as the French or the Italian disease.
105	more men distinguished for position, talents and merits.

| 109 | *command* | have her to himself. |
| 112 | *constantly* | Compare l. 11. |

SATIRE 3

This satire (subtitled 'Of Religion' and 'Upon Religion' in two manuscripts) was probably written in 1594 or 1595, when Donne was himself considering the rival claims of Roman Catholicism and Anglicanism, and before his participation in the Cadiz and Islands expeditions.

1–3   My natural (*kind*) pity chokes my scornful laughter (produced in the *spleen*); my vaunting (*brave*) scorn forbids me to weep. If I am to be wise, I must neither deride sins nor lament them.

4   *railing*   using vigorous reproaches.
     worn   ingrained.

7   *the first . . . age*   the pre-Christian (and therefore *blinded*, pagan) era.

9, 10   *them*   the virtuous pagans, *blind philosophers* (l. 12).

10   *means*   the Christian religion.

11   *end*   salvation.

12–13   *whose merit . . . faith*   whose strictly moral living may be reckoned by God to be an allowable substitute for the faith which was not available to them.

17   *mutinous Dutch*   Compare Elegy 20, 'Love's war', ll. 5–6. English soldiers had aided the Dutch since 1586.

20   *dungeons of the earth*   mines or caves.

22   *frozen north discoveries*   the search for a north-west and a north-east sea-route to the Pacific.

23   *salamanders*   newt-like amphibians, once supposed able to live in fire or to put out fire.

23–4   *divine / Children*   Shadrach, Meshach and Abednego, cast into a 'burning fiery furnace' by Nebuchadnezzar (see Daniel 3).

24   *fires of Spain*   the fires in which the Spanish Inquisition burned heretics.
     the line   the equator.

25	*limbecks* alembics. In equatorial countries our bodies are distilled through sweating.
27–8	*draw ... words* draw his sword for a duel, or swallow your deadly insult (of cowardice).
28	*of straw* worthless.
29	*desperate* in a state of despair; ready for damnation.
30, 33	*foes* the world, the flesh and the Devil.
30	*his* God's.
33–5	*the foul ... quit* The foul Devil, whom you strive to please, would willingly – for hate, not love, of you – grant you his whole kingdom (hell) to repay you (for serving him).
36–8	*The world's ... wane* all earthly things are perishable, and the earth itself is nearing its end (a leading theme of *The First Anniversary*).
40	*itself's death* self-destroying (through self-indulgence).
43	*Mirreus* like the other proper names (ll. 49, 55, 62, 65), invented to typify a group, here the Roman Catholic: perhaps 'myrrheus' (perfumed with myrrh, often spelled 'mirre').
44, 47	*here* in England.
47	*her rags* empty ceremonies.
47–8	*obey / The statecloth* reverence the canopy over the throne.
49	*Crants* the Calvinist. Donne has invented a name with Dutch, German or Swiss associations (*Kranz* (German), a garland).
53	*humours* fancies.
55	*Graius* the Anglican. *Graius* (Latin), a Greek, has no evident point.
59	*godfathers* word-play: (1) baptismal sponsors; (2) those who assume spiritual authority.
60	*tender* word-play: (1) (verb) offer; (2) (adjective) immature.
62	*values* fines imposed upon wards for refusing marriages arranged by their guardians; figuratively alluding to the fine for not attending one's parish church.
	Phrygius the free-thinker, *careless* because indifferent to religion. *Phryges* (Greek), freemen, was the original name

for the inhabitants of what became known as Phrygia in Asia Minor.

65   *Gracchus* the relativist. Gracchus was the name of a Roman family devoted to democracy, hence possibly relevant to equality.

69   *too much light* the idea (which causes his spiritual blindness) that all religions equally have the light of truth.

70   *Of force* of necessity.
       forced when put under pressure (compare ll. 89–110).

71–3 The idea is to return to primitive Christianity.

75   *none . . . worst . . . best* The implied word is 'religion'.

76   to be a Roman Catholic, or an anti-Catholic, or a Protestant.

77   *in strange way* on an unfamiliar road.

84   *that night* 'The night cometh, when no man can work' (John 9: 4).

85   *To will implies delay* When one is determining to do a thing, one is not doing it.

86–7 *Hard deeds . . . reach* As the body's labours achieve difficult deeds, those of the mind achieve difficult knowledge.

90   *here* on earth.

91   *blank-charters* properly, blank cheques which Richard II forced his wealthy subjects to give him; here, figuratively, blank death-warrants (see l. 92).

92   *vicars* deputies. Kings who persecute believers are not acting *as* Fate (here meaning God's will) but merely *for* it (that is, they can kill the body, but they send the soul to heaven, not to hell as they would like to do).

96–7 *Philip* II of Spain, Pope *Gregory* (VII, XIII or XIV), Henry (*Harry*) VIII, *Martin* Luther.

98   *mere contraries* absolute opposites.

103–10 The 'calm' water corresponds to legitimate authority, the 'rough' to the tyrannous abuse of power.

The Progress of the Soul

Subheading *Infinitati sacrum* sacred to infinity: (1) because the story, and therefore the poem, can never be finished, the soul being *deathless* (l. 1); (2) because the poem will be immortal (ll. 9–10).

Metempsychosis   transmigration of the soul.

Poema satyricon   a satiric poem.

2	*my picture* not literally, but by an account of my purpose.
3	*through-light* word-play: (1) transparent; (2) thoroughly frivolous (compare *through-vain*, l. 473).
5	*tax* criticize.
8	sine talione without retaliation.
10	*Trent Council* the Council of Trent (1542), a Counter-Reformation assembly.
26	*works this* causes this discrepancy between the soul's powers in its different incarnations (as is immediately illustrated).
30–1	*for poison* Spiders were thought to make poison, and to be poisonous when swallowed.
34	*her first making* her creation.
35	*is he* unidentified, as the story is unfinished; perhaps therefore a joke (see note on subheading). See also ll. 61–70.

THE PROGRESS OF THE SOUL: FIRST SONG

2	*Fate* chance.
3–4	*all times ... since* The *law* is the Ten Commandments, so the three ages are before Moses, through the rest of Old Testament history, and since the birth of Christ.
7–8	The periods of world history were traditionally called the Golden, Silver, Bronze and Iron Ages. They are described in Ovid's *Metamorphoses*, I, 89–150. The Golden Age was one of innocence and plenty; the Iron Age is one of violence and competitive greed.
8	*this one* this one *work* (l. 9).

9	*Seth's pillars* pillars (one of brick, one of stone) supposedly erected by the children of Seth (the son of Adam) to perpetuate his astronomical discoveries.
11	*Thee* the sun.
16	*Danow* Danube.
19	See Genesis 1: 11–13, 14–19.
21–30	Not even Noah's ark contained so many creatures as this soul has inhabited.
21	*holy Janus* Noah, like the two-faced Roman god, looked two ways by seeing the world before and after the Flood.
33	*where we offspring took* at the instant of our conception.
41	*lustres* five-year periods.
47	*this* composition of this poem.
48	*launch out* set to work. The metaphor is continued in the next stanza.
55	make my obscure difficult poem easy to understand and pleasant to read.
56–60	The story begins in the Garden of Eden and finishes in modern England.
61–70	This seems to point to Elizabeth I (ll. 61–3) – an extraordinarily daring implication, virtually accusing her of heresy – though l. 66 is inconsistent because Elizabeth's life overlapped Luther's and the soul could not be in two places at once.
68	*th' Empire and late Rome* the ancient Roman Empire and the contemporary Church of Rome.
70, 71, 77	*room* Used in two senses: (1) (figurative) station; (2) (literal) location. For the belief stated in ll. 71–8, see p. 286.
78	*learnèd tree* Tree of Knowledge.
80	*from pulling free* exempt from plucking (and therefore *in security*, not apprehensive).
90	*sweat* See Genesis 3: 19: 'In the sweat of thy face shalt thou eat bread.'
97	*turning . . . fled* returning to paradise.
119–20	*not liberties . . . heresies* Donne here argues that heresies cannot be eradicated by argument but must be suppressed by law.

124–5	*fled away . . . day* this freed soul, two days old, fled away.
130	*a plant* as the poem later explains, a mandrake, a root vegetable shaped somewhat like a human being.
150	The mandrake (*Atropa mandragora*) was used as an aphrodisiac (to *kindle*) and to cause abortion.
165	*moist red eyes* The name Cain was thought to mean 'lamentation, constant weeping'.
167–8	Poppy and mandragora are used in soporifics (compare *Othello*, III. iii. 335–8).
188	*Meat fit for men* corn, bread, etc.
200	*both kinds* males and females.
201–3	See note on 'The relic', ll. 29–30.
205	The verb 'is' must be supplied.
212	*gummy blood* sticky sap.
217	'Ten dozen of sparrows' and 'potato-roots' are among the ingredients of an 'elixir' in Massinger's *A New Way to Pay Old Debts*, II. ii. 17–24.
257	*but . . . get* but to catch a few, big enough for food.
262	*Once* for once.
267–8	*faith / Cares not* is not an article of faith (and so can be left to speculation).
270	*board* tack (as of a ship's course).
274	*sea pie* sea magpie, i.e. oystercatcher.
294	*Fat gluttony's best orator* Because his latest meal has given him strength he is an argument in favour of gluttony.
300	*officer* official of state, here satirized for destructiveness and greed.
302	*thrown out* delivered (whales are viviparous).
303–5	*if . . . swum* The Peloponnese (*Morea*) is visualized as fastened (*manacled*) to Greece by a chain (the isthmus of Corinth).
306–7	The Cape of Good Hope has a mountain (Table Mountain) upon it.
309–10	The (young) whale is compared to a ship in a storm (*when all hopes fail*), capsized (*overset*) or floating dismasted (*without sail / Hulling*).
315	*bark* hide like tree-bark.

320	*seas above the firmament* See Genesis 1: 7, 9, for these heavenly waters.
321–3	Like a state official (see l. 300), he lets his prey (*suitors* whom he exploits) come to him.
328	*states* kingdoms.
336–7	*The sun ... / Parchèd* The sun has been to both tropics (Cancer and Capricorn) twenty times: twenty years have passed.
340	*period* end.
	station permanence.
345	*outstreat* exude.
346–7	*undo / The plot of all* ruin the ground-plan of the whole scheme.
350	*them* tyrants.
351	*flail-finned thresher* The fox-shark, or thresher, has a long tail (which it actually uses to beat the sea when rounding up shoals of fish) like a flail.
353	*backs him* gets behind the whale.
360	*his own dole* the food he himself gives as alms.
369	*of their own* some of the love due to them.
385–6	It was a popular error that the elephant had no knee-joints, and it was thought that it slept leaning against a tree.
390	*remissly* The elephant was remiss in not having knotted its trunk to prevent mice from climbing up inside it (another popular error).
398	*room* station.
400	A fanatic who has no interest in surviving (see ll. 397–8) can assassinate anyone.
405–6	*in that trade ... type* By being a shepherd Abel prefigured priests and kings in charge of other people.
416	*Attached ... grips* seized her in a tight grasp.
419	*resist* resistance.
	straiten so hold so tightly.
421	*engaged her* won her over.
431	By marrying their daughters they have (previously) begotten their wives; by having sexual relations with their mothers they have (subsequently) begotten their sisters.

432   *emperors*   Nero and Domitian.
437   *A riddling lust*   a paradoxical embodiment of lust.
       schoolmen   medieval theologians.
439   *Moaba*   This and the other names of Adam's non-scriptural
       children (except Tethlemite) are either taken from or cor-
       rupted from rabbinical tradition.
459   *tumbles*   performs *somersaults* (l. 465).
471   *proved*   tried (made love to).
473   *through-vain*   thoroughly foolish.
480   *Nature . . . gaol*   The law of nature (according to the 'liber-
       tine' view) was not restrictive like the laws of God and
       man; compare 'The relic', ll. 29–30.
489   *who, thus prevented, flew*   who was fleeing, having been
       thwarted by Tethlemite's arrival.
494   *chemics' equal fires*   the even heat applied by alchemists.
499   *thicker*   i.e. than the other organs.
500   *life's spirits*   Compare 'The ecstasy', ll. 61–4.
502   *well-armed*   i.e. by the skull, considered as a headpiece.
503–5 Compare 'The funeral', ll. 9–11.
510   *plough*   See Genesis 4: 2.
516   *Cain's race*   See Genesis 4: 17–22.
517   Compare l. 9. *Astronomy* and astrology (the sense intended
       here) were interchangeably used in Donne's time.
518   *simply*   purely (all earthly things being mixed).
519–20 *Comparison* must measure how much good any mixed thing
       contains, and *opinion* (an exploratory mental state between
       knowledge and ignorance) must judge its value.

Verse Letters

THE STORM: TO MR CHRISTOPHER BROOKE

Title   Christopher Brooke (*c.* 1570–1628) was one of Donne's
         closest lifelong friends. They shared a chamber at Lincoln's
         Inn from May 1592 when Donne arrived there. Brooke
         gave away the bride at Donne's clandestine marriage and

was imprisoned for doing so. He became a Bencher and the Treasurer of Lincoln's Inn and was a Member of Parliament from 1604 to 1626.

In 1597, like many other young men, Donne joined the Earl of Essex's expedition which aimed at attacking the Spanish navy at Ferrol. The ships sailed on 10 July, but a few days later encountered the great storm described in the poem, and most of them had to return to Plymouth.

2 *these* these *lines* (l. 7).

4 *Hilliard* Nicholas Hilliard (1547–1619), the famous court miniaturist.

13–16 *From out ... again* Winds were supposed to issue from caverns in the earth, and the middle region of the air was supposed to be intensely cold.

18 *prisoners ... fees* Debtors whose creditors had discharged them were still kept in prison if they could not pay the gaoler's fees.

22 *as Sara ... see* Sarah, Abraham's wife, said 'God hath made me to laugh' (Genesis 21: 6) when she bore Isaac in her old age.

23–4 To see departing friends off by sharing the first part of their journey was a custom.

33–4 The prophet Jonah, fleeing from his duty to God, was overtaken by a storm at sea. The mariners woke him and charged him with the disaster (Jonah 1).

52 *fear away fear* frighten away fear itself.

53 *sicknesses* the *ague* (l. 54) and *dropsy* (l. 55) caused by the buffeting wind and the overflowing sea-water.

58 The bodies of hanged pirates were customarily gibbeted in chains beside the Thames.

65 *qualm* passing discomfort.

66 *lightsome* cheerful.
 Bermuda The Atlantic around Bermuda was 'a hellish sea for thunder, lightning, and storms', according to Ralegh (1596).

67 *light's elder brother* See Genesis 1: 2–4.

69–71 *All ... cover* All things are reduced to a single nothing, since a single *deformity* (ugly darkness) hides the form of all things. Note the play on *forms*, *uniform*, *deformity*.

72   *Another* Fiat   another *Fiat lux* (Latin, 'Let there be light').

74   *I wish not thee*   I do not wish you here.

THE CALM

Title   On 15 August the fleet set out again from Plymouth, and was again dispersed by bad weather. On the way to a rendezvous at the Azores Ralegh's squadron, with which Donne was serving, was becalmed for two days (9 and 10 September) in very hot weather. It is probable that this poem was also addressed to Christopher Brooke.

3–4   This alludes to Aesop's fable, in one version of which the frogs petition Zeus for a king; he sends them a log, and, when they are dissatisfied with that, a stork. Donne compares the motionless ship to the log (*block*) and the storm to the stork.

9   *those isles*   the Azores.

15   The seamen have hung their washed clothes in the area between foremast and mainmast where the soldiers were posted in sea-fights.

16   The tackling is also hung with clothes and looks like a secondhand-clothes shop (*frippery*).

17   *No use of lanterns*   There is no need of lanterns (*OED*, use, *sb.*, 21) because there is not enough wind to blow out a naked candle.

19–20   Compare 'The storm', ll. 13–16. The *upper vault* of the air is calm because winds cannot penetrate the middle region.

23   *calenture*   a fever afflicting sailors in the tropics, a symptom of which is the delusion that the sea is green fields.

27   *Who live*   those who remain alive.

28   *walkers ... ovens*   Shadrach, Meshach and Abednego (see Satire 3, ll. 23–4).

29   *these*   the *great fishes* (l. 24), sharks.

30   *brimstone bath*   Sulphur baths were a treatment for syphilis.

33   In Marlowe's *Tamburlaine*, Part I, IV. ii, Tamburlaine the

whom he has defeated and imprisoned in a cage.

34 Samson lost his strength when his hair was shaved off (Judges 16), and languished in slavery.

35–6 *as a myriad ... invade* The emperor Tiberius had a pet snake which was eaten by ants, a fact which he interpreted as an omen of the power of the people.

37 The galleys *crawl* because (1) they are slow, (2) the oars look like the legs of a centipede; they are *sea-gaols* because they are rowed by chained prisoners, and resemble small *chips* of wood moved by fins (the oars).

38 *Might brave our Venices* The Atlantic is as calm as the Mediterranean, in which galleys could operate, and where Turkish ones might defy Venice, with which (as a city fixed in the sea) the English ships are compared. Some texts have 'pinnaces' for *Venices*.

49–50 This couplet explains why sailors *forget to pray* to be spared a calm (l. 48).

52 *before he was* before he existed.

54 *disproportion it* unfit us for what we want to do.

TO SIR HENRY WOTTON

Title Henry Wotton (1568–1639) was a close friend of Donne from their arrival at Oxford in 1584. He travelled widely in Europe (1589–94), entered the Middle Temple in 1595, became a secretary of the Earl of Essex, and like Donne went on the expedition to Cadiz (1596) and the Azores (1597). In 1603 he was knighted, and in 1604 went as ambassador to Venice. This poem dates from 1597–8, when several members of Essex's circle were engaging in friendly debate about the merits of court, city and country life.

5–6 A humorous version of the biblical commonplace that human life is like grass (Psalm 90: 5–6).

8 *remoras* sucking-fish. See Elegy 18: 'Love's progress', l. 58.

10	Compare Ecclesiasticus 13: 1: 'He that touches pitch shall be defiled.' Proverbial.
11	*the even line* the equator.
12	*adverse* opposite to each other.
13	*two ... regions* the temperate regions of the northern and southern hemispheres, lying between the extremes of equator and pole.
17–18	examples showing that two bad things cannot combine into one good thing.
18	*torpedo* electric ray, a fish emitting an electric shock when handled.
22	*no such* no such people (as if their souls had fled).
24	*one end* death.
25–6	The country is a wilderness, where no good quality acquired by habit (such as good manners) is understood, and people are content to remain as they were born.
28	*blocks* logs; blockheads.
34	Falsehood has become a naturalized citizen. Virtue is exiled to remote places.
46	*Utopian* idealistic (from *Utopia*, Sir Thomas More's ideal commonwealth).
	old Italian 'Inglese italianato e un diavolo incarnato' (an Italianate Englishman is an incarnate devil: proverbial). Word-play in *old*: (1) advanced in years; (2) absolute.
48	*Inn* lodge for a short time.
55	*a lead without a line* a lead weight for testing the water's depth – but without the cord to draw it up again.
59–62	alluding to two contrasting schools of medicine. *Galen* (second century AD) held that illness was caused by excess or deficiency of the 'humours' (hot, cold, moist, dry) and was to be cured by *correctives* that restored the balance. Paracelsus (1493–1541) and the 'chemists' (*chemics*) held that illness was to be *purged* away, by analogy with the purifying of metals.
65–8	Wotton had travelled in these countries in 1589–94.
70	*I have ... Donne* I have ended, and I am, yours, Donne. Compare the word-play in 'A hymn to God the Father'.

Title   Lucy Russell (born Harrington), Countess of Bedford
        (1581–1627), was Donne's chief patroness. She married the
        Earl of Bedford in 1594 (she being 13 and he 22). Soon after
        James I's accession (1603) she met the queen, and became a
        Lady of the Bedchamber and the queen's closest friend, per-
        forming with her in the court masques of Jonson and Inigo
        Jones. She was prominent in court society until her retire-
        ment in 1620. At her estate of Twickenham Park from 1607
        she gathered around her a circle of literary friends including
        Donne and Jonson.
1   *sublime* purified (like *refined*, a term from alchemy).
4   *elements*   Those underfoot are earth and water, those over-
        head air and fire.
11   *stilling* distillation.
12   *dung* used by chemists to produce a steady warmth.
15   *Te Deums' melody* 'Te Deum laudamus' ('We praise thee,
        O God'), a hymn at morning prayer, often elaborately set.
18   *Sicil Isle* Sicily, location of the volcano Mount Etna.
19   *darker* in more obscurity.
21   *But one* God alone excepted.
23   *souls' stuff* the material of which souls are made.
26   *discovers* uncovers.
        quick living.
27   *your through-shine front* your transparent face.
29   *specular stone* See 'The undertaking', l. 6.
33   *know and dare* know good and dare to do it.
34–6   Aristotle and scholastic philosophers held that plants have a
        soul of growth, that animals also have a soul of sense, and
        that human beings also have a soul of reason. The first two
        souls exist before the third is added, so they possess the
        elder's *birthright*, but do not therefore claim superiority (*seek
        precedence*) nor give up their functions (*fly*) when the reason-
        able soul arrives.
37–9   Similarly *discretion*, though first acquired, must coexist with
        religion (synonymous with *zeal*).

| 42 | *her* the soul's (combining discretion and religion). |

| 43–4 | *Nor . . . break them* Nor must we dare to break these two apart, wrongly imagining that we can solder and join them together again. |

| 46 | *types* emblems. The circle was regarded as the perfect figure. |

| 47–8 | The circles' *centres* are indivisible (*pieceless*) because in geometry a point has position but no dimensions. They are emblems (*types*) of *religion* because they *flow* into all the radii (*lines*) which *go* in all directions (*ways*). |

| 51 | *ways* means. |

| 52 | *thither* in the right direction. |

| 53–4 | Those who wish to change their lives either covet something that they do not possess or repent something that they have done. Neither motive can apply to you, for you are great and good. |

The First Anniversary: An Anatomy of the World

Donne had written two important funeral elegies in 1609. In December 1610 Elizabeth Drury, the subject of this much longer poem, died; she was not quite 15 years old. Her father, Sir Robert Drury (1575–1615), was a landowner with a town house in what is still Drury Lane and a family estate in Suffolk, on which Donne's sister Anne was living after her second marriage. Donne stated that he had never met Elizabeth Drury, and perhaps he did not meet her parents until after her death; a funeral elegy of 106 lines, written directly after she died, may have started the acquaintance. The Drurys invited Donne to accompany them on a tour of Europe, and *The First Anniversary* must have been written between the invitation and the departure in November 1611; it was published, with the funeral elegy, before the end of the year. Donne immediately began a *Second Anniversary* (subtitled *Of the Progress of the Soul*), which was published early in the following year. In September 1612 they returned from Europe, and Donne and his family moved into a house in Drury Lane.

In *An Anatomy* (that is, a dissection) *of the World* Donne points out, in ingenious detail, how the world has been declining ever since the Fall of Man and may now be considered dead. Elizabeth Drury's death is hyperbolically taken as proof of the fact: Donne turns her into a paragon of beauty and virtue, and asserts that her life held the world together – an assertion that defies common sense but allows him to draw a vivid contrast between purity and corruption and to direct the reader away from the world and towards heaven.

6	may house a guest soul but does not have a soul which he can truly call his.
7–8	The soul is metaphorically called a *queen* who has been on a *progress* and has now returned to her *standing house* (compare Elegy 9, 'The autumnal', ll. 19–20).
12–13	The underlying metaphor is of suicide by bleeding into a warm bath, but it is not pursued in the following lines.
21	*physic* remedial medicine. The hot and cold *fits* (l. 20) of *ague* (synonymous with *fever*, l. 19) were thought to counteract such diseases as cramp.
24	*in a lethargy* at the point of death. For the symptoms, see ll. 28–31.
48	the loss of an example (of conduct) so strong that it served as a law.
57	*balm* the preserving and healing element thought (by Paracelsus' followers in medicine) to exist in human bodies.
73	*shut in all day* She is the sun which, having set, has taken daylight away.
75–6	*Which . . . new world* which creates a new world, free from the carcass of the old one (because her virtue, not the world's elements, supplies the material, ll. 77–8).
76	*new creatures* virtuous beings.
78	*the form our practice is* by imitating her virtue we give it existence in the world that she has left.
79	*thus elemented* composed of her virtue.
92	*a neutrality* a state of being neither well nor ill.

95 *ruinous* rushing headlong forward (the root meaning); *headlong* (l. 97) and *precipitation* (l. 98) continue the idea.

103–4 They (women) were originally, and are still, only accessories (helpers) in good purposes, but principals in bad ones.

106 i.e. because the Fall of Man brought death into the world.

107–10 alluding to the supposition that sexual activity shortens life. Compare *The Progress of the Soul*, ll. 204–10.

115 Pliny's *Natural History* sceptically reports the tradition that stags live thirty-six times longer than human beings, and ravens three times longer than stags. Jonson, in a poem, estimates an oak's life as 300 years.

122 Man's growth witnessed to the quality of the food (*meat*), and was directly proportioned to (*recompensed*) it.

128 *Methusalem* Methuselah lived 969 years (Genesis 5: 27).

134 *to have three lives* to obtain a long lease.

136 *span* about 9 inches.

145 only when we are laid out do we appear at full length.

149–50 *disposed . . . was* brought into a smaller bottle the concentrated essence of their quality, which was diffused through their bulk.

151 *not retired, but damped* The imagery is not clear: *damped* suggests *shrinking* (l. 153), but *retired* does not suggest *close weaving* (l. 153) but rather the 'shrinking' of a snail into its shell.

159 *new diseases* particularly syphilis, known in Europe since the fifteenth century.

160 *new physic* fatal 'remedies' which ignorant physicians are continually inventing; perhaps also a satirical thrust at Paracelsian medicine (see p. 269).

161 *vice-emperor* God's deputy (Genesis 1: 26–8).

172–3 *Help . . . wants* even if one should grant (*allow*) that his other deficiencies (*wants*) might be (medically) helped, or at least their wasting effects retarded.

173–4 *depart / With* part with.

176 In Greek and Latin the names of virtues are of the feminine gender.

180 *tincture* essence (a term of *alchemy*, l. 182).

187   *banquet*   take a snack (OED, banquet, *sb.*²).

195   *the angels*   those who rebelled with Lucifer.

205   *new philosophy*   modern science.

206   In the old 'philosophy' there was a sphere of *fire* beyond the sphere of air encircling the earth.

207–8   Copernicus and others had asserted that the earth goes round the sun, not the sun round the earth. Thus the earth has lost its old place as centre of the universe.

212   *to his atomies*   into its component atoms.

214   all proper mutual support and all proper relationship.

216–18 It is a paradox to speak of '*a* phoenix' because there is only one (see p. 215); hence the power of the image of universal arrogance and selfishness.

221   *magnetic force*   William Gilbert asserted in 1600 that the earth was a magnet (an early form of gravitational theory).

228–9   *the general / Steward to Fate*   she who dispensed to the world what God had willed.

234   *single money*   small change.

235–6   She is the city of which the world is the mere outskirts; the world is merely the miniature version of her (a paradox, as the human body is called the *microcosm* of the world).

251–62 The old belief was that the stars were fixed to the concentric spheres encircling the earth; but observation shows that deviations (*eccentric parts*) occur, and these are mapped on charts with vertical (*downright*) and horizontal lines (*overthwarts*). Observation also divides the stars into forty-eight constellations, and notes the appearance and disappearance of particular stars.

265   *the goat and crab*   the tropics of Capricorn and Cancer.

268–72 Instead of continually describing the same (supposed) circle around the earth, the sun continually alters its position relative to the earth.

274   *nearer us*   a false supposition based on the difference between Ptolemy's calculations and those of his successors.

278–80 lines of celestial longitude and latitude (as in l. 256).

286   *Tenerife*   Tenerife, an island in the Canaries, has a mountain over 12,000 feet high.

294	*Antipodes* those who dwell on the opposite side of the globe.
295	*a vault infernal* hell, traditionally located in the centre of the earth.
299	then the round world, supposed solid, has a great cavity in it.
311	*that ancient* not definitely identified; perhaps Pythagoras.
317	*great doctors* St Augustine and St Ambrose.
319–21	*that might be . . . peace* the Ark (*that*) might be an emblem (*type*) of her in peacefully combining mutually hostile animals, as she harmonized conflicting elements and conflicting passions.
337	*well* fitting, seemly.
338	To lack moral wisdom is almost as bad as to be wicked.
343–4	a popular superstition.
345	An amalgam of gold and quicksilver (*mercury*, known in alchemy as *serpens mercurialis*, whence *stung*) is pale in colour.
358	*our souls are red* i.e. like our scarlet sins (Isaiah 1: 18).
365–6	i.e. because *all colour* would seem to contradict *all diaphanous*.
380	*The father* is the sky (*the heaven*, l. 378), *the mother* the earth (the *elements* of earth and water, l. 379).
388	*what they be* i.e. because of their frightful unaccustomed forms.
389	*worms* serpents. Aaron and the Egyptian magicians (*mages*) contended by turning their rods into serpents (Exodus 7: 10–12).
391	*artist* astrologer, alchemist, or other practiser of occult arts.
392	*constellate* use the power of a favourable constellation for.
396	*correspondence* the *commerce* (l. 399) or *traffic* (l. 400) between heaven and earth.
404	*yea ashes too* even their ashes.
407	*dying swan* Swans were supposed to sing when at the point of death.
418	*states* kinds of people (see ll. 419–24).
421–2	*some people . . . crave* some subjects have some restraint

(*stay*), so that they crave no more than kings should give them.

426   *our age was iron*   The four *ages* of the world, in chronological and descending order, are gold, silver, bronze and *iron*.

436   *to have read*   long enough to permit a lecture to be given.

440   *Were punctual*   dealt with it point by point.

449   *feast*   saint's day.

456   *concoction*   purification (alchemical term).

460   *chronicle*   historiography.

461–5   Deuteronomy 31: 19–21; 32: 1–43.

469   *incomprehensibleness*   her being too great to be confined within limits.

Religious Poems

HOLY SONNETS

1 (*'Thou hast made me'*)

6   *doth cast*   The singular verb is governed by both nouns *despair* and *death*. In l. 7, *doth waste* is governed by *flesh*.

9   *Only*   but.

11   But Satan so strongly tempts me to despair.

13–14   May thy grace give me wings to frustrate his craft, and mayst thou, like a magnetic lodestone (*adamant*), draw mine iron heart to thee. Compare *A Midsummer Night's Dream*, II. i. 195–8.

2 (*'As due by many titles'*)

1   *titles*   legal entitlements (as listed in ll. 2–8).

3   *decayed*   ruined (by the Fall of Man, which, with the Redemption, is referred to in l. 4).

5   *son*   word-play: (1) son; (2) sun (Matthew 13: 43).

6   *pains*   labours.

3 ('O might those sighs and tears')

2   *spent* i.e. on women, as a lover, in *idolatry* (l. 5).

6   *rent* rend.

7   My past suffering was a sinful one which I now repent. Some texts have 'my sin, now I repent' ('My past suffering was a sinful one, but now I repent').

8   The metre has been read in two ways: (1) by discounting the first syllable (some texts have 'Cause'); (2) by stressing *did* and *must*.

9   *hydroptic* swollen with drink (as in dropsy).
          night-scouting spying by night.

10   *itchy* itching to satisfy his lust.
          self-tickling self-caressing.

4 ('O my black soul')

3–4   Human life was traditionally called a pilgrimage (compare Holy Sonnet 6, l. 2). The analogy here is with a pilgrim who, while abroad, has committed treason against his own king.

5   *death's doom* sentence of death.

7   *damned* condemned.

13–14 Compare Isaiah 1: 18.

5 ('I am a little world')

2   of matter (the four *elements*) and spirit (such as the angels wholly consist of); of body and soul.

5   *You* astronomers and geographical discoverers.

9   *drowned no more* as God promised to Noah after the Flood (Genesis 9: 9–17).

10   *burnt* There was expectation (based on 2 Peter 3: 10–12) that the world would end by a general conflagration. Compare Holy Sonnet 7, l. 5.

12   *fouler* uglier (because the *fire* – here twofold, hence the plural verb *have* – of lust and envy has blackened it).

13–14   Compare Psalm 69: 9:'The zeal of thine house hath eaten me up.'

6 ('This is my play's last scene')

5   *unjoint*   divide from each other.
7   *that face*   God's, as judge.
9   *her first seat*   Compare Holy Sonnet 4, l. 4.
13   Even when the penitent soul has *purged* the *evil* of its sins, it still bears the hereditary sin of Adam and must therefore be *imputed righteous* (have righteousness attributed to it) by the merit of Christ.

7 ('At the round earth's imagined corners')

1   *corners*   Compare Revelation 7: 1: 'And after these things I saw four angels standing on the four *corners* of the earth'; but these angels have no *trumpets* (l. 2), which enter the poem from 1 Corinthians 15: 52 ('for the trumpet shall sound, and the dead shall be raised incorruptible').
7   *Despair . . . slain*   Those slain by *despair* are suicides, those slain by *law* have been executed, and those slain by *chance* have died in accidents.
7–8   *and you . . . death's woe*   those human beings who are alive when the Last Judgement is announced.
9   *a space*   for a time (relating to both *sleep* and *mourn*).
12   *there*   in God's presence.
13–14   True repentance will assure the sinner that God has confirmed his pardon with his (Christ's) blood. The image is of a royal pardon with the king's seal upon it.

9 ('If poisonous minerals')

10   *only worthy*   alone having value.
11   *Lethean*   like Lethe, the river of oblivion in Hades.
13–14   Some people ask thee to remember them (that is, be good to them) as recompense for their faithful service (*as debt*); I

think it mercy in thee if thou wilt forget me (that is, forget what a sinner I am). The point is in the paradox of the last line, since to forget the sinner absolutely would be not mercy but the severest justice: compare p. 172.

10 ('Death, be not proud')

7	referring to the proverb that the good die young.
8	Death gives rest to their bodies (*bones*) and is a freeing (*delivery*) of their souls from the prison of the body.
9–10	Compare Holy Sonnet 7, ll. 6–7.
11	*poppy or charms* opium or hypnosis.
12	*why swell'st thou then?* why do you puff yourself up with pride?
14	Compare 1 Corinthians 15: 26: 'The last enemy that shall be destroyed is death.'

11 ('Spit in my face, ye Jews')

2	*scoff* mock.
5	*satisfied* atoned for.
7	*inglorious* of low rank; in antithesis to *glorified* (l. 8), ascended into heaven (see John 7: 39).
8	*Crucify him daily* i.e. by sinning; compare Hebrews 6: 6: 'They crucify to themselves the Son of God afresh.'
9	*admire* wonder at.
10	*pardon* remit our punishment.
11–12	See Genesis 27: 16, 21–3, 36. Jacob supplanted his elder brother Esau by obtaining the firstborn's blessing from their blind father Isaac, whom he deceived by having his hands and neck covered with kids' skins in order to feel hairy like Esau.

13 ('What if this present were the world's last night?')

1	What if this present night were to bring the end of the world?

5	*amazing* terrifying.
9	*idolatry* worship of women.
10	*profane* secular (as contrasted with spiritual); compare Holy Sonnet 19, l. 6.
11–12	*Beauty . . . rigour* Beauty is a sign of pity, only ugliness is a sign of rigour.
12	*thee* the soul.

14 ('Batter my heart, three-personed God')

1–4	The dominant imagery is of repairing a metal utensil: tinkering is unfavourably contrasted with reforging.
1	*three-personed* the Trinity of Father, Son and Holy Spirit.
5	*to another due* owing duty to somebody other than whoever has *usurped* it.
11	The verbs *untie* and *break that knot* are increasingly vivid synonyms for *divorce*.
14	*ravish* in two senses: (1) carry off; (2) violate (this second sense making a strong paradox with *chaste*; compare *enthral* and *free*, l. 13).

17 ('Since she whom I loved')

1–4	Donne's wife Ann died on 15 August 1617, in her thirty-third year, five days after giving birth to their twelfth child.
2	*and to hers . . . dead* and is dead to her good and to mine (is incapable of doing good to herself or me).
6	*head* source.
8	*dropsy* here an immoderate thirst for love (compare ll. 7, 9), which *melts* (emotionally affects) the poet.
10	*for hers offering all thine* offering all thy love to replace hers.
12	*saints and angels* the poet's deceased wife in heaven.
13–14	God is here said to fear (*doubt*) that the three foes of mankind (compare Satire 3, ll. 33–42) – even the ugliest of them, the Devil – may supplant him (*put thee out*) in the poet's affections.

18 ('Show me, dear Christ')

1   *Show me*   Compare l. 12, but contrast the plurals in ll. 9–11, 14.

        thy spouse   the church (compare Revelation 19: 7–8, and Song of Solomon 2, heading).

2–3   *she . . . painted*   the Church of Rome (*the other shore* being particularly that of France).

3–4   *which . . . here*   either (1) extreme Protestantism (including English Puritanism), characterized by a contempt for ceremonial; or (2) moderate Protestantism (including English Anglicanism), which suffered a heavy reverse with the Elector Palatine's defeat in Bohemia in October 1620 (see pp. 254–5).

5   alluding satirically to the claims of some Protestant sects (with a short expectation of life: *one year*) to have rediscovered long-lost primitive Christianity.

6   *self truth*   truth itself.

8   Solomon's temple was built on Mount Moriah (2 Chronicles 3: 1), Rome is a city built on *seven* hills, and Geneva is *on no hill*.

11–14   The theme (implicit in the whole sonnet) is the wish for unity in the church. The expression is paradoxical and daring. For Christ as husband and the church as bride and *dove*, compare Song of Solomon 5: 2 ('Open to me, my sister, my love, my dove, my undefiled'); but there is also a suggestion of a complaisant (*kind*) husband who will prostitute (*betray*) his wife to other men, by whom she will be *embraced* and to whom she will be *open*.

11   *Betray*   word-play: (1) betray; (2) reveal.

19 ('O, to vex me')

5   *humorous*   changeable (subject to humours).

8   *none*   non-existent.

13   *ague*   fever, with bouts of heat and cold (compare ll. 7, 14).

Title   The poem may have been suggested by *De Cruce* (Antwerp, 1595), a treatise by the Belgian scholar Justus Lipsius (1547–1606) in which the cross-like objects mentioned in ll. 17–24, already traditional, were collected and pictured. Donne is also evidently reacting against Puritan hostility to the image of the Cross, and defending his right as a private person to possess a cross.

5   *It bore all other sins*   The Crucifixion atoned for the sins of mankind.

9–10   alluding to Puritan preaching, legislation and expressions of outrage.

12   *another cross*   an affliction (therefore a *cross* in *another* sense).

13   *Better were worse*   To have no affliction, though apparently *better*, would be a *worse* condition than to be afflicted.

15–16   Who can blot out the cross which the priest made on my forehead with consecrated water at my baptism?

21   *small things*   for example, straws, or the rushes strewing a floor.

22   *crossèd wings*   the wings being at a right angle to the body and tail.

23–4   The *globe* is a terrestrial globe, the *sphere* a celestial globe, and the *meridians* and *parallels* the lines of longitude and latitude.

27   *These*   spiritual crosses (afflictions).
    extracted chemic medicine   remedies extracted by chemical processes according to Paracelsus's system of medicine (see p. 269); *stilled* (distilled) and *purged* (purified), l. 30, continue the metaphor.

31   *ungrudged, unto you sticks*   is accepted by you without grudging.

33–4   Michelangelo expresses this idea in one of his sonnets.

36   *not his, but he*   not merely his image but his true self.

37   *coiners*   forgers of counterfeit money (instead of makers of gold).

38   This charge was often levelled at the Puritans.

41   *cross*   check.

42	*double loss* To the actual misfortunes (*crosses*) is added the sin of self-righteousness.
45–6	*take / No cross* endure no hardship.
46	*a snake* the danger lurking in the pleasure of the eye.
47	*the rest* the rest of the senses (*th' others*, l. 50).
48	*Make them indifferent* treat all these unpleasant things as neither good nor bad.
52	The heart (as conventionally represented) has its point below, therefore not turned to heaven; it trembles, and is therefore not firm.
53	*dejections* castings-down.
53, 54	*it* the heart.
55	*vent* breathe.
56	The upper bones of the skull are separated by fine cracks which form a cross.
58	*concupiscence of wit* the lust to be clever.
59	*fall* escape.
63	*pictures* representations.
64	*That Cross's children* those miniature crucifixions.

GOOD FRIDAY, 1613. RIDING WESTWARD

Title	As some of the manuscripts indicate, Donne did ride westward on Good Friday (3 April) 1613, while journeying from Sir Henry Goodyer's house at Polesworth, Warwickshire, to Sir Edward Herbert's at Montgomery.
1–2	As each heavenly sphere is moved by the angel (or *intelligence*) dwelling within it, so a human soul is moved by devotion.
3–8	As the heavenly spheres' movements are affected by other forces, particularly that of the utmost sphere or 'first mover', almost every day of the year, so our souls allow pleasure or business to divert them from their course. Their natural motion was from west to east (compare ll. 9–10).
10	*bends* word-play: (1) directs its course; (2) bows.
11	*a sun* Christ (with a pun on sun/son).
	by rising set die by being raised on the Cross (l. 13).

12	*endless day* eternal life for all mankind (ll. 13–14).
17	See Exodus 33: 20: 'Thou canst not see my face: for there shall no man see me, and live.'
	that is self life who is life itself.
19	*lieutenant* deputy.
20	The death of Christ was preceded by three hours of darkness, and accompanied by an earthquake (Matthew 27: 45, 51).
	footstool Compare Isaiah 66: 1: 'The heaven is my throne, and the earth is my footstool.'
	wink close its eye.
22	*turn* This is the reading of some texts; other texts read 'tune'.
23–4	God is equally the *zenith* (highest point) to us and to those who live on the opposite side of the globe (*antipodes*).
25–6	*that blood . . . his* It was debated whether the soul resided in the blood. Whether or not Christ's soul did so during his incarnation, his blood is *the seat of all our souls* because it gives us life.
27	*Make dirt of dust* mingle with the *dust* and convert it into *dirt* (mud).
32	*that sacrifice* Christ as the sacrificial victim.
36	*the tree* the Cross.
38	*Corrections* punishment by blows.
41–2	Make me look like thee again, by thy grace, to such an extent that thou mayst recognize me, and I'll turn my face.

A HYMN TO CHRIST, AT THE AUTHOR'S LAST GOING INTO GERMANY

Title	Donne travelled to Germany, as chaplain to Viscount Doncaster's diplomatic mission, in May 1619. On 18 April he had preached a farewell sermon at Lincoln's Inn which anticipated the imagery of this poem's opening stanza.
1	*torn ship* Donne dramatizes the situation (as in ll. 3 and 5): he was in fact about to cross the English Channel (*our seas*, l. 10) in a highly seaworthy vessel.

15	*control* restrain.
19	*more* others (ll. 23–8).
20	*whoever gives, takes liberty* whoever gives another the freedom to love elsewhere takes the liberty to do likewise himself (compare l. 21).
25	*hopes* of advancement.
26–8	This is not a prayer for death but a resolution to die to the world and its *stormy days* by concentrating on God (compare ll. 12–14).

HYMN TO GOD MY GOD, IN MY SICKNESS

Title	The sickness was probably the serious fever which attacked Donne in November 1623 and which he describes in his *Devotions* (see pp. 159–68), though his biographer Izaak Walton (1640) ascribed it to his last illness in March 1631. For the evidence, see Helen Gardner, *Divine Poems*, pp. 132–5, and R. C. Bald, *Life*, pp. 453–4.
6	*love* care.
7	*Cosmographers* makers and interpreters of maps.
9	*my south-west discovery* The south is the hot quarter, the west the quarter where the sun declines; here used figuratively for death by fever (l. 10).
10	**Per** fretum febris, *by these straits* bilingual word-play: *fretum* (Latin) (1) raging heat; (2) strait (the phrase means 'by the raging heat/strait of fever'); straits (1) narrow sea-passages; (2) hardships.
16–17	All three places are used figuratively for the same thing, heaven. *Pacific* means 'peaceful'; *Jerusalem*, besides meaning 'vision of peace', is the 'heavenly Jerusalem' of Revelation 21: 10–27; 22: 1–5; the *eastern riches*, besides the wealth of China, suggests 'treasure in heaven' (Matthew 6: 19–21).
18	*Anyan* a supposed strait (*Streto de Anian*) first marked on a map of 1566 as dividing North America from eastern Asia, and called by an old name for Annam.
19	The (heavenly) places of ll. 16–17 can be reached only by passing through *straits* (l. 10, sense 2).

285

20	whether in Europe, Africa or Asia. The descendants of Noah's three sons repopulated the world after the Flood.
21–2	Here (as in *The Progress of the Soul*, ll. 71–8) Donne's poetical idea requires the Tree of Knowledge and the Cross to have occupied the identical place, though this was inconsistent with the traditional location of paradise between the Tigris and Euphrates in Mesopotamia, near Damascus. See Helen Gardner, *Divine Poems*, pp. 135–7, for further discussion.
23–5	Christ is *the last Adam* (see 1 Corinthians 15: 45; Romans 5: 12–21).
24	*sweat* See Genesis 3: 19: 'In the sweat of thy face shalt thou eat bread, till thou return unto the ground.'
	surrounds overflows (the original meaning).
26	*his purple* Christ's saving blood, considered as a cloak.
27	By this crown of thorns (which he wore at his Crucifixion) give me his crown of glory (see 1 Peter 5: 4).
30	Not an actual biblical text.

A HYMN TO GOD THE FATHER

Title	Donne's biographer Izaak Walton (1640) ascribed this poem to his illness of 1623.
1–2	This sin is original sin, the sin *done before* by Adam and inherited by all human beings at birth (*where I begun*).
3	*run* ran (a common form of the past tense).
5	A paradox and (in the second *done*) a pun (on the poet's name).
7–8	This sin is perhaps the writing of licentious poetry.
13–14	*spun / My last thread* The 'thread of life' is a traditional expression.
14	*perish on the shore* be (figuratively) shipwrecked within sight of land.
15	*sun* word-play on 'Son'. In a sermon Donne speaks of 'the Son of God, the sun of glory'. Some texts have 'son' here and 'he' for 'it' in l. 16.

Devotions

At the end of November 1623 Donne contracted 'spotted fever' (relapsing fever, as it is now called), then epidemic in the City of London. The disease is of sudden onset and rapid development, reaching its crisis within a week; if the patient survives, recovery is slow. The patient, in spite of insomnia and prostration, remains fully conscious. Donne, who was out of danger by 6 December, composed the *Devotions upon Emergent Occasions and Several Steps in my Sickness* during his convalescence. He completed the work during December and it was published in January 1624.

The twenty-three 'devotions' consist of 'meditations upon our human condition, expostulations and debatements with God, and prayers upon several occasions to him'. Each 'devotion' is in these three parts, and marks a stage in the process of sickness and recovery. Only six of the meditations are given (in full) in this selection.

DEVOTIONS, 1

Title	*grudging* symptoms.
4	*We study health* in such books as Sir Thomas Elyot's *The Castle of Health* (1541) and Thomas Coghan's *The Haven of Health* (1584).
10	*disorder* bad living (physically).
22	*urine* Observation of urine's discoloration was a method of diagnosis.
28	*quickened* given life. It was believed that the rational soul (see 'To the Countess of Bedford', ll. 34–6 and note) was acquired by human beings some time later than conception.
31–4	*these lightnings ... exhalations* The *flashes* are before the eyes, the *noises* in the ears; *offuscations* is synonymous with *darkenings*; *exhalations* are eruptions on the skin.

DEVOTIONS, 6

8	*ill affections* disorders.
29	*put her measure* set her limits.

31   *damp*   dangerous chilling mist.

         stupefaction   torpor of the senses.

34   *murmuring*   complaining.

DEVOTIONS, 7

6–7   *his candour and his ingenuity*   his frankness and his openness.

12   *derive*   delegate.

14–15   *two consuls*   when Rome became a republic (509 BC).

15   *one dictator*   Julius Caesar (49 BC).

26   *a watch*   a group of watchmen led by a constable.

32   *Dionysius*   Dionysius the elder (who ruled Syracuse, 405–367 BC) died after celebrating the success of a tragedy he had written by a drinking-bout; but it was his son, not he, who was deposed.

36   *live of a little*   live upon little means.

43–4   *the greatest man of style*   the man of greatest title.

44–6   *the Conqueror . . . a grave*   William the Conqueror (King of England, 1066–87). When he died, at Rouen, his attendant nobles fled to their estates, abandoning his body and taking his valuables.

49   *proctor*   agent.

54   *receipt*   prescription.

64   *the bill*   Bills of mortality, listing the number of deaths in each London parish, were published weekly from 1592.

69   *visited*   as contrasted with having regular medical attendance.

75   *julep*   a cooling drink made of distilled waters and syrups.

76   *bezoar*   a stony concretion found in the stomachs of some kinds of goat, used in medicine particularly as an antidote to poison.

DEVOTIONS, 16

1   *a convenient author*   an author appropriate to the present subject. Gerolamo Maggi (*c.* 1523–72), an Italian engineer, whose book was published in 1608.

2   *enlarged himself* increased his book (also word-play on *enlarged*, freed).

4   *that steeple* i.e. of St Paul's cathedral.

5   *is more heard* ironical understatement. The music of the heavenly concentric spheres is inaudible.

6–7   *I have heard . . . ordnance* Donne heard ordnance when he served under Essex on the Cadiz expedition of 1596.

8   *a steeple* This steeple was at Antwerp, which Donne visited in 1611–12 with Sir Robert Drury. The other (*another*, 1.9) was at Rouen on the same journey.

15   *correcting* punishing. A 'whipping boy', who thus obtained the benefit of a good education, was kept for this purpose.

21   *a monastery* at Salerno (the story is told by Angelo Rocca, *De Campanis Commentarius*, a treatise on bells, 1612).

30–1   *by attorney* by proxy.

31   *preferred* promoted.

38–40   *To be an incumbent . . . by dying* word-play on *incumbent* ((1) beneficed clergyman; (2) one who lies in something), *doctor* ((1) of divinity; (2) one who teaches) and *mortification* ((1) spiritual dying to worldly things; (2) physical dying).

DEVOTIONS, 17

1   *for whom this bell tolls* The bell was tolled slowly and softly while a person was known to be dying (the passing-bell); at his or her death it was rung loudly a few times (the death-knell). Devotion 18 begins: 'The bell rings out: the pulse thereof is changed; the tolling was a faint and intermitting pulse upon one side; this stronger, and argues more and better life.' (In sounding the passing-bell the clapper struck one side of the bell; in sounding the death-knell it struck both sides.)

21–2   (*in which . . . mingled*) This anecdote of the lawsuit may be Donne's invention.

36   *main* mainland.

38   *friends'* The original (as was usual) has no apostrophe, so

either *friends'* or *friend's* may have been intended, and *friend* in either sense ((1) close relation; (2) friend in the modern sense).

DEVOTIONS, 23

2   *to cover your fire*   The curfew bell was rung in order to reduce accidental fires.

6   *a* meum *and* tuum   a mine and thine (Latin: legal terms).

28   *one natural unnatural day*   A *natural* day (of 24 hours) would be an *unnatural* one if it combined the longest period of daylight (18 hours) with the longest period of darkness (18 hours).

Sermons

SERMONS, EXTRACT 1

1   *I am not all here*   This passage follows a statement that at the general resurrection both the body and the soul will be completely present.

9–10   *predestination and reprobation*   The doctrine of the Elizabethan Protestant Church (which was mainly Calvinist in its doctrine, though much of its common prayer was translated from Catholic services) on this difficult theological subject is briefly set out in number 17 of the Thirty-Nine Articles of Religion agreed in 1562 and thereafter to be found in the Book of Common Prayer.

14   *a private visit*   (by implication) to a woman. Most of Donne's congregation would be young men.

SERMONS, EXTRACT 2

1–2   A *close prisoner* is confined to a cell; in less strict imprisonment one is confined to the prison and its grounds.

11–12   Quis homo   what man.

1–2   *is death*   is punishable with death.

2–4   *As soon . . . death*   See Genesis 3: 21–3.

8–9   On *tolls* and *will ring out*, see *Devotions*, 17, l. 1 and note.

10–11   Quotidie . . . putamus   We die every day, and yet we think we are eternal.

16   *the moral man*   any moral philosopher.

19   Mors . . . mortalium   Death is the law, the tax, the duty of moral men.

29   incivile, inofficiosum   anti-social, undutiful.

1   *When all is done*   Donne has been discussing speculations as to whether hell is an actual place with a material fire, and has concluded that, since the facts are unknowable, what matters is the spiritual use that we make of our idea of hell.

4   *the apostle*   Paul (Hebrews 10: 31).

5   *David*   See 2 Samuel 24: 14.

34–6   'Quare . . . *but live*'   The quotations are from Ezekiel 18: 31 and Psalm 118: 17.

39   *standing and knocking*   See Revelation 3: 20.

42   *calentures*   here synonymous with *fevers*.

52   *Tophet*   hell.

53   *the worm*   Mark 9: 44: 'Where their worm dieth not, and the fire is not quenched.'

61–2   For the *pillar of fire* and the *pillar of the cloud*, see Exodus 13: 21.

3   *David*   In Psalm 101: 1.

       fix . . . modulation   determine to think and sing.

25   *God is love*   1 John 4: 16.

34   *that prayer*   the penultimate verse of the hymn 'Te Deum laudamus' ('We praise thee, O God'), which is repeated daily at the service of morning prayer.

36	*cloud of quails* See Exodus 16: 13.
38	*gomer* measuring-container.
55	*Fool . . . soul* See Luke 12: 20.
58	*Lord . . . us* This prayer, which precedes the Lord's Prayer at morning and evening prayer, was written on the door of any house visited with the plague.
63	*Balaam* See Numbers 22: 28–30.
64	*one thief* at the Crucifixion. See Luke 23: 40.
66	*the Devil* See Acts 19: 13–16.
73	*illness* sinfulness.
77	*elected* chose me for salvation; predestined me to salvation. See *Sermons*, extract 1, ll. 9–10.
87	*today . . . voice* a quotation from Psalm 95, which is repeated in entirety almost daily at morning prayer.
100	*illustrate* lighten.

SERMONS, EXTRACT 6

2	*prison* debtors' prison.
4	*spital* hospital, especially for venereal diseases.
25–6	*because . . . stand for me* Compare the response at morning and evening prayer to 'Give peace in our time, O Lord': 'Because there is none other that fighteth for us but only thou, O God.'
32	*humours* physical constitution.
38	*that pondus gloriae* that weight of glory (2 Corinthians 4: 17).

SERMONS, EXTRACT 7

1	*when we consider* Donne is maintaining that there is nothing in the world either perfect or permanent.
14	*chimera* synonymous with *fancy*.

SERMONS, EXTRACT 8

Title	*the fast* Charles 1 (acceded 1625) had ordered a public fast

292

because of England's reverses in the war against France and Spain.

1   Stipendium . . . est   Romans 6: 23: 'The reward of sin is death.'

9   *told over*   reckoned up.

15–16   statutum est . . . semel mori   Hebrews 9: 27: 'it is appointed unto men once to die.'

18   *impotent*   unrestrained.

31   miserationes . . . opera   Psalm 145: 9.

35   *emblems of tribulation*   As in Psalm 124: 4–5.

SERMONS, EXTRACT 10

1   *this chapter*   Genesis 1.

9   *after him*   after Lactantius.

11   *compassed*   circumnavigated. This was first done in 1519–22 by the expedition led by the Portuguese explorer Ferdinand Magellan (who was killed during it, 1521).

24   *Livy* and *Guicciardini* were Roman and Italian historians respectively.

45–6   *Throw . . . raise it*   See John 2: 19.

Glossary

Abbreviations: *adj.*, adjective; *adv.*, adverb; *conj.*, conjunction; *n.*, noun; *pa.p.*, past participle; *pr.p.*, present participle; *prep.*, preposition; *v.*, verb.

able (*v.*)   make capable
acquittance (*n.*)   receipt
admiration (*n.*)   wonder
adulterate (*v.*)   commit adultery
affect (*v.*)   impress; please
affection (*n.*)   emotion
ague (*n.*)   fever
allay (*n.*)   alloy
allow (*v.*)   admit
amaze (*v.*)   terrify
anatomy (*n.*)   dissection
angel (*n.*)   gold coin
antic (*adj., n.*)   grotesque; fantastic
approve (*v.*)   commend; admit; try
article (*v.*)   negotiate
assumed (*pa.p.*)   taken up

atomy (*n.*)   atom
attend (*v.*)   await

ballast (*v.*)   steady by loading
bare (*adj.*)   needy
become (*v.*)   befit
benight (*v.*)   darken
bent (*pa.p.*)   inclined
betray (*v.*)   reveal
blast (*v.*)   blight
board (*n.*)   table; tack (in sailing)
boot (*v.*)   profit
bottle (*n.*)   bundle
brave (*adj.*)   courageous; fine; showy
break (*v.*)   become bankrupt
broker (*n.*)   pawnbroker
busy (*adj.*)   officious; prying

carcanet (*n.*)   necklace
chafe (*v.*)   soften; anger
chaw (*v.*)   chew
chemic (*n.*)   alchemist
civility (*n.*)   politeness
clog (*n.*)   encumbrance
close (*n.*)   secret
college (*n.*)   society
compact (*v.*)   hold together
compass (*v.*)   attain
conceit (*n.*)   wit; intelligence
conceited (*adj.*)   ingenious
concoction (*n.*)   purification
conduit (*n.*)   water-pipe
confound (*v.*)   confuse
consort (*v.*)   accompany
consumption (*n.*)   wasting
  disease
content (*n.*)   contentment
control (*v.*)   overcome
corse (*n.*)   corpse
country (*n.*)   nation; district;
  countryside
courtesy (*n.*)   salutation
cozen (*v.*)   deceive
curious (*adj.*)   artfully made;
  over-inquisitive

day (*n.*)   daylight
decay (*v.*)   deteriorate; fade
  away
deformity (*n.*)   ugliness
denizened (*pa.p.*)   naturalized
desperate (*n.*)   person in
  despair
determined (*pa.p.*)   ended
device (*n.*)   ingenuity

devicefully (*adv.*)
  significantly
dint (*n.*)   indentation
discover (*v.*)   reveal
disuse (*v.*)   unaccustom
divining (*pr.p.*)   foretelling
doubt (*n.*, *v.*)   fear

earthly (*adj.*)   earth-like
ecstasy (*n.*)   rapture
elemented (*pa.p.*)   composed
embar (*v.*)   forbid
embayed (*pa.p.*)   in harbour
emblem (*n.*)   symbol
empery (*n.*)   empire
engine (*n.*)   machine; long-
  range weapon
enlarge (*v.*)   extend
enow (*adj.*)   enough
equal (*adj.*)   even
escape (*n.*)   misdeed
even (*adj.*)   equal
except (*conj.*)   unless
excess (*n.*)   over-indulgence
exhaled (*pa.p.*)   evaporated

fall (*v.*)   befall; escape
fame (*n.*)   reputation; rumour
fantasy (*n.*)   fancy
fling (*v.*)   hurry
flout (*v.*)   scorn
foggy (*adj.*)   marshy
fond (*adj.*)   foolish
forbear (*v.*)   refrain
foreign (*adj.*)   external
foul (*adj.*)   ugly

friend (*n.*)   friend; relative; lover

frolic (*adj.*)   cheerful

front (*n.*)   face

frustrate (*v.*)   defeat

furnished (*pa.p.*)   equipped

gallery (*n.*)   antechamber

get (*v.*)   obtain; beget

giddiness (*n.*)   changeableness

glass (*n.*)   mirror

glorious (*adj.*)   full of glory; full of light

grace (*n.*)   mercy

gull (*n., v.*)   fool

habit (*n.*)   costume

hardly (*adv.*)   with difficulty

harmless (*adj.*)   blameless

heart's-bane (*adj., n.*)   heart's poison

heavy (*adj.*)   mournful

hoise (*v.*)   set (sails)

hoiting (*pr.p.*)   frolicsome

hospital (*n.*)   refuge

humour (*n.*)   one of the physical humours (blood, phlegm, black bile, yellow bile); disposition

hungerly (*adv.*)   hungrily

husband (*n.*)   married man; farmer

hydroptic (*adj.*)   dropsical

ideate (*v.*)   conceive

illude (*v.*)   deceive

impale (*v.*)   fence in

increpation (*n.*)   reproachful exclamation

ingenuity (*n.*)   ingenuousness

ingle (*v.*)   pet

ingress (*v.*)   enter

inmate (*n.*)   temporary resident

jointure (*n.*)   joint estate of husband and wife

jolly (*adj.*)   bold

kind (*adj.*)   natural; affectionate

lame (*adj.*)   defective

lank (*adj.*)   thin

late (*adj.*)   recent

leave (*v.*)   cease

leese (*v.*)   lose

let (*n.*)   hindrance

lie (*v.*)   lie down; reside; tell a lie

light (*adj.*)   clear; easy; slight; unchaste

limbeck (*n.*)   alembic

lock (*n.*)   wisp

main (*n.*)   mainland

manacled (*pa.p.*)   handcuffed

manna (*n.*)   honeydew

means (*n.*)   possessions

meat (*n.*)   food

mere (*adj.*)   absolute

mew (*v.*)   enclose

minion (*n.*)   darling

minority (*n.*)   youth

monster (*n.*) freak
motion (*n.*) movement;
   incitement
muddy (*adj.*) dirty; coarse
murmur (*v.*) complain

near (*adj.*) direct
nephew (*n.*) descendant
neutral (*adj.*) neuter
next (*adj.*) nearest
nice (*adj.*) delicate
nill (*v.*) will not
nurse (*v.*) nourish

o'erpower (*v.*) outlast
offspring (*n.*) birth
ordnance (*n.*) cannon
overfraught (*pa.p.*)
   overloaded

pain (*n.*) suffering; labour;
   penalty
pensionary (*adj.*) paid
physic (*n.*) medicine
pinnace (*n.*) light sailing
   boat
place (*n.*) position
play (*n.*) gambling
politic (*adj.*) crafty
powder (*n.*) gunpowder
prefer (*v.*) promote
prince (*n.*) ruler (of either
   sex)
prize (*v.*) assess
prove (*v.*) experience; become
pule (*v.*) whine

quick (*adj.*) living
quicken (*v.*) give life to
quintessence (*n.*) the
   supposed fifth element (in
   alchemy)

rags (*n.*) fragments
rare (*adj.*) thin
refrain (*v.*) restrain
remora (*n.*) sucking-fish
remorse (*n.*) pity
rent (*v.*) rend
repair (*v.*) proceed
resolved (*pa.p.*) dissolved
rest (*v.*) remain
roomful (*adj.*) spacious

scape (*n.*) evasion
season (*n.*) time
sense (*n.*) physical senses
senseless (*adj.*) insensible
several (*adj.*) separate
shiver (*v.*) break in pieces
silly (*adj.*) simple
since (*adv.*) now; when
singular (*adj.*) unique
sojourn (*v.*) temporarily
   reside
sophistry (*n.*) ingenuity
sound (*v.*) express
sovereign (*adj.*) supreme
span (*n.*) 9 inches
spent (*pa.p.*) exhausted
spill (*v.*) destroy
spital (*n.*) hospital
state (*n.*) status
stay (*n.*) support; delay
stay (*v.*) wait

stews (*n.*)   brothels
still (*adv.*)   continually
still (*n.*)   distilling apparatus
stilling (*n.*)   distillation
store (*n.*)   abundance
straight (*adv.*)   immediately
straiten (*v.*)   tighten
strict (*adj.*)   narrow
style (*n.*)   title
'suage (*v.*)   assuage
sublunary (*adj.*)   beneath the
   moon
subtle (*adj.*)   fine; abstruse
sudden (*adj.*)   hasty
supply (*n.*)   support
supply (*v.*)   fill
surround (*v.*)   overflow
swoll (*pa.p.*)   swelled

tell (*v.*)   count
temper (*n.*)   discretion
thorough (*prep.*)   through
throughly (*adv.*)   thoroughly
tincture (*n.*)   essence
torpedo (*n.*)   electric ray (fish)
tottered (*pa.p.*)   tattered
toyful (*adj.*)   playful
travail (*n.*)   labour
trill (*v.*)   trickle
try (*n.*)   test

turn (*v.*)   return
turtle (*n.*)   turtle-dove
type (*n.*)   symbol

undo (*v.*)   ruin
unite (*pa.p.*)   united
unthrift (*n.*)   prodigal
use (*n.*)   habit

valiant (*adj.*)   powerful
vapour (*v.*)   evaporate
very (*adj.*)   true
vivary (*n.*)   vivarium

want (*v.*)   lack
wanton (*v.*)   frolic
waste (*v.*)   decay; be destroyed
watch (*v.*)   keep awake
water (*n.*)   urine
weal (*n.*)   pustule
wink (*v.*)   close the eye or
   eyes; flicker
witty (*adj.*)   crafty
woodbine (*n.*)   honeysuckle
worm (*n.*)   snake
worth (*adj.*)   valuable

zone (*n.*)   girdle